VISIONS OF POLITICS

The first of three volumes of essays by Quentin Skinner, one of the world's leading intellectual historians. This collection includes some of his most important philosophical and methodological statements written over the past four decades, each carefully revised for publication in this form. In a series of seminal essays Professor Skinner sets forth the intellectual principles that inform his work. Writing as a practising historian, he considers the theoretical difficulties inherent in the pursuit of knowledge and interpretation, and elucidates the methodology which finds its expression in his two succeeding volumes. All of Professor Skinner's work is characterised by philosophical power, limpid clarity and elegance of exposition. These essays, many of which are now recognised classics, provide a fascinating and convenient digest of the development of his thought.

QUENTIN SKINNER is Regius Professor of Modern History in the University of Cambridge and a Fellow of Christ's College. He has been the recipient of several honorary degrees, and is a Fellow of numerous academic bodies including the British Academy, the American Academy and the Academia Europea. His work has been translated into nineteen languages, and his many publications include *The Foundations of Modern Political Thought* (two volumes, Cambridge, 1978), *Machiavelli* (Oxford, 1981), *Reason and Rhetoric in the Philosophy of Hobbes* (Cambridge, 1996) and *Liberty before Liberalism* (Cambridge, 1998).

VISIONS OF POLITICS

Volume 1: Regarding Method

QUENTIN SKINNER

Regius Professor of Modern History
University of Cambridge

CAMBRIDGE
UNIVERSITY PRESS

CAMBRIDGE
UNIVERSITY PRESS

University Printing House, Cambridge CB2 8BS, United Kingdom

One Liberty Plaza, 20th Floor, New York, NY 10006, USA

477 Williamstown Road, Port Melbourne, VIC 3207, Australia

4843/24, 2nd Floor, Ansari Road, Daryaganj, Delhi - 110002, India

79 Anson Road, #06-04/06, Singapore 079906

Cambridge University Press is part of the University of Cambridge.

It furthers the University's mission by disseminating knowledge in the pursuit of education, learning and research at the highest international levels of excellence.

www.cambridge.org
Information on this title: www.cambridge.org/9780521589260

First published 2002
Fourth printing 2006

A catalogue record for this publication is available from the British Library

ISBN 978-0-521-58105-9 Hardback
ISBN 978-0-521-58926-0 Paperback

Contents

General preface

Several of the chapters in these volumes are appearing in print for the first time. But most of them have been published before (although generally in a very different form) either as articles in journals or as contributions to collective works. Revising them for re-publication, I have attempted to tread two slightly divergent paths at the same time. On the one hand, I have mostly allowed my original contentions and conclusions to stand without significant change. Where I no longer entirely endorse what I originally wrote, I usually indicate my dissent by adding an explanatory footnote rather than by altering the text. I have assumed that, if these essays are worth re-issuing, this can only be because they continue to be discussed in the scholarly literature. But if that is so, then one ought not to start moving the targets.

On the other hand, I have not hesitated to improve the presentation of my arguments wherever possible. I have corrected numerous mistranscriptions and factual mistakes. I have overhauled as well as standardised my system of references. I have inserted additional illustrations to strengthen and extend a number of specific points. I have updated my discussions of the secondary literature, removing allusions to yesterday's controversies and relating my conclusions to the latest research. I have tried to make use of the most up-to-date editions, with the result that in many cases I have changed the editions I previously used. I have replied to critics wherever this has seemed appropriate, sometimes qualifying and sometimes elaborating my earlier judgments. Finally, I have tinkered very extensively with my prose, particularly in the earliest essays republished here. I have toned down the noisy polemics I used to enjoy; simplified the long sentences, long paragraphs and stylistic curlicues I used to affect; taken greater pains to make use of gender-neutral language wherever possible; and above all tried to eliminate overlaps between chapters and repetitions within them.

I need to explain the basis on which I have selected the essays for inclusion in these volumes. I have chosen and grouped them – and in many cases supplied them with new titles – with two main goals in mind. One has been to give each volume its own thematic unity; the other has been to integrate the volumes in such a way as to form a larger whole.

The chapters in volume 1, *Regarding Method*, are all offered as contributions to the articulation and defence of one particular view about the reading and interpretation of historical texts. I argue that, if we are to write the history of ideas in a properly historical style, we need to situate the texts we study within such intellectual contexts and frameworks of discourse as enable us to recognise what their authors were *doing* in writing them. To speak more fashionably, I emphasise the performativity of texts and the need to treat them intertextually. My aspiration is not of course to perform the impossible task of getting inside the heads of long-dead thinkers; it is simply to use the ordinary techniques of historical enquiry to grasp their concepts, to follow their distinctions, to recover their beliefs and, so far as possible, to see things their way.

The other volumes are both concerned with leading themes in early-modern European political thought. In volume 2, *Renaissance Virtues*, I focus on the fortunes of republicanism as a theory of freedom and government. I follow the re-emergence and development from the thirteenth to the sixteenth century of a theory according to which the fostering of a virtuous and educated citizenry provides the key to upholding the liberty of states and individuals alike. My concluding volume, *Hobbes and Civil Science*, examines the evolution and character of Thomas Hobbes's political thought, concentrating in particular on his theory of the state. I consider his views about the power of sovereigns, about the duties and liberties of subjects and about the grounds and limits of political obedience. I attempt in turn to relate these issues to Hobbes's changing views about the nature of civil science and its place in his more general scheme of the sciences.

While stressing the unity of each volume, I am anxious at the same time to underline the interrelations between them. I have attempted in the first place to bring out a general connection between volumes 2 and 3. As we turn from Renaissance theories of civic virtue to Hobbes's civil science, we turn at the same time from the ideal of republican self-government to its greatest philosophical adversary. Although I am mainly concerned in volume 3 with the development of Hobbes's thought, much of what he has to say about freedom and political obligation can also be read as a

critical commentary on the vision of politics outlined in volume 2. The
linkage in which I am chiefly interested, however, is the one I seek to
trace between the philosophical argument of volume 1 and the historical
materials presented in volumes 2 and 3. To put the point as simply as
possible, I see the relationship as one of theory and practice. In volume 1
I preach the virtues of a particular approach; in the rest of the book I try
to practise what I preach.

As I intimate in my general title, *Visions of Politics*, my overarching historical interest lies in comparing two contrasting views we have inherited
in the modern West about the nature of our common life. One speaks of
sovereignty as a property of the people, the other sees it as the possession
of the state. One gives centrality to the figure of the virtuous citizen, the
other to the sovereign as representative of the state. One assigns priority
to the duties of citizens, the other to their rights. It hardly needs stressing
that the question of how to reconcile these divergent perspectives remains a central problem in contemporary political thought. My highest
hope is that, by excavating the history of these rival theories, I may be
able to contribute something of more than purely historical interest to
these current debates.

Full Contents: Volumes 1–3

Acknowledgements

I remain deeply obliged to the large number of colleagues who supplied
me with detailed comments on the original versions of the chapters in
these volumes, and I am very glad of the chance to renew my thanks to
them here. This is also the moment to single out a number of friends
who have given me especially unstinting support and encouragement
in my work over the years. I list them with the deepest gratitude: John
Dunn, Clifford Geertz, Raymond Geuss, Fred Inglis, Susan James, John
Pocock, John Thompson, Jim Tully. My debt to them can only be
described – in the words of Roget's indispensable *Thesaurus* – as immense,
enormous, vast, stonking and mega.

I also owe my warmest thanks to those friends who have helped to
give the individual volumes in this book their present shape. For advice
about the argument in volume 1 I am particularly grateful to Jonathan
Lear, Kari Palonen, Richard Rorty and the late Martin Hollis. For numerous discussions about the themes of volume 2 I am similarly indebted
to Philip Pettit and Maurizio Viroli. As will be evident from my argument
there, I also learned a great deal from chairing the European Science
Foundation workshop 'Republicanism: A Shared European Heritage'.
Special thanks to Martin van Gelderen and Iain Hampsher-Monk for
many instructive and enjoyable conversations, and for helping to make
our meetings such a success.[1] For advice about volume 3 I owe an overwhelming debt to Kinch Hoekstra, Noel Malcolm and Karl Schuhmann,
all of whom have shown a heartwarming readiness to place at my disposal
their astounding knowledge of early-modern philosophy. A number of
my recent PhD students have likewise helped me by commenting on
individual chapters or on my project as a whole. My thanks to David
Armitage, Geoffrey Baldwin, Annabel Brett, Hannah Dawson, Angus

---

[1] The papers read and discussed at our meetings have now been published in two volumes: Martin
van Gelderen and Quentin Skinner (eds.), *Republicanism: A Shared European Heritage* (Cambridge
University Press, 2002).

Gowland, Eric Nelson, Jürgen Overhoff, Jonathan Parkin and Richard Serjeantson.

As well as receiving so much assistance from individual scholars, I owe at least as great an obligation to the institutions that have sustained me throughout the long period in which I have been working on the materials presented here. The Faculty of History in the University of Cambridge has provided me with an ideal working environment throughout my academic career, and I have benefited immeasurably from my association with Christ's College and Gonville and Caius College. I never cease to learn from my colleagues and from the many brilliant students who pass through the Faculty, and I owe a particular debt to the University for its exceptionally generous policy about sabbatical leave. This is the first piece of work I have completed while holding my current post as a Leverhulme Major Research Fellow. I hope that other publications will follow, but in the meantime I already owe the Leverhulme Trust my warmest thanks for its support.

I need to reserve a special word of appreciation for the owners and custodians of the paintings and manuscripts I have examined. I am indebted to the Marquis of Lansdowne for permission to consult the Petty Papers at Bowood, and to the Duke of Devonshire and the Trustees of the Chatsworth settlement for allowing me to make extensive use of the Hardwick and Hobbes manuscripts at Chatsworth. I am similarly grateful for the courtesy and expertise I have encountered in the manuscript reading rooms of the Bibliothèque Nationale, the British Library, the Cambridge University Library, the Bodleian Library and the Library of St John's College Oxford. I am likewise grateful for the friendly helpfulness of the custodians of the Cappella degli Scrovegni in Padua and the Palazzo Pubblico in Siena.

For permission to reproduce photographs my thanks are due to Alinari (Florence), the Warburg Institute (University of London) and Dost Kitavebi (Ankara). For permission to make use of material that originally appeared in their pages I am grateful to the following journals and publishers: Blackwells and Co., The British Academy, *Comparative Studies in Society and History*, *Essays in Criticism*, Europa Publications, *The Finnish Yearbook of Political Thought*, *The Historical Journal*, *History and Theory*, *History of Political Thought*, *The Journal of Political Philosophy*, *The Journal of the Warburg and Courtauld Institutes*, Macmillan and Co., *New Literary History*, *Politics*, *Prose Studies*, The Royal Historical Society, Stanford University Press and The University of Pennsylvania Press.

I have benefited from an extraordinary amount of patient and resourceful assistance in the final stages of preparing these volumes for the press. Richard Thompson amended the quotations in several articles in which I had originally modernised the spelling of early-modern texts. Alice Bell devoted an entire summer to checking transcriptions and references with wonderful meticulousness. Anne Dunbar-Nobes undertook the enormous labour of assembling the bibliographies, rewriting them in author-date style, reformatting all the footnotes and checking them against the bibliographies to ensure an exact match.

While these volumes have been going through the Press I have received a great deal more in the way of technical help. Anne Dunbar-Nobes agreed to serve as copyeditor of the book, and saw it into production with superb professionalism as well as much good cheer. Philip Riley, who has for many years acted as proofreader of my work, generously agreed to perform that task yet again, and duly brought to bear his matchless skills, patience and imperturbability.

I cannot speak with sufficient admiration of my friends at Cambridge University Press. One of my greatest pieces of professional good fortune has been that, throughout my academic career, Jeremy Mynott has watched over the publication of my books with infallible editorial judgement. Richard Fisher has likewise been a pillar of support over the years, and has edited the present work with characteristic enthusiasm, imagination and unfaltering efficiency. My heartfelt thanks to them both, and to their very able assistants, for so much goodwill and expertise.

I cannot end without acknowledging that, if it were not for Susan James and our children Olivia and Marcus, I could not hope to manage at all.

The reprinting of these volumes has provided me with a welcome opportunity to weed out some small inaccuracies. I am very grateful to Richard Westerman for helping me to recheck the text.

Conventions

Abbreviations. The following abbreviations are used in the footnotes:

BL: British Library
BN: Bibliothèque Nationale
DNB: Dictionary of National Biography
OED: Oxford English Dictionary

Bibliographies. These are simply checklists of the primary sources I have actually quoted and the secondary authorities on which I have relied. They make no pretence of being systematic guides to the ever-burgeoning literature on the themes I discuss. In the bibliographies of printed primary sources I list anonymous works by title. Where a work was published anonymously but its author's name is known, I place the name in square brackets. In the case of anonymous works where the attribution remains in doubt, I add a bracketed question-mark after the conjectured name. The bibliographies of secondary sources give all references to journal numbers in arabic form.

Classical names and titles. I refer to ancient Greek and Roman writers in their most familiar single-name form, both in the text and in the bibliographies. Greek titles have been transliterated, but all other titles are given in their original language.

Dates. Although I follow my sources in dating by the Christian era (CE and BCE), I have had to make some decisions about the different systems of dating prevalent in the early-modern period. The Julian Calendar ('Old Style') remained in use in Britain, whereas the Gregorian ('New Style') – ten days ahead of the Julian – was employed in continental Europe from 1582. When quoting from sources written or published on the Continent I use the Gregorian style, but when quoting from

British sources I prefer the Julian. For example, I give Hobbes's date of birth as 5 April rather than 15 April 1588, even though the latter date is technically correct from our point of view, given that the Gregorian calendar was adopted in Britain in the eighteenth century. A further peculiarity of early-modern British dating is that the year was generally taken to start on 25 March. I have preferred to follow the continental practice of treating the year as beginning on 1 January. For example, I treat Hobbes's translation of Thucydides – entered in the Stationers' register with a date of 18 March 1628 – as entered in 1629.

Gender. Sometimes it is clear that, when the writers I am discussing say 'he', they do *not* mean 'he or she', and in such cases I have of course followed their usage rather than tampered with their sense. But in general I have tried to maintain gender-neutral language as far as possible. To this end, I have taken full advantage of the fact that, in the British version of the English language, it is permissible for pronouns and possessives after *each, every, anyone,* etc. to take a plural and hence a gender-neutral form (as in 'to each their need, from each their power').

References. Although I basically follow the author-date system, I have made two modifications to it. One has been rendered necessary by the fact that I quote from a number of primary sources (for example, collections of Parliamentary debates) that are unattributable to any one author. As with anonymous works, I refer to these texts by their titles rather than the names of their modern editors and list them in the bibliographies of primary sources. My other modification is that, in passages where I continuously quote from one particular work, I give references so far as possible in the body of the text rather than in footnotes. Except when citing from classical sources, I generally give references in arabic numerals to chapters from individual texts and to parts of multi-volume works.

Transcriptions. My rule has been to preserve original spelling, capitalisation, italicisation and punctuation so far as possible. However, I normalise the long 's', remove diphthongs, expand contractions, correct obvious typographical errors and change 'u' to 'v' and 'i' to 'j' in accordance with modern orthography. When quoting in Latin I use 'v' as well as 'u', change 'j' to 'i', expand contractions and omit diacritical marks. Sometimes I change a lower-case initial letter to an upper, or vice versa, when fitting quotations around my own prose.

Translations. When quoting from classical sources, and from early-modern sources in languages other than English, all translations are my own except where specifically noted. I make extensive use of the editions published in the Loeb Classical Library, all of which contain facing-page versions in English. But because these renderings are often very free I have preferred to make my own translations even in these instances. I must stress, however, that I remain grateful for the availability of these editions, and have generally been guided by them in making my own translations, even to the extent of adopting turns of phrase.

I

Introduction: Seeing things their way

'Facts alone are wanted in life', Mr Gradgrind assures us at the start of *Hard Times*.[1] Many historians appear to share Mr Gradgrind's sentiment, but some of the most powerful voices in recent philosophy have questioned whether there are any indisputable facts to be acquired. I am concerned in the chapters that follow with three principal aspects of this sceptical challenge. I shall mainly be writing as a practising historian reflecting on the task in hand. But I shall nevertheless have the temerity to suggest that there are good reasons in each instance for joining the sceptical camp.

One assault on the world of facts was launched some time ago from the direction of the theory of knowledge. This campaign was primarily waged by those who aimed to discredit the empiricist belief that our world consists of sense data capable of being directly perceived and un-contentiously described. It would not be too much to say that by now this particular dogma of empiricism has fallen into very general dis-repute. Scarcely anyone nowadays believes in the possibility of build-ing up structures of factual knowledge on foundations purporting to be wholly independent of our judgements.

I seek in chapters 2 and 3 to explore some implications of this post-empiricist critique, implications that seem to me of special relevance for practising historians. My aim in chapter 2 is to reconsider the familiar view that our goal as historians should be to assemble all the facts about a given problem and recount them as objectively as possible. I try to show that this approach is untenable, and to sketch an alternative and more realistic vision of the relationship between historians and their evidence.

In chapter 3 I turn to examine a more specific question about the world of facts. The issue here is one that cannot be evaded by anyone interested in understanding the beliefs of alien cultures or earlier societies. When we

---

[1] Dickens 1985, p. 47.

I

examine such beliefs, we often find that they are not merely unfamiliar but appear in many cases to be obviously false. What role should our sense of their truth or falsity play in our attempts to explain them? One influential answer has been that, since false beliefs point to failures of reasoning, we need to begin by considering the truth of the beliefs we study as an indispensable guide to explaining why they were held. My aim in chapter 3 is to demonstrate that this approach, although frequently recommended, is fatal to good historical practice, and I defend the view that the concept of truth is irrelevant to the enterprise of explaining beliefs.

Besides being assailed by epistemologists, the world of facts has been undermined in recent times by developments within the theory of meaning. The cardinal assumption of positivistic philosophies of language was that all meaningful statements must refer to facts, and thus that the meanings of sentences must be given by the method of verifying the assertions contained in them. Quine cast doubt on this whole approach with his insistence that there is no such 'unvarnished news' to report. So did Wittgenstein when he first emphasised the multifarious ways in which languages are actually used, and went on to argue that we should stop asking about the 'meanings' of words and focus instead on the various functions they are capable of performing in different language games.

These powerful critiques were subsequently extended in two related directions. J. L. Austin, John Searle and others proceeded to examine in detail what might be meant by investigating the uses as opposed to the meanings of words. Isolating the concept of a speech act, they pursued the implications of the fact that, whenever we use language for purposes of communication, we are always doing something as well as saying something. Meanwhile H. P. Grice and a number of theoretical linguists went on to reconsider the concept of meaning at issue when we ask what someone may have meant by saying or doing something. This related contribution likewise had the effect of shifting attention away from 'meanings' and towards questions about agency, usage and especially intentionality.

I attempt in chapters 4, 5 and 6 to explore the relevance of these developments for historians of philosophy and intellectual historians more generally. When I originally wrote the article republished here as chapter 4, I was working against a backdrop of assumptions about the importance of the 'perennial issues' in the history of Western thought. It was widely agreed that the question of whether the so-called classic texts remain worthy of study depends on the extent to which they can be shown to address these perennial issues in a 'relevant' way. I protested that this approach is insensitive to the possibility that earlier thinkers may have been interested in a range of questions very different from our own. More specifically, I objected that, by appropriating the past in this fashion, we leave ourselves no space to consider what earlier philosophers may have been *doing* in writing as they wrote. I began, in other words, to invoke some insights derived from the theory of speech acts to criticise prevailing practices and to plead for a more historically-minded approach to the history of ideas.

My resulting discussion was mainly polemical, although I should add that, in reprinting this early article, I have softened the polemics as well as excising some clumsy formulations and repetitious arguments. While this essay remains more a critique than a programme, it already adumbrates the view of textual interpretation I go on to develop in chapters 5 and 6. In chapter 5 I engage in a ground-clearing exercise, looking for a pathway through the tangled debates about intentionality and the interpretation of texts. In chapter 6 I lay out my own approach to interpretation, attempting at the same time to protect it from a number of misunderstandings and to respond to a number of objections that have subsequently been levelled against it. As I have already intimated, the nerve of my argument is that, if we want a history of philosophy written in a genuinely historical spirit, we need to make it one of our principal tasks to situate the texts we study within such intellectual contexts as enable us to make sense of what their authors were doing in writing them. My aspiration is not of course to enter into the thought-processes of long-dead thinkers; it is simply to use the ordinary techniques of historical enquiry to grasp their concepts, to follow their distinctions, to appreciate their beliefs and, so far as possible, to see things their way.

As will be clear from my stress on the need to recapture what past writers were doing, I mark a strong distinction between what I take to be two separable dimensions of language. One has conventionally been described as the dimension of meaning, the study of the sense and reference allegedly attaching to words and sentences. The other is perhaps best described in Austin's terms as the dimension of linguistic action, the study of the range of things that speakers are capable of doing in (and by) the use of words and sentences. Traditional hermeneutics has generally concentrated almost exclusively on the first of these dimensions. I concentrate at least as much on the second, as will become clear to any reader of volumes 2 and 3 of the present work. One way of summarising my approach would thus be to say that I try to take seriously the implications of the contention that, as Wittgenstein expresses it in his *Philosophical Investigations*, 'words are also deeds'.[2]

Reflecting on the idea that speech is also action, I came to the conclusion that the theory of speech acts might have something to tell us about the philosophy of action more generally, and in particular about the role of causality in the explanation of behaviour. I originally explored this suggestion at the end of the article reprinted here as chapter 4, but soon came to see that my argument was seriously confused. Later I decided to try again, and the outcome was the article that appears here (in a much revised and truncated form) as chapter 7. The thesis I defend is that, even if we agree that motives function as causes, there can nevertheless be non-causal explanations of action. This conclusion still seems to me tenable, and certainly represents a big improvement on my original argument. This being so, I have deleted from chapter 4 the section in which I initially tried to mount this case.

Having stumbled into studying the philosophy of action, I found myself confronting yet further questions that seemed to me of great importance for practising historians. What exact role is played by our beliefs in explaining our behaviour? What does it mean to speak of our beliefs as rationally held? What role should be assigned to assessments of rationality in the explanation of beliefs and behaviour? I first tried to broach these questions at the end of the article reprinted here as chapter 7, but again my initial effort was a failure. Here too I decided to try again, and eventually wrote the more extended treatment of these issues to be found in chapters 2 and 3. These discussions supersede my original account, so I have truncated and rewritten the closing sections of chapter 7 in which I first tried to address these themes.

The approach I follow in these chapters reflects my acceptance of the kind of holism we encounter in the philosophies of Quine, Davidson and especially the later Wittgenstein. One of my principal aspirations is to point to the relevance and importance of this movement in post-analytical philosophy for the interpretation of texts and the study of conceptual change. I seek to elucidate concepts not by focusing on the supposed 'meanings' of the terms we use to express them, but rather by asking what can be done with them and by examining their relationship to each other and to broader networks of beliefs. I assume in turn that the question of what it is rational to believe depends in large measure on the nature of our other beliefs. I attempt to interpret specific beliefs by

---

[2] Wittgenstein 1958, para. 546, p. 146.

placing them in the context of other beliefs, to interpret systems of belief by placing them in wider intellectual frameworks, and to understand those broader frameworks by viewing them in the light of the *longue durée*.[3]

So far I have been speaking of post-empiricist theories of meaning and knowledge and their role in destabilising the positivistic world of facts. I next want to consider a third way in which our traditional view of language as a vehicle essentially for expressing and communicating our thoughts has of late been extended and rendered more complicated. One of the most salutary achievements of post-modern cultural criticism has been to improve our awareness of the purely rhetorical aspects of writing and speech, thereby heightening our sensitivity to the relations between language and power. As we have increasingly been made to see, we employ our language not merely to communicate information but at the same time to claim authority for our utterances, to arouse the emotions of our interlocutors, to create boundaries of inclusion and exclusion and to engage in many other exercises of social control.

I proceed in chapters 8, 9 and 10 to address some questions about these textual strategies. It goes without saying that there is much more to be said and done along these lines. My own contribution is confined to the study of one particular range of rhetorical techniques, those concerned with exploiting the power of words to underpin or undermine the construction of our social world. Chapter 8 attempts, by reference to a specific historical example, to illustrate the dependence of social action on the normative descriptions available to us for legitimating our behaviour. This chapter is largely new, although the germ of it can be found in an article I published as long ago as 1974.[4] Chapter 9 presents a typology of the strategies available for redescribing our social world in such a way as to re-evaluate it at the same time. Chapter 10 investigates in greater detail the specific rhetorical techniques by means of which these ideological tasks are capable of being performed.

Critics have persistently complained that my approach to the history of philosophy robs the subject of its point. If we cannot learn from the perennial wisdom contained in the classic texts, what is the value of studying them? To many of my critics it seems that, by treating these texts as elements in a wider discourse, whose contents change with changing

---

[3] This means that, when I read in Bevir 2001, p. 188 that the holism espoused by Quine and Wittgenstein 'has had little impact on the philosophy of history', I feel that I have lived in vain. I imagine that colleagues such as James Tully must feel the same.

[4] See Skinner 1974, pp. 289–301.

circumstances, I leave them bereft of anything except 'the dustiest anti-
quarian interest'.[5] I foresaw this depressingly philistine objection and
originally tried to counter it at the end of the article reprinted here
as chapter 4. My response was far from sufficient to satisfy my critics,
however, and I therefore tried to spell it out in greater detail at the end
of the article reprinted here as chapter 6. But even that was not enough,
and the objection that my work is purely historical, and that nothing can
be learned from it, continues to be made.[6]

Perhaps it may be worth trying to restate my argument in a more
forthright style. It is true that my work is as historical as I can make it.
But it is nevertheless intended at the same time as a contribution to the
understanding of our present social world. As I have elsewhere argued,[7]
one of the uses of the past arises from the fact that we are prone to
fall under the spell of our own intellectual heritage. As we analyse and
reflect on our normative concepts, it is easy to become bewitched into
believing that the ways of thinking about them bequeathed to us by the
mainstream of our intellectual traditions must be *the* ways of thinking
about them. Given this situation, one of the contributions that historians
can make is to offer us a kind of exorcism. If we approach the past with a
willingness to listen, with a commitment to trying to see things their way,
we can hope to prevent ourselves from becoming too readily bewitched.
An understanding of the past can help us to appreciate how far the values
embodied in our present way of life, and our present ways of thinking
about those values, reflect a series of choices made at different times
between different possible worlds. This awareness can help to liberate
us from the grip of any one hegemonal account of those values and how
they should be interpreted and understood. Equipped with a broader
sense of possibility, we can stand back from the intellectual commitments
we have inherited and ask ourselves in a new spirit of enquiry what we
should think of them.

There is also much to be learned from reflecting on what we uncover
when we begin to investigate the texture of moral, social and political
thinking as it was actually carried on in the past. We encounter endless
disputes about the application of evaluative terms; we witness continual
struggles to win recognition and legitimacy; and we gain a strong sense
of the ideological motivations underlying even the most abstract systems

---

⁵ Tarlton 1973, p. 314; Gunnell 1982, p. 327.
⁶ See, for example, Wokler 2001, pp. 156–7. But for a more sympathetic appraisal see Hampsher-
Monk 2001, pp. 168–74.
⁷ I draw in this paragraph on the discussion in Skinner 1998, pp. 116–17.

of thought. We find, in short, that philosophical argument is often deeply intertwined with claims to social power.

As I indicate in chapter 10, there are several implications one might feel inclined to draw from this spectacle. One is that the principles governing our moral and political life have generally been disputed in a manner more reminiscent of the battlefield than the seminar room. (Or perhaps the moral is that seminar rooms are really battlefields.) A further and connected implication is that it may be right to view with a certain irony those moral and political philosophers of our own day who present us with overarching visions of justice, freedom and other cherished values in the manner of dispassionate analysts standing above the battle. What the historical record strongly suggests is that no one is above the battle, because the battle is all there is. A final moral to be drawn is perhaps that agency deserves after all to be privileged over structure in social explanation. Language, like other forms of social power, is of course a constraint, and it shapes us all. As I try to show in chapters 8 and 9, however, language is also a resource, and we can use it to shape our world.

There is thus a sense in which the following chapters, far from reflecting a depoliticised stance,[8] may be said to culminate in a political plea. The plea is to recognise that the pen is a mighty sword. We are of course embedded in practices and constrained by them. But those practices owe their dominance in part to the power of our normative language to hold them in place, and it is always open to us to employ the resources of our language to undermine as well as to underpin those practices. We may be freer than we sometimes suppose.

[8] The progressive depoliticisation of the professional study of political theory over the past two generations is the theme of Wokler 2001.

2

The practice of history and the cult of the fact

I

British historians are notoriously suspicious of philosophical reflections about the nature of their craft. The charge is no doubt exaggerated, but it is hard to deny that they have sometimes gloried in presenting themselves as straightforward empiricists for whom the proper task of the historian is simply to uncover the facts about the past and recount them as objectively as possible. Despite the inroads of post-modernist culture, this characterisation continues to hold good for many practitioners,[1] and lately their outlook has been defended anew in recent theoretical work.[2] Among those who have not only adopted this stance but have offered a theoretical justification of it, by far the most eminent in recent times has been Sir Geoffrey Elton, who always combined his large and distinguished output as an historian of early-modern Europe with a forthright willingness to reflect on the nature of historical enquiry, a topic on which he published no fewer than three books.[3] While this readiness to come forward as a philosopher of history was unusual, Elton's actual philosophy was a reassuringly familiar one: he presented himself at all times as an unashamed exponent of the cult of the fact.[4] Elton's theoretical writings may thus be said to offer a particularly illuminating means of assessing the strengths and weaknesses of this approach, and it is accordingly on his vision of the historian's task that I shall concentrate in what follows.

This chapter is a revised and extended version of an article that originally appeared under the title 'Sir Geoffrey Elton and the Practice of History' in *Transactions of the Royal Historical Society*, 6th series, 7 (1997), pp. 301–16.

[1] A point well emphasised in Roberts 1996. For the analogous place of what Peter Novick has called 'hyperobjectivism' in the American historical profession, see the fascinating details in Novick 1988, esp. pp. 573–629.

[2] See, most notably, Evans 1997, esp. pp. 75–102.

[3] For the three main statements of Elton's creed see Elton 1969a, Elton 1970 and Elton 1991.

[4] I owe this phrase to Liam Hudson, who originally applied it more generally to the methods of British social science. See Hudson 1972.

8

II

If we begin with Elton's first and fullest consideration of the methods and purposes of historical study, his book entitled *The Practice of History*, we find a revealing metaphor running through the argument. The aspiring historian is pictured as an apprentice – at one point specifically as an apprentice carpenter – who is aiming to produce a first piece of work to be inspected and judged by a master craftsman.[5] Elton repeatedly speaks of the need for the young scholar to undergo 'a proper apprenticeship'. He must acknowledge that 'his life is that of an apprentice learning a craft'; that he needs to 'train himself to his trade'; and thus that he needs to be 'instructed, guided, and trained'.[6]

One assumption worth noting is that both teacher and pupil are always assumed to be male. A further and pivotal assumption is that teachers and writers of history are best viewed as practitioners of a *techne*, as craftsmen who have mastered a distinctive set of skills and are thus in a position to pass on what Elton describes as 'the truths of practice and experience'.[7] This commitment is strongly reinforced by the authorial voice we hear throughout Elton's writings on historical method. The tone is very much that of someone who has rules to impart, rules that an apprentice will do well to read, mark and learn if he is to be 'thoroughly and properly trained'.[8]

The first important lesson that the apprentice learns from the opening chapter of *The Practice of History* is that 'history deals in events, not states; it investigates things that happen and not things that are'. From this it is said to follow that historians must think of their analyses 'as steps in a chain of events, as matters explanatory of a sequence of happenings'. They must therefore 'concentrate on understanding change, which is the essential content of historical analysis and description'.[9] Subsequently this activity is equated with providing explanations of events. The historian's basic duty is 'to consider and explain change', and this ability is identified with the process of 'deducing consequences from disparate facts'.[10]

I am not sure how much headway we are to imagine that the apprentice may already have made in his historical studies. But he will not need to have read very much to know that all these contentions are highly debatable. Suppose he has at least turned the pages of some works in the

---

[5] For the aspiring historian as an apprentice, see Elton 1969a, pp. 34–5, 144, 159, 216; as an apprentice carpenter, p. 214.

[6] Elton 1969a, pp. 103, 113, 213, 221.   [7] Elton 1969a, pp. 15, 19, 160, 187.

[8] See Elton 1969a, p. 219, and for the theme of teaching more generally cf. pp. 178–221.

[9] For these quotations see Elton 1969a, p. 22.   [10] Elton 1969a, pp. 37, 128–9, 166.

history of art or philosophy. In that case he will know that by no means all historians are preoccupied with explanation, especially if by that process we mean (in Elton's formula) the deducing of consequences. Some are instead concerned with the provision of interpretations, and thus with the process of placing texts and other such objects within the fields of meaning from which their own individual meanings can arguably be inferred. If, in addition, the apprentice has read any religious or economic history, he will know that even historians concerned with explanation are by no means always interested in explaining events. Some are interested in accounting for such matters as the prevalence of particular belief-systems or the ways in which past systems of production and exchange have worked.

I suppose we are not to imagine that the apprentice will have read any works in the philosophy of history. Certainly he will not have done so if he has been following the lessons of the master, for Elton explicitly assures us in the Preface to *The Practice of History* that 'a philosophic concern with such problems as the reality of historical knowledge or the nature of historical thought only hinders the practice of history'.[11] Nevertheless, our imagined apprentice might surely be a sufficiently reflective person to wonder how it can possibly be the case that, as Elton maintains, the way in which historians explain events is by 'deducing consequences from disparate facts'.[12] It is true that a knowledge of consequences may sometimes lead an historian to reconsider the significance of an event. But the result of doing so will not be to explain it; it will merely be to re-identify what stands to be explained. When it comes to explanation, the historian surely needs to focus not on the outcome of events but on the causal conditions of their occurrence.

These considerations might lead one to conclude that Elton must simply have made a slip at this point, and that what he must have meant to write was that historians explain events by way of assigning their causes. Since he insists, however, that 'to suppose that causal relationships are the main content of history is an error', he apparently has no wish to be rescued in this way.[13] But in that case I cannot make sense of his view of historical explanation, simply because I cannot see how the act of tracing the consequences of an event has any bearing upon the explanatory task of giving an account of why it occurred.

If we turn, however, to Elton's second book on the study of history, we encounter a more sophisticated and extended analysis of historical

<hr>

[11] Elton 1969a, p. vii; cf. also p. 129, where the theoretical literature on historical explanation is dismissed as 'quite remarkably barren and irrelevant'.
[12] Elton 1969a, p. 129.   [13] Elton 1969a, p. 23.

explanation in which the emphasis is placed entirely on causes rather than consequences. I am referring to *Political History: Principles and Practice*, which Elton originally published in 1970. The first three chapters are largely given over to a more genial if less incisive development of a number of claims already advanced in *The Practice of History* about the alleged primacy of politics in historical studies. But in chapter 4, entitled 'Explanation and Cause', Elton breaks a considerable amount of new ground. He also breaks a considerable number of lances, tilting at the entire philosophical literature on historical explanation with breathtaking self-confidence.

While the outcome is polemically spectacular, the argument is weakened by Elton's insistence that good theory in this area amounts to nothing other than a reflection and restatement of practice.[14] Since it is historians who provide historical explanations, he repeatedly proclaims, it is for them to tell us what makes a good explanation, rather than listening to what he describes as philosophers' nonsense. What is needed is an account of 'what the historian does', an analysis of 'the historian's concept of cause', an investigation into 'what the historian might mean by talking about causes'.[15]

Elton may well be right to stress the pragmatic element in the notion of explanation, an element perhaps best captured by saying that good explanations are those which succeed in removing puzzles about the occurrence of facts or events. But it hardly follows that good historical explanations will consist of anything that practising historians may care to offer us in the way of attempting to resolve such puzzles. Historical explanations cannot be immune from assessment as explanations, and the question of what properly counts as an explanation is inescapably a philosophical one. The question cannot be what historians say; the question must be whether what they say makes any sense.

This is not to deny that Elton may be justified in claiming that the philosophers he discusses imposed too stringent a model by making it a requirement of good historical explanations that they be nomological in form, such that the task of the historian is held to be that of explaining facts and events by reference to empirical laws of which they can be shown to be instances.[16] Nevertheless, the philosophers in question were surely right to insist that the provision of causal explanations in history must

---

[14] See Elton 1970, esp. p. 135, and cf. Elton 1991, esp. pp. 3, 34, 51, 54, 61.

[15] Elton 1970, pp. 125, 136, 145; on philosophers' nonsense see p. 129.

[16] See Elton 1970, esp. pp. 124–30 for his attack on attempts to apply hypothetico-deductive models of explanation to history. His target is the kind of argument put forward in Hempel 1942.

to some extent depend on our capacity to relate particular instances to wider generalities. Elton strongly disagrees, arguing that generalisations are 'no help at all' in the search for historical explanations, since historians are always concerned with 'the particular event'.[17] But the *non sequitur* is blatant: even if it were true that historians are only concerned with particular events, it certainly does not follow that they are under no obligation to investigate causal uniformities in order to explain them. Despite Elton's assurances, moreover, I cannot myself see how historians can hope to solve any puzzles about the occurrence of facts or events without making some attempt to relate such particulars to a broader explanatory background.

If we now return, however, to the point at which we left Elton's argument in *The Practice of History*, we find that none of these considerations greatly matters to him after all, since these are not the questions that he chiefly wants the apprentice to address. At the end of chapter 1 he suddenly introduces a new and different claim about the objectives of history. The apprentice is now told that history, 'to be worthy of itself and beyond itself, must concentrate on one thing', namely the extraction from all the available evidence of what Elton later calls 'the true facts'.[18] This is not perhaps a very felicitous way of introducing the argument, since it subsequently emerges that, for Elton, a true statement *is* a statement of fact, so that the concept of a true fact turns out to be a pleonasm.[19] Nevertheless, the new and contrasting claim he wishes to advance is not in doubt: it is that historians are basically engaged in the assembling of facts with the aim of arriving at the truth.[20] Announcing this commitment, Elton declares his unswerving allegiance to the cult of the fact. There can be no doubt, he insists, that 'the truth can be extracted from the evidence' and thus that, by uncovering the facts of history, the historian can aspire to discover 'the true reality of the past'.[21]

Elton's later pronouncements about historical method admittedly involve some shifting back and forth between these two perspectives. His inaugural lecture at the University of Cambridge, delivered in 1968 and reprinted in his book *Return to Essentials* in 1991, begins by reverting to the claim that 'the essence of all history is change'.[22] His second inaugural

---

[17] See Elton 1970, pp. 132, 151–2, and cf. the attack on the place of generalisations in explanation at pp. 126–31.

[18] Elton 1969a, pp. 68, 86.   [19] Elton 1969a, pp. 86, 133.

[20] Elton 1969a, p. 70. Thereafter the point is continually reiterated; see pp. 74, 97, 101, 117, 123.

[21] Elton 1969a, pp. 79, 97.   [22] Elton 1991, p. 80.

lecture, delivered as Regius Professor of Modern History in 1983 and reprinted in the same volume, speaks in even more emphatic tones about 'the inadequacy of any historical analysis which is not predominantly directed towards an understanding of change through time'.[23] But on the whole it is the alternative idea of extracting the truth from the assembling of facts that wins the day. The first inaugural lecture insists that historians must engage in 'the proper assessment and proper study of evidence', adding that this is because they are 'concerned with one thing only: to discover the truth'.[24] Chapter 3 of *Political History*, which is actually entitled 'Evidence', likewise speaks about the bodies of material studied by historians and promises that 'something like the truth can be extracted from them'.[25] The second inaugural lecture ends by repeating once more that the sole aim of the historian is that of 'telling the truth about the past'.[26] Finally, these are precisely the 'essentials' to which Elton recalls us in his *Return to Essentials* of 1991. The apprentice must acquire 'a professional training' in 'the treatment of the historical evidence' about every event he investigates, with the eventual aim of arriving at 'the truth of the event and all that surrounds it'.[27]

The second chapter of *The Practice of History* adds some examples to clarify what Elton means by speaking about items of historical evidence.[28] The sort of thing he has in mind, he says, is something like a financial account, or the record of a court case, or one of the material relics of the past, such as a house. These are 'far and away the most important and common' types of evidence that the apprentice can expect to encounter, and these are the sorts of documents and factual materials out of which he must extract the truth.[29]

I imagine the apprentice exhibiting a certain surprise at this point. Perhaps these forms of evidence are the most common, but is it obvious that they are 'far and away the most important'? What about the major works of theology, philosophy and science that adorn our libraries? What about the heritage of great paintings and other works of art that fill our museums and galleries? Elton gives his answer in the concluding chapter of *The Practice of History*. The apprentice must learn to distinguish between optional aspects of historical study and 'real' or 'hard' history.[30] The 'hard outline' of historical research and teaching 'must consist of the actions of governments and governed in the public life of the time', this being the

---

[23] Elton 1991, p. 120.   [24] Elton 1991, pp. 89, 91.   [25] Elton 1970, p. 84.
[26] Elton 1991, p. 125.   [27] Elton 1991, pp. 30, 54.
[28] The examples are repeated in Elton 1970, pp. 12–13.   [29] Elton 1969a, p. 101.
[30] Elton 1969a, pp. 190, 197, 199. On 'real' history see also Elton 1970, esp. pp. 22, 32.

only theme 'sufficiently dominant to carry the others along with it'.[31] But as long as this forms the 'backbone' of our historical studies,[32] there is no harm in adding such optional extras as intellectual history or the history of art, although the latter admittedly encourages 'woolliness and pretence'.[33] Elton even allows that some kinds of intellectual history – for example, the history of political theory – may have a positive value, since the study of people's thinking about politics 'bears directly on a main part of the student's "hard" history' through its connection with 'the problem of political organisation and action'.[34] By the time Elton came to publish *Return to Essentials*, however, he had noticed with evident dismay that in the meantime the history of ideas had been 'suddenly promoted from the scullery to the drawing room'.[35] To cope with this unforeseen impertinence, he takes greater care in his later work to warn the apprentice that intellectual history is not 'real' history at all. 'By its very nature' it is 'liable to lose contact with reality', and is indeed 'removed from real life'.[36]

The apprentice is thus left with some very definite instructions about what to study and how to study it. He must concentrate on 'hard' history, and thus on the type of evidence originally singled out in chapter 2 of *The Practice of History*: the evidence provided by such things as the record of a court case or a material relic such as a house. He should then make it his business to extract the facts, and thus the truth, from such forms of evidence. He must remember, as chapter 2 puts it, that 'historical method is no more than a recognised and tested way of extracting from what the past has left the true facts and events of that past'.[37] Nor need the apprentice have any doubt 'that the truth can be extracted from the evidence by the application of proper principles of criticism'.[38] Provided that he follows his instructions properly, the goal can unquestionably be achieved. As with all successful cults, the cult of the fact promises to guide us towards a final truth, 'a truth which', as Elton somewhat gnomically intones, 'is more absolute than mere truthfulness'.[39]

By this stage I imagine the apprentice beginning to feel slightly bewildered. Elton has offered him the example of a house as an instance

---

[31] Elton 1969a, p. 172. The point is still more emphatically made in Elton 1970, esp. pp. 7, 65, 157, 177.

[32] Elton 1969a, p. 197. Cf. also Elton 1970, where he insists (p. 73) on the 'primacy' of political history and singles it out (p. 68) as 'the most important' subject of historical research.

[33] Elton 1969a, p. 190.

[34] Elton 1969a, p. 190. For a repetition and enlargement of the argument, see Elton 1970, pp. 43–53.

[35] Elton 1991, p. 12.   [36] Elton 1991, pp. 27, 60.   [37] Elton 1969a, p. 86.

[38] Elton 1969a, p. 97.   [39] Elton 1969a, pp. 73–4.

of the type of evidence from which he is expected to extract the facts in such a way as to arrive at the truth. But how can one hope to set about seeking the truth, *simpliciter*, about such a thing as a house? Will it not be necessary to approach the study of the house with some sense of why I am studying it, why it might be of interest, before I can tell how best to go about examining it?

Elton has of course foreseen the anxiety and offers an interesting response. The opening chapter of *The Practice of History* introduces a distinction between 'real' historians and amateurs.[40] Amateurs such as Lord Acton or G. M. Trevelyan (who was 'a really fine amateur') intrude themselves and their enthusiasms upon the past.[41] By contrast, real historians wait for the evidence to suggest questions by itself. As Elton later puts it, the questions a real historian asks are never 'forced by him upon the material'; rather they are forced by the material upon the historian. The real historian remains 'the servant of his evidence', of which he 'should ask no specific questions until he has absorbed what it says'.[42] The distinction recurs in chapter 3, in which we are again informed that the questions we ask as historians must 'arise out of the work' and 'not be sovereignly imposed on it'.[43]

This kind of injunction has been central to the German tradition of hermeneutics, and is prominent in the writings of Hans-Georg Gadamer, especially his *Wahrheit und Methode* of 1960.[44] It is true that Gadamer's name makes no appearance in *The Practice of History*, and that when Elton later invokes him in *Return to Essentials* it is only to dismiss him as ponderous and confused.[45] It seems to me, however, that Elton is not only echoing one of Gadamer's most characteristic themes, but that the argument they are both putting forward embodies a salutary reminder about the need to be aware of our inevitable tendency towards pre-judgement and the fitting of evidence into pre-existing patterns of interpretation and explanation.[46] Moreover, the warning seems all the more valuable in view of the fact that the premature consignment of unfamiliar evidence to familiar categories is so hard to avoid, as even apprentice historians know.

There remain some difficulties about applying this rule in practice. Gadamer would certainly not approve, in the first place, of the positivistic confidence with which Elton asserts it. Consider again Elton's example of a house as an instance of the kind of raw evidence that an apprentice

---

[40] Elton 1969a, pp. 29–36.   [41] Elton 1969a, p. 31.   [42] Elton 1969a, p. 83.
[43] Elton 1969a, p. 121.   [44] See Gadamer 1960 and cf. Gadamer 1975.
[45] Elton 1991, pp. 29, 38.   [46] Gadamer 1975, esp. pp. 235–74.

might confront. Gadamer would point out that Elton has already begged the question by characterising the object under investigation as a house. It will be unwise for Elton to retort that the object under investigation must be a house because it is described as such in all relevant documents. The House of Commons is described as a house in all relevant documents, but it is not a house. Nor will Elton fare any better if he replies that the object must be a house because it looks like a house. On the one hand, an object might look nothing like a house and nevertheless be a house. (Think of lighthouses now used as houses.) On the other hand, an object might look very like a house and nevertheless not be a house. (Think of the mausoleums designed by Sir John Vanbrugh.) As Gadamer always stresses, we are already caught up in the process of interpretation as soon as we begin to describe any aspect of our evidence in our own words.[47]

A second and more intractable problem arises as soon as we ask how far we can hope to carry Elton's idea of confronting a piece of evidence such as a house and allowing it, as he repeatedly demands, to force its questions upon us. Elton is adamant that 'the only proper ambition' for an historian is 'to know all the evidence', with the result that the task of the apprentice historian must be to begin by acquiring 'total acquaintance with the relevant material' if he is to end up by telling the truth about it.[48] The underlying aspiration to arrive at a definitive reading of a body of evidence dies surprisingly hard. Elton's commitment has more recently been echoed, for example, by Peter Gay, who has written of his regret at his decision to entitle his major work on the eighteenth century *The Enlightenment: An Interpretation*. Gay remarks that while ' "*the* Interpretation" would have sounded immodest' this would nevertheless 'have been what I meant'.[49]

But what would it mean to offer *the* interpretation of the Enlightenment? It would mean, at the very least, offering an analysis sufficiently comprehensive to enable us either to incorporate or to set aside every rival reading of every piece of evidence that might be thought relevant to the provision of a total picture of the high culture of the eighteenth century. Not merely is such a project of doubtful intelligibility, but the mere attempt to undertake it would consume endless lifetimes. Any analysis

---

[47] On language as the medium in which all interpretative activity is carried on, see Gadamer 1975, esp. pp. 345–66.

[48] See Elton 1969a, pp. 87, 96 and cf. pp. 88, 92, 109.

[49] Gay 1974, p. 211 n. But Gay generally pleads for a perspective more akin to the one I am defending here; see, for example, Gay 1974, pp. 210–13, 217. For a discussion of Elton's and Gay's arguments see Novick 1988, pp. 610–12.

of the phenomenon of the Enlightenment will inescapably be based on a series of prior judgements about the nature of its most characteristic preoccupations, together with a further series of judgements about how best to illustrate them. But to engage in such judgements is already to recognise that we are, of course, offering only *an* interpretation. Our resulting survey may be a model of fairminded inclusiveness, but it cannot possibly include everything, and will therefore be open to continuous reinterpretation both by scholars who discover new facts and by scholars who offer new interpretations of the significance of existing ones.

The same objections apply even in the case of Elton's seemingly more modest demands upon the apprentice historian. As we have seen, Elton's basic suggestion is that, when confronting an item of evidence such as a house, the apprentice should begin by acquiring 'total acquaintance' with it if he is to end up by telling the truth.[50] Again, however, the question is how we can hope to render intelligible the idea of seeking total acquaintance with an item of evidence such as a house. Consider, for example, the project of acquiring total acquaintance with Chatsworth House, and thereby arriving at the truth about that principal residence of the Dukes of Devonshire. A complete study of all the facts about Chatsworth would be literally endless. It would take a lifetime for the apprentice to accumulate anything like a full description (whatever that may mean) of the house itself. (How many windows does it have? How many panes of glass? How big is each pane? How much do they weigh? Where did they come from? How much did they cost?) So far the apprentice has not even entered the muniment room to stare glassily at the scores of manuscript volumes devoted to the lives of Chatsworth's owners and the process of building it. (How many volumes? How many pages in each volume? How many words on each page? What sort of ink was used?)

As Elton's discussion proceeds, however, he evidently begins to see the difficulty, or at least begins to shift his ground. In chapter 3 of *The Practice of History* he is still assuring us that historians 'can discover something fairly described as the truth' about the objects of their research.[51] But in chapter 4 he frequently replaces this contention with the very different and vastly more modest claim that historians can hope to arrive at some particular truths. Whereas chapter 2 had spoken of recovering 'the truth' about 'past realities', chapter 4 prefers to speak of the historian's capacity

[50] See Elton 1969a, pp. 87, 96 and cf. pp. 88, 92, 109.
[51] See Elton 1969a, p. 117; but cf. pp. 179, 221, where he continues to insist on his earlier claims about 'the truth'.

to find out 'solid truths' and thereby to 'establish new footholds in the territory of truth'.[52]

It subsequently turns out that this more modest account of the historian's task is what really matters to Elton. The aim of the 'real' historian is that of arriving at new truths by way of adding to the number of incontrovertible facts. It is because of his sense that, as he puts it in chapter 3 of *The Practice of History*, there are many things that historians 'know beyond doubt' and 'can say with certainty'[53] that Elton later savages the deconstructionists and their scepticism about facts with such assurance. Elton knows beyond question 'who the eldest surviving child of Henry VIII was'; this is one of an 'enormous number' of historical facts 'on which no dispute is possible'.[54] It follows that, when he finds himself obliged to confront such deconstructionist critics as Dominick LaCapra with their claim that 'there cannot be any ascertainable certainties in history', Elton is in no doubt about how to respond.[55] Although he does not know how to spell Professor LaCapra's name, he knows for a fact that LaCapra is merely exhibiting 'the mindless arrogance of the self-satisfied' if he is attempting 'to deny the existence of facts'.[56]

It is true that Elton betrays himself into some blank contradictions in the course of mounting this argument. The earlier chapters of *The Practice of History* are emphatic that 'a great deal of history' is 'knowable and known beyond the doubt of anyone qualified to judge', and thus that 'some historical writing is simply and obviously right'.[57] But in the final chapter, and again in *Return to Essentials*, Elton is no less emphatic that the historian 'must be a professional sceptic',[58] and that one of the main functions of 'real' historians must be 'to cast doubt upon the possibility that in historical studies anyone will ever be finally "right"'.[59]

Elton's restatement of his ideal is far from coherent, but his ideal itself is surely clear and unexceptionable. If we now return to Chatsworth with no higher ambition than to say a number of true things about it, we can surely hope to succeed. We may be able to determine such factual matters as its overall height, the size of its grounds and perhaps even the number of its rooms with absolute finality, so long as we take care to avoid any problems of an interpretative kind (such as, for example, what is to count as a room). If this is all that is meant by the quest for

---

[52] Elton 1969a, pp. 168, 177.   [53] Elton 1969a, p. 111.   [54] Elton 1969a, p. 80.

[55] For the discussion of LaCapra's views see Elton 1991, pp. 58–61.

[56] Elton 1991, p. 59.   [57] Elton 1969a, pp. 107, 123.   [58] Elton 1991, pp. 23–4.

[59] Elton 1969a, p. 206. On the need for 'sceptical thinking' and 'critical scepticism' on the part of historians see also pp. 55, 103, 205.

the truth – that is, the capacity to uncover and state a number of facts – then it can certainly be granted to Elton that, as he puts it in chapter 3 of *The Practice of History*, historians are often able to end up by offering statements 'of manifest and incontrovertible truth'.[60]

Unlike his initial demand, Elton's more modest proposal at least has the merit of suggesting a research programme that could in principle be carried out. It is not clear, however, that this will necessarily alleviate the anxiety originally expressed by our imagined apprentice. He now knows that his job is to find out a number of facts about Chatsworth with the aim of stating a corresponding number of truths about it. But he also knows that the facts about Chatsworth are so numerous that he will never be able to find out more than a very small fraction of them. (If he stupidly decides, for example, to start by finding out how many stones went into its construction, he will certainly never finish his dissertation on time.) Moreover, since every fact he discovers will have to be expressed in words, and since Michel Foucault has by now familiarised even apprentice historians with the thought that all classificatory schemes are subject to endless challenge and revision, he may even begin to wonder how many genuinely incontrovertible facts he can hope to state. Suppose, for example, he decides to catalogue the works of art contained in Chatsworth. He wants to know whether he should include the furniture. The correct answer, obviously, is that he should include only those items of furniture which are also works of art. But what is required for something to be a work of art? On the one hand, the question clearly has no simple answer, perhaps no answer at all. But on the other hand, the apprentice needs an immediate answer if he is going to be able to state as a matter of incontrovertible fact how many works of art Chatsworth contains. Perhaps there are fewer incontrovertible facts than he has been led to believe.

The apprentice need not despair, however, for Elton is on hand to reassure him that (as he remarks in speaking of my own writings on this subject) these are unduly high-falutin doubts.[61] But even if the apprentice feels duly reassured, he is still in need of some advice about how to start work on his thesis about Chatsworth. What sort of incontrovertible facts should he be looking for? What sort of facts should he be trying to find out?

One obvious way of replying would be to revert to the somewhat Socratic approach I initially proposed. What first attracted you, one

---

[60] Elton 1969a, p. 176.   [61] Elton 1991, p. 42.

might ask in return, to the idea of making a study of Chatsworth? What made you think that a dissertation on this particular mansion of the late seventeenth century might be of interest? I think this would certainly be my own response. I would expect the apprentice to have some views about why it might be of some value – here and now, to himself and others – to know more about Chatsworth and its history. Just as the value of factual information depends on what the historian wants to understand, I would argue, so the attempt to uncover new facts needs to be guided by a sense of what appears to be worth understanding.[62] I would urge the apprentice, in other words, to solve the problem of how to study Chatsworth by first asking what might be the purpose of studying it at all.

If our imagined apprentice is expecting some such answer from Elton, however, he is in for a rude shock. It is Elton's view that asking such questions is the quickest way of revealing that you have failed to understand the nature of the historian's craft. He insists in *The Practice of History* that our historical studies must be kept entirely separate from any such concerns,[63] and in *Return to Essentials* he reiterates the point with even greater vehemence. 'The fundamental questions we put to the evidence' must remain 'independent of the concerns of the questioner'.[64] We must recognise that Chatsworth – or any other relic of the past – must be studied 'in its own right, for its own sake', and that this constitutes 'the first principle of historical understanding'. What distinguishes 'real' practitioners of history is their willingness to grant the past 'full respect in its own right'.[65]

It might be supposed that what Elton means is that, once we have selected a topic for investigation, we must be sure to treat it in its own terms, even though the topic will of course have been selected on the grounds that it seems to us to possess some inherent value and interest. This would be to say – to cite an epigram of John Dunn's – that the historian should be Whig as to subject matter, Tory as to truth.[66] But to assume that this is Elton's position would be seriously to underestimate the sweep of his argument in *The Practice of History* about the need to approach the past 'in its own right, for its own sake, and on its own terms'.[67] It is Elton's view that we must take the greatest care *not* to select our topics on the grounds that they seem to us to have some current interest or (worse still) some contemporary social relevance or importance. The point is made with ferocious emphasis, and with Elton's

---

[62] For a classic account of a similar view of factual evidence see Carr 1961, pp. 1–24.
[63] Elton 1969a, p. 65.   [64] Elton 1991, p. 55.   [65] Elton 1969a, pp. 18, 66, 86.
[66] Dunn 1980, p. 26.   [67] Elton 1969a, p. 86.

habitual repetitiousness, in every chapter of his book. The historian must avoid any attempt 'to justify his activity as a social utility'. To proceed in this way is to commit 'the cardinal error'. He must recognise that his entire pursuit 'involves, above all, the deliberate abandonment of the present'.[68] The same point is made yet again in *Return to Essentials*. We are now assured that the entire project of historical research ('all of it') must be completely divorced from the 'needs and concerns of the present'.[69]

By this stage I imagine the apprentice becoming seriously worried, perhaps even a touch desperate. Does this mean that all the facts I might discover about Chatsworth are of equal interest? Am I just to go there and start making a list of anything it occurs to me to say about it? If this is all I am expected to do, might I just as well be studying something else, perhaps anything else?

If the apprentice is insolently attempting a *reductio ad absurdum* he is in for another rude shock, for it turns out that this is exactly what Elton believes. When he addresses the question of teaching in the closing chapter of *The Practice of History*, he goes so far as to declare that the actual content of what we teach, and *a fortiori* what we study as historians, 'matters in essence very little' and is indeed 'of no importance'.[70] Real historians, as he had earlier put it, are not distinguished by the problems they study but by 'the manner of their study'; their problems may appear 'narrow or petty', but they gain their importance from 'the techniques of study' they impart.[71] This is a truth that needs to be grasped not merely by teachers of history but by 'anyone concerning himself with historical studies in any form'. The purpose of our studies must be sought 'in the intellectual training they provide', and it is because 'all history, properly deployed' can equally well supply this training that 'it matters in essence very little what particular sections of it are taught'.[72]

I imagine the apprentice stunned at this point into incredulity. So it doesn't matter in the least what facts I find out about Chatsworth, so long as I employ the right techniques to find them out? This is precisely Elton's point. 'The University', as he patiently explains, 'must train the mind, not fill the untrained mind with multi-coloured information and undigested ideas, and only the proper study of an identifiable discipline according to the rules and practices of that discipline can accomplish that fundamental purpose.'[73] But what of our ability to learn from the past about unfamiliar social structures, about developments in art, religion and philosophy, about the conditions and mechanisms of political and

---

[68] Elton 1969a, pp. vii, 66, 86.   [69] Elton 1991, p. 72.   [70] Elton 1969a, pp. 187, 188.
[71] Elton 1969a, pp. 34, 69.   [72] Elton 1969a, pp. 186, 188.   [73] Elton 1969a, p. 199.

economic change? Some of these examples are Elton's, but they leave him unmoved. 'This is nothing to do with the framing of courses for study and examination, with the real work of intellectual training.'[74] But what about his earlier insistence that it matters very much what kind of history we learn and teach, since 'the actions of governments and governed' alone provide us with a backbone of 'real' or 'hard' history? Here I do not know what to say, for as far as I can see Elton makes no effort to reconcile this argument with his yet more strongly voiced belief in the overriding importance of technique.[75]

III

It is surely worth pausing at this sensational moment to reflect on the completeness of the disjunction that Elton eventually draws between the content and the justification of our historical studies. What could have prompted so great a scholar to paint himself into such a dark and dismal corner? The clue lies, I believe, in considering the nature of the intellectual crisis so painfully reflected in the pages of *The Practice of History*. By the time Elton came to publish the original version of this manual in 1967, he had issued some of his best-known technical scholarship as well as two of his most widely used textbooks. As *The Practice of History* makes clear, he not only thought highly of this *oeuvre*[76] but had managed to persuade himself that the kind of research in which he himself specialised called for the exercise of exceptional human powers. He speaks of the need for a searching intelligence, for sympathy and judgement, for 'imagination controlled by learning and scholarship'.[77] He even speaks in an uncharacteristic moment of pomposity of the historian's 'obligations as an artist' as well.[78]

Elton was acutely aware, however, that a number of prominent historians had meanwhile ceased to believe in the validity or importance of the sort of administrative and political history in which he had made his name. Among those particularly singled out in *The Practice of History* for

---

74 Elton 1969a, p. 200.

75 One possible reconciliation might take the form of saying that the required technical skills can best be gained from studying certain types of document, and that the most suitable types on which to practise are those concerned with English central government. So far as I am aware, Elton never explicitly suggested this reconciliation, although he arguably hinted at it in Elton 1969b, p. 33.

76 See, for example, Elton 1969a, pp. 174–6.

77 See Elton 1969a, pp. 112, 177 and cf. Elton 1970, p. 108 on the exceptional skills needed to write political history.

78 See Elton 1969a, pp. 158–9 and cf. p. 124.

arguing that such preoccupations have 'ceased to be valid' are Richard Southern and Keith Thomas.[79] As Elton concedes, both acknowledge that political history retained its importance so long as the teaching of history in British universities remained closely tied to the training of a political elite and a civil service capable of running a great empire. With the loss of these social conditions, however, Southern and Thomas were led to conclude that the justification for singling out this kind of history had come to an end as well. Both accordingly enter what Elton describes as unacceptable pleas for a new sense of why history might matter to our society, together with a call for the cultivation of new forms of historical enquiry – a call for more intellectual history in the case of Southern, more social history in the case of Thomas.[80]

A surprising feature of *The Practice of History* is that Elton makes no attempt to respond to these arguments by seeking to vindicate the social value or cultural significance of his own very different kind of research. He could surely have attempted – as several of his admiring obituarists did – to convey some sense of why the study of administrative and constitutional history might still be thought to matter even in a post-imperial culture dominated by the social sciences. It is true that, a couple of years later, he made some gestures in this direction in his first inaugural lecture. But it is striking that he almost instantly stopped short, apologising for starting to speak in such a 'very vague and rather vapoury' way.[81] Faced with the question of how a knowledge of history might help the world, he preferred to advise historians to 'abandon and resign' such aspirations altogether.[82]

Why was Elton so doubtful about assigning any social value or utility to his own brand of history? I am not altogether sure, although the answer must certainly be connected with his curious but persistent belief that any attempt to vindicate the usefulness of studying the past must include a demonstration of the historian's capacity to issue predictions.[83] This is particularly a theme of Elton's first inaugural lecture. 'We are told', he confides, that what historians must do if they are to be socially useful is to answer the question 'What help can the past offer to the future?'[84]

---

79 Elton 1969a, pp. 17–18, 185.
80 For a discussion of these claims see Elton 1969a, esp. pp. 17–18, 185–6.
81 Elton 1991, p. 93.   82 Elton 1991, p. 96.
83 The same anxiety afflicted J. H. Hexter at much the same time, but he instead responded by attempting to vindicate the historian's predictive powers. See Hexter 1971, esp. pp. 36–42. But Hexter appears to miss his own point, for the predictions he discusses – although presented as those of an historian – are not issued in virtue of his being an historian at all.
84 Elton 1991, p. 84.

But who tells us this? It is hard to think of any contemporary historian or philosopher of history who has advanced this argument, and Elton himself mentions no names. He can scarcely have in mind his two *bêtes noires*, Southern and Thomas, both of whom are exclusively concerned with the question of how the past might be made relevant to the present. Nor can he be thinking of the Marxist historian he most frequently attacks, Christopher Hill, for while it was undoubtedly an aspiration of classical Marxism to make use of historical materials to formulate predictive social laws, Christopher Hill has never exhibited anything more than a passing interest in that aspect of Marxist philosophy.

There remains something of a mystery surrounding the sources of Elton's scepticism about the broader educational value of his own studies. About the fact of his scepticism, however, he leaves us in no doubt. His second inaugural lecture robustly declares that 'we should not trouble ourselves too much' about the alleged lessons of history, since this would be to study the past for an 'inappropriate and usually misleading purpose'.[85] Eight years later, in the version of his Cook Lectures published in *Return to Essentials*, his mood had become even more dismissive. He begins by stigmatising the nineteenth-century belief in the lessons of history as little more than an influential absurdity, and goes on to warn us against the 'temptation' of believing that the study of history is of any relevance to our future or present state.[86]

Elton clearly recognised, however, that these commitments left him with only two possible ways of convincing us – as he always remained anxious to do – that the study of history should nevertheless be recognised as a vocation 'appropriate to the highest abilities of the human reason'.[87] One alternative would be to abandon any attempt to vindicate the social value of his own kind of history in favour of claiming that the value of the subject somehow lies in the study of the past as a whole. This is the line he begins to follow in *Return to Essentials*, and especially in the three Cook Lectures included in that book. The first lecture opens by informing us that 'history teaches a great deal about the existence of free will'. The second adds that a professional assessment of the past can be used to demolish a number of comfortable myths. The third concludes that history can tell us about the unexpected and, again, about the reality of human freedom.[88]

These are not perhaps very promising lines of thought, and it is surely to Elton's credit that he never made any effort to explain or develop them.

---

[85] Elton 1991, p. 114. [86] Elton 1991, pp. 4, 9.
[87] Elton 1969a, p. 16n. [88] Elton 1991, pp. 7–8, 45–6, 73.

He was undoubtedly aware that the past has always been studied for a myriad of changing reasons, and that any attempt to summarise them will almost inevitably degenerate into just such a string of clichés. But this leaves him with only one means of vindicating the importance of his own studies. As we have already seen, he is forced into arguing that any attempt to offer a social justification of history is an irrelevance, the reason being that what matters in history is not the content of our studies but the range of techniques we deploy in practising them. This is the conclusion which, in effect, supplies him with the theme of both inaugural lectures reprinted in *Return to Essentials.* The second proclaims that the value of historical study lies entirely in the 'mind-training capacity' it provides. Even more bluntly, the first concludes that what historians 'are here to teach the world' is nothing other than 'the proper assessment and proper study of evidence'.[89]

We can now see what makes Elton's image of the historian as a master carpenter such a revealing one. What matters, he believes, is not whether we are engaged in making tables, chairs or wooden spoons; what matters is the nature of the craft skills equally required for engaging in any of these activities. Like Mr Gradgrind, Elton believes that 'facts alone are wanted'. It follows, in Elton's philosophy, that the most important task must be to learn how best to find them out.

By now I should expect the apprentice to have given up trying to write his dissertation on Chatsworth, perhaps devoting himself instead to a career in retailing (as Elton appears to recommend at one point).[90] I fear that some such feeling of discouragement would certainly have been my own response, although Elton's outstanding success as a teacher suggests that there must be some way in which I am failing to respond with adequate appreciation to his advice to neophytes. Be that as it may, I should like to end by summoning my imagined apprentice once more to ask Elton if he doesn't fear that something of broader educational significance may have been forfeited by his unrelenting insistence on technique at the expense of content. It turns out, however, that Elton has no regrets, since he is not sure about the value of a broader liberal education in any case. This darkest vein of scepticism surfaces – without preamble or explanation – in his first inaugural lecture, in the course of which Sir Richard Morison, one of Henry VIII's propagandists, is approvingly cited for the view that education is a great cause of sedition and other mischiefs in commonwealths. Elton follows up the quotation with a disconcerting flurry of questions. 'Should we', he suddenly asks,

---

[89] Elton 1991, pp. 89, 108.   [90] Elton 1991, p. 94.

'really be practising education? Are we not overestimating it as a power for good, or possibly underestimating it as a power for evil? Ought we not sometimes to stand away from the whole question of education?' Even more disconcerting is his response. Education 'is a livelihood', he concedes, 'but it may be a folly', and it is undoubtedly a cause of mischief in commonwealths.[91]

Elton's fundamental reason for wishing to emphasise technique over content appears to have been a deeply ironic one: a fear that historical study might have the power to transform us, to help us think more effectively about our society and its possible need for reform and reformation. Although it strikes me as strange in the case of someone who spent his life as a professional educator, Elton clearly felt that this was a consummation devoutly to be stopped. Much safer to keep on insisting that facts alone are wanted.

[91] Elton 1991, p. 85.

3

Interpretation, rationality and truth

I

Many historians make it a principal part of their business to investigate and explain the unfamiliar beliefs we encounter in past societies. But what is the relationship between our provision of such explanations and our assessment of the truth of such beliefs? The question is obviously a highly intractable one, but no practising historian can hope to evade it, as many philosophers have recently and rightly pointed out. Within the Anglophone tradition, the most eminent philosopher to highlight these issues of late has been Charles Taylor, and it is on his formulation of the question that I shall begin by focusing as I try to work my way towards my own answer to it.

II

The key issue for historians, as Taylor states it, is whether they should seek to avoid 'taking a stand on the truth of the ideas' they investigate.[1] Is it desirable, or even possible, to 'bracket' the question of truth, 'to insulate questions of historical explanation from those of truth'?[2] My first response is that I am not altogether clear what Taylor means by the 'bracketing' of truth. Sometimes he seems to be asking whether historians should somehow seek to discount or set aside the fact that they themselves hold certain beliefs to be true and others false. If this is Taylor's question, then my answer is that I am sure no historian can ever hope to perform such an act of forgetting, and that in any case it would be most unwise to try.

This chapter has been adapted and developed from the central section of my 'Reply to my Critics' in *Meaning and Context: Quentin Skinner and his Critics*, ed. James Tully (Cambridge, 1988), pp. 235–59.

[1] See Taylor 1988, p. 224 and cf. Shapiro 1982, esp. p. 537.
[2] Taylor 1988, pp. 220, 223.

Consider the fact that so great a political philosopher as Jean Bodin believed there to be witches in league with the devil.[3] Or the fact that so great a student of nature as Aristotle believed that bodies change quality whenever they change place.[4] Living in the twenty-first century, we are likely to feel – and unlikely to be able to repress the feeling – that these claims are simply false. But we are also likely to find our interest quickened by the discovery that such eminent authorities, capable of saying so many things that seem straightforwardly true, were also capable of entertaining such apparent absurdities. If we begin by focusing on such beliefs, we shall provide ourselves with a good starting-point for investigating the structure of Aristotle's or Bodin's thought. For here at least we come upon something that cries out to be explained. We shall also provide ourselves with a good means of ensuring that our eventual explanation takes a sympathetic and non-anachronistic form. For whatever account we provide will have to include an explanation of the fact that such admittedly bizarre beliefs nevertheless commended themselves to such unquestionably distinguished minds.[5]

At other points in his discussion Taylor seems to be asking a different question: whether the views that historians take about the truth-value of the beliefs they expound ought to affect the types of explanation they give of them.[6] My answer here is that this depends on what is meant by speaking about the truth-value of beliefs, a topic on which Taylor writes in a somewhat ambiguous way.

Sometimes the issue he raises is whether our explanations ought to vary – or are sure to vary – with our sense of whether the beliefs we investigate are 'true or valid in relation to the needs of the people who live under them'.[7] This question – seemingly inspired by the hermeneutics of Gadamer – appears to me to embody an unhelpfully wide, even a metaphorical, extension of the concept of a true belief. But if this is the issue on which historians are asked to pronounce, then my own answer would be that of course our explanations are bound to vary with whatever judgements we make about truth in this extended sense. If we encounter an ideology that we judge to be true to the needs of the society living under it, we are sure to treat that fact as part of our explanation for its success. If we come upon an ideology that seems demonstrably untrue

---

[3] Bodin 1595, p. 49. For a denunciation of Bodin for holding these beliefs see Anglo 1973. For a defence see Monter 1969 and for a full reconstruction of Bodin's demonology and its associated vision of politics see Clark 1997, pp. 668–82.

[4] For this formulation of Aristotle's belief see Kuhn 1977, p. xii.

[5] Kuhn 1977, pp. xi–xii.   [6] Taylor 1988, p. 213.   [7] See Taylor 1988, p. 223 and cf. p. 226.

in this extended sense, we shall certainly be obliged to explain its success in a very different way. (But unless we find that the society in question is on the point of dissolution, we are surely more likely to conclude that we cannot hope to explain such a phenomenon at all.)

At most points in his discussion, however, Taylor speaks about true beliefs in a more familiar and restricted way. When he asks whether historians should take account of the fact that a particular belief is true when seeking to explain it, what he generally seems to be asking is whether we should take account of the fact that the belief in question accords with our own best current beliefs about the matter at issue. I am not of course (nor is Taylor) offering this as a definition of truth. I am only observing that this is how we generally use the term.[8] (Though the moral of this, as Donald Davidson has suggested, is perhaps that we ought not to ask for a definition.)[9] I take it, accordingly, that the question with which Taylor is principally occupied is this: whether we as historians can or ought to avoid asking ourselves whether we endorse the beliefs we are seeking to explain.

Taylor himself maintains that it is undesirable and probably impossible to bracket truth in this way,[10] a conclusion that aligns him with a large number of Anglophone philosophers writing about the topic of social explanation.[11] Taylor himself remains deliberately tentative about this commitment,[12] but if we turn to some of these other philosophers we find two main reasons usually given for espousing it. One line of argument, stressed in particular by Graham Macdonald and Philip Pettit, derives from Donald Davidson's theory of radical interpretation.[13] The suggestion is that, unless we begin by assuming that the holding of true beliefs constitutes the norm among the peoples we study, we shall find ourselves unable to identify what they believe. If too many of their beliefs prove to be false, our capacity to give an account of the subject matter of those beliefs will begin to be undermined. Once this starts to happen, we shall find ourselves unable even to describe what we hope to explain. The implication, as Davidson himself puts it, is that 'if we want to understand others, we must count them right in most matters'.[14]

---

[8] For the suggestion that the moral of this is that we should adopt a pragmatic concern with solidarity at the expense of our traditional quest for objectivity see Rorty 1985.

[9] Davidson 1986.   [10] Taylor 1988, p. 220.

[11] See, for example, MacIntyre 1962, p. 62 (a passage cited with approval in Hollis 1972, p. 101); Jarvie 1970, esp. pp. 245–7; Lukes 1973, p. 247; Newton-Smith 1981, pp. 252–7; Macdonald and Pettit 1981, pp. 33–4; Graham 1981, pp. 173, 177; Shapiro 1982, pp. 556, 577; Hollis 1988.

[12] Taylor 1988, pp. 218, 220.

[13] Macdonald and Pettit 1981, pp. 186–7. For their application of Davidson's theory see esp. pp. 18–29.

[14] Davidson 1984, p. 197.

I cannot see that this view of radical interpretation possesses the relevance for historians that some of Davidson's more enthusiastic followers, such as Macdonald and Pettit, have supposed. Davidson is merely proposing a general strategy for using assertions to get at underlying beliefs, the strategy of beginning by assuming general agreement. It may well be that we need to start with some such assumption if we are to find another culture intelligible. If I am to identify the nature of Bodin's beliefs about witches, or even to establish that they are beliefs about that particular subject-matter, it certainly seems plausible to assume that Bodin and I must share a considerable number of ancillary beliefs. It is arguable, however, that Davidson has overemphasised the significance of this consideration and too comfortably ridiculed the notion of radically different conceptual schemes.[15] Certainly it does not follow that I need to assume that Bodin's beliefs specifically about witches are mainly true before I can be sure of identifying them as beliefs about witches. It may be that practically everything Bodin says about that particular topic strikes me as obviously false. But by learning his language (an easily recognisable form of French) and by seeing what concepts he uses and how he reasons with them, I can nevertheless hope to identify without much difficulty where he is talking about witches and what he thinks about them. It is true that, if I am to keep up with his arguments, it may be necessary for him to reassure me at various points that he is still talking about witches. As long as he continues to make it clear that this is so, however, there seems no reason to fear that I may suddenly feel obliged to conclude that he must be talking about something else, even if practically everything he is saying strikes me as patently absurd.[16]

I turn to the second reason often given for supposing that the issue of truth must never be bracketed. False beliefs, it is said, point to failures of reasoning, and failures of reasoning require additional explanations of a kind not needed in the case of true beliefs. This appears, for example, to be the thought underlying Keith Graham's contention that we shall be acting 'in a spirit of ill-judged humility' as historians if we fail to consider the points at which the social beliefs we investigate are 'flawed or inadequate'.[17] A similar thought underlies Steven Lukes's discussion of the special explanatory problems he takes to arise in connection with the need to 'identify the mechanisms that prevent men from seeing the falsity' of their beliefs.[18] The same commitment likewise emerges from

---

[15] A claim powerfully argued in Forster 1998.
[16] See McGinn 1977 and cf. Hacking 1982, esp. p. 60.
[17] Graham 1981, p. 177.   [18] Lukes 1973, p. 242.

Macdonald and Pettit's more extended analysis of the way in which judgements about truth and falsity are bound to enter into 'the kind of explanation one gives' of alien beliefs.[19] When a belief under investigation proves to be true, they assert, no further explanation is required. But when a belief is 'manifestly false' or 'obviously incorrect' there is something further to be explained. We need in particular to consider the kinds of 'social function or psychological pressure' that could have prevented the agent in question from recognising 'the mistaken nature of the belief'.[20]

If this is the argument on which historians are asked to take a stand, then my own response is a simple and emphatic one. It is I think nothing less than fatal to good historical practice to introduce the question of truth into social explanation in this way. To do so is to assume that, whenever an historian encounters a belief which he or she judges to be false, the explanatory problem must always be that of accounting for a lapse of rationality.[21] But this is to equate the holding of rational beliefs with the holding of beliefs that the historian judges to be true. And this is to exclude the obvious possibility that, even in the case of beliefs that nowadays strike us as manifestly false, there may have been good grounds in earlier historical periods for holding them to be true.

Having gestured at the concept of rationality, I ought to stress that I intend nothing very grand or precise by that much abused term.[22] When I speak of agents as having rational beliefs, I mean only that their beliefs (what they hold to be true) should be suitable beliefs for them to hold true in the circumstances in which they find themselves. A rational belief will thus be one that an agent has attained by some accredited process of reasoning. Such a process will in turn be one that, according to prevailing norms of epistemic rationality, may be said to give the agent good grounds for supposing (as opposed to merely desiring or hoping) that the belief in question is true.[23] A rational agent will thus be someone who, as David Lewis excellently summarises, believes what he or she ought to believe.[24]

---

[19] Macdonald and Pettit 1981, p. 34.   [20] Macdonald and Pettit 1981, pp. 9, 34, 42.

[21] For explicit statements to this effect see Lukes 1977, pp. 121, 132, 135.

[22] My attempt to construe the concept in an informal way is indebted to Putnam 1981, pp. 150–200.

[23] To speak of rationality simply in terms of having good reasons for our beliefs is to run the danger of eliding the distinction between epistemic and practical rationality. For examples of this elision see Laudan 1977, p. 123 and Stout 1981, pp. 165–6. It is true that the distinction is one that pragmatists bid us elide. See for example Rorty 1979, pp. 328–9. As I emphasise below, however, I do not see how historians can hope to operate satisfactorily without it. For a helpful analysis of the distinction itself see Mortimore and Maund 1976.

[24] Lewis 1974, p. 336.

None of this implies that rational agents need to hold any specific beliefs, save for those which may be indispensable to bare survival.[25] So this means in effect that a rational agent will be someone whose beliefs are held in the light of a certain attitude towards the process of belief formation itself. This attitude must certainly include an interest in consistency. Rational agents want their reasons for holding their beliefs to bear upon their truth. But to espouse a given belief as well as its contradictory is to hold at least one belief that must be false. A rational agent will thus be concerned, at least in seriously troubling cases, to identify and eliminate any such obvious inconsistencies. Above all, rational agents must be interested in the justification of their beliefs.[26] They must be concerned with the kinds of coherence, and where appropriate the kinds of evidence, that give them grounds for concluding that their affirmations of belief can in fact be justified. They will thus be concerned to view their own beliefs critically, to consider whether they really can be justified by considering the degree to which they may be said to fit with each other and with perceptual experience.

It seems difficult to go further. In particular, it seems positively erroneous to try to arrive at a single criterion, and hence a method, for discriminating rational beliefs. The relations between the ideal of rationality and the practices embodying it seem too complex and open-ended to be captured in the form of an algorithm.

It is true that recent epistemology has been much concerned to discover such procedures or sets of rules. Among positivist philosophers, this at first gave rise to the proposed test of verifiability. But this seems much too strict. Apart from other difficulties, it provides the historian with a potentially anachronistic – and in any case a far from perspicuous – notion of direct observational evidence as the basis for justifying beliefs. This in turn appears to overlook the fact that it may be rational to hold a given belief, even in the absence of any such evidence, as long as it can be plausibly inferred from other rationally held beliefs.[27] The enemies of positivism later proposed an alternative criterion, that of falsifiability. But this seems even less satisfactory. As I have suggested, it appears a minimal characterisation of rational agents to say that the reasons they give for their beliefs should be reasons for holding them to be true. But

---

[25] Putnam 1981, pp. 38–40 calls these 'directive' beliefs. But in spite of what some commentators have implied (for example, Macdonald and Pettit 1981, pp. 26–8), this class seems to me of vanishingly small significance from the point of view of the historian.

[26] See Putnam 1981, esp. pp. 54–6, 155–68 and cf. McCullagh 1984.

[27] Putnam 1981, pp. 105–13; Mortimore and Maund 1976, pp. 14–20.

on the one hand, the fact that a given hypothesis may have resisted attempts to falsify it scarcely gives us any grounds for supposing it to be true.[28] And on the other hand, the application of such a test has the effect of excluding as irrational a number of otherwise well-confirmed and well-justified beliefs.[29]

These remarks seem to me as much as it is appropriate to try to say about rationality in general terms. I now turn to explain why it seems to me fatal to satisfactory social explanations to exclude the possibility of holding a false belief in a wholly rational way. My reason is an obvious and familiar one. It is simply that the kinds of explanations we offer for beliefs we judge to be rationally held are of a different order from the kinds of explanations we feel obliged to offer if we come to doubt whether a given belief is held in a rational way. To equate the holding of false beliefs with lapses of rationality is thus to foreclose, in advance of knowing whether this is appropriate, on one type of explanation at the expense of another.

This is not to claim, as some philosophers have done, that rational belief is its own explanation.[30] This thesis has been vigorously espoused by Martin Hollis and others, but one obvious problem with this approach is that it overlooks the gap between demonstrating the rationality of a belief and explaining why it was held. Even if we can show that it was rational for some particular historical actor to espouse a certain belief, the explanation of why he or she espoused it may always be independent of that fact.[31] Hollis's formulation also conveys the impression that, once a given belief is exhibited as rational, there will be nothing further to explain. It is certainly true that we find the phenomenon of rational belief less puzzling than blatant lapses from rationality. But therein lies the danger. For it remains true that the attainment of rationality will always be an achievement. So an enquiry into the conditions that enable us to attain that state will never be any the less legitimate, and may in some cases be no less necessary, than an enquiry into the conditions that may prevent us from attaining it.

To say all this is not to claim – as Martin Hollis, Alasdair MacIntyre and others have done – that the forms of explanation appropriate to rational and irrational belief must differ because 'rational belief cannot

---

[28] For this point see Stove 1982.

[29] This claim has often been made in relation to both Freud's and Darwin's theories. See Putnam 1981, esp. pp. 196–200. For a restatement see Lakatos 1978, esp. pp. 8–101.

[30] See, for example, Hollis 1974; Hollis 1988, pp. 140, 144.

[31] I urge this objection against Hollis in Skinner 1978a, pp. 61–3. See also Elster 1982.

be explained in causal terms'.[32] I see no reason to doubt that, if there is a sufficient reason for an agent to accept a given belief, that reason may function as a cause of its acceptance. I agree, that is, with the proponents of the so-called 'strong programme' that it seems appropriate to adopt what David Bloor has called a requirement of impartiality in the explanation of beliefs, a requirement that they should all be approached and explained in the same causal terms.[33] But I see no reason to add, as the exponents of the strong programme have done, that this requirement is incompatible with making judgements about rationality.[34] To insist on the relevance of such judgements is not to deny that we ought to be looking for causal explanations of the capacity to achieve rationality no less than of failures to achieve it.

When I insist on the need to ask whether a given belief is or is not rational as a preliminary to explaining it, my reason is rather that the different cases raise explanatory puzzles of different kinds. Even if we assume that our explanations will in each case be causal in form, the causes of someone's following what are taken to be the relevant norms of reasoning will nevertheless be of a different order from the causes of their violating them. It follows that, unless we begin by enquiring into the rationality of the belief concerned, we cannot be sure of correctly identifying what it is that needs explaining, nor in consequence of directing our investigations along appropriate lines. If the belief proves to be one that it was rational for the agent to have held, we shall need to investigate the conditions of that achievement. If it was less than rational or palpably absurd to have held it, we shall need to enquire into the very different sorts of conditions that may have inhibited or prevented the agent from following accepted canons of evidence and argument, or perhaps supplied the agent with a motive for defying them.[35]

To reject this line of argument, as the advocates of the strong programme have done, it is necessary to insist not merely on a requirement of impartiality in the explanation of beliefs, but also on what David Bloor has called a requirement of symmetry.[36] This further principle, as Barry Barnes expounds it, requires that we reject any contention to the effect that one belief can be stigmatized as more 'ideological' than another

<hr>

[32] See MacIntyre 1971, pp. 255, 246–7 and cf. Hollis 1988, esp. pp. 140, 145. See also Hollis 1982, esp. pp. 80, 85 for the distinction between 'rational' and 'structural' explanations of belief.

[33] Bloor 1976, p. 5. See also Barnes 1974, p. 43; Barnes and Bloor 1982, p. 23.

[34] See, for example, Barnes and Bloor 1982, p. 25.

[35] Laudan 1977, pp. 188–9; Stout 1981, pp. 170–1; Newton-Smith 1981, pp. 253–7. But for a critique of my attempt to turn the concept of rationality into a tool for historians see Bartelson 1995.

[36] Bloor 1976, p. 5.

in consequence of being in some way 'unsatisfactory' or insufficiently grounded.[37] We have to recognise that all our beliefs are socially caused in such a way that, to some degree, their objects remain masked from us. It follows that all of them must be approached and explained in one and the same way.

If this is nothing more than a stipulation about how we ought to use the term 'ideological', then perhaps it will do no harm. But if it is a proposal about how historians ought to set about the business of explaining beliefs, then it seems to me fatal for just the reasons I have sought to give. It refuses to recognise that one of the reasons why someone may hold a certain belief is that there is good evidence in favour of it, that it fits well with their other beliefs, and so on – in a word, that it is rational for them to hold it. If we refuse to speak in these terms, we deprive ourselves of an indispensable means of identifying the most appropriate lines of enquiry to follow in any given case.

It may be helpful to offer an illustration of what I mean by speaking of the fatal consequences of failing to ask in this way about the rationality of beliefs. Consider the influential explanation of witchcraft beliefs offered by Emmanuel Le Roy Ladurie in his classic study, *The Peasants of Languedoc*.[38] Ladurie starts by stressing that such beliefs were of course manifestly false, a mere product of 'mass delirium'.[39] He proceeds to infer that they could never have been rationally held. As he explicitly asserts, those who espoused them were simply 'slipping savagely into the irrational in belief and behaviour'.[40] The effect of this commitment is to direct Ladurie's attention as an historian in one particular way. He assumes that what he must be looking for is an explanation for a breakdown in normal reasoning, a situation in which 'the peasant consciousness suddenly broke loose from its moorings'.[41] The question, as he puts it, is how to account for such an upsurge of obscurantism, such an epidemic of pathological beliefs.[42]

One element in Ladurie's answer is that, with the progress of the Reformation, the peasantry began to fear a loss of their traditional spiritual help. 'Far from their priests, the peasants found themselves alone with

---

[37] Barnes 1974, pp. 43, 128–30.

[38] For the suggestion that the study of witchcraft beliefs offers a good illustration of the role played by rationality postulates in historical study I remain much indebted to MacIntyre 1971, pp. 244–59. For a full account of the specific example I discuss see James 1984, pp. 166–71, an analysis to which I am also much indebted.

[39] Ladurie 1974, pp. 203–5. For a full discussion see James 1984, pp. 166–71.

[40] Ladurie 1974, p. 210.   [41] Ladurie 1974, p. 208.

[42] Ladurie 1974, pp. 203–4, 206–7. Cohn 1976, p. 258 makes similar claims about witchcraft beliefs as a 'collective fantasy'.

their anxieties and their primordial fears – and abandoned themselves to Satan.'[43] But Ladurie's principal hypothesis is that they felt a deep sense of frustration at the collapse of the social upheavals associated with the Reformation itself. With the failure of social reform, their continuing desire to improve their lot took on a 'mythical dress', and was forced to express itself in the 'chimerical and fantastic revolt of the witches' Sabbath, an attempt at demonic forms of escape'.[44]

I am not concerned with Ladurie's actual explanations, although it hardly seems an incidental consequence of his approach that they turn out to be so dizzyingly speculative.[45] I am solely concerned with the fact that, by treating it as self-evident that a certain set of beliefs could never be rationally held, Ladurie leaves himself no space to consider a quite different sort of explanation.[46] He cannot allow that the peasants may have believed in the existence of witches as a result of holding a number of other beliefs from which that particular conclusion might reasonably have been held to follow.

To consider only the simplest possibility, suppose that the peasants also held the belief – widely accepted as rational and indeed indubitable in sixteenth-century Europe – that the Bible constituted the directly inspired word of God. If this was indeed one of their beliefs, and if it was rational for them to hold it, then it would have been the height of irrationality for them to have disbelieved in the existence of witches. For the Bible not only affirms that witches exist, but adds that witchcraft is an abomination and that witches must not be suffered to live.[47] To announce one's disbelief in the existence of witches would thus have been to announce a doubt about the credibility of God's word. What could have been more dangerously irrational than that?

Ladurie excludes in advance the possibility that those who believed in witches may have done so as a result of following out some such recognisable chain of reasoning. But this not only means that he puts forward an explanation of witchcraft beliefs which, for all he knows, may be completely irrelevant. It also means that he bypasses a range of questions about the mental world of the peasants which it may be indispensable to answer if their beliefs and behaviour are to be satisfactorily understood.[48]

---

[43] Ladurie 1974, p. 207.   [44] Ladurie 1974, p. 203.

[45] As Clark 1997, pp. 25–6 observes, they also require Ladurie to make even less plausible claims about what was going on in the minds of individual witches.

[46] The type of explanation explored in Clark 1997.

[47] See, respectively, Deuteronomy 13.10–12; Galatians 5.20; Exodus 22.18.

[48] For two classic studies in which the mental world of witchcraft beliefs is sympathetically recovered see Thomas 1971, pp. 435–583 and Clark 1997.

A common objection to the above line of argument has been that it presupposes an excessively objectivist conception of rationality. Disciples of the later Wittgenstein such as Peter Winch, as well as exponents of the strong programme such as Barry Barnes and David Bloor, have all converged on this point. As Barry Barnes puts it, echoing and endorsing Peter Winch's case, to claim that we can assess and criticise the rationality of beliefs is to presuppose 'external standards' of rationality of an 'objective' kind.[49] But we have no access to any such 'super-cultural norm', and in consequence no prospect of being able to 'discriminate existing belief-systems or their components into rational and irrational groups'.[50] The very idea of assessing the rationality of beliefs is thus dismissed as nothing better than an intrusion, a forcible imposition of our own epistemic standards on an alien 'universe of discourse' or 'form of life'.

This objection is I think totally misconceived. But my reason for saying so is not that I imagine – as Martin Hollis does – that we can hope to vindicate a substantial and objective conception of reason and employ it in the assessment of beliefs.[51] It is rather that the abandonment of any such project does not preclude the idea of assessing beliefs for their rationality. If an historian stigmatises the upholding of a particular belief within a particular society as irrational, this judgement need never flow from the application of an allegedly objective conception of what can or cannot properly count as rationality. The historian need only be claiming that he or she has uncovered the prevailing norms for the acquisition and justification of beliefs in that particular society, and that the belief in question appears to have been upheld in the face of, rather than in the light of, those norms themselves. The historian need only be claiming that the agent in question fell short of – or perhaps abandoned, manipulated or in some other way deliberately defied – some generally accepted standard of epistemic rationality.

If historians were to adopt this approach, they would be engaging in the assessment of beliefs in just the manner I have recommended. But at no point would they be applying an 'external' standard of rationality in an 'intrusive' way. They would not be asking themselves whether the belief in question was rational according to their own standards (still less *the* standards) of epistemic rationality. They would merely be reporting that

---

[49] Barnes 1974, pp. 69–70, 130. Cf. Winch 1970. But Lear 1982 shows that Wittgenstein's argument cannot be assimilated to that of the sceptical relativist.

[50] See Barnes and Bloor 1982, p. 27 and cf. Barnes 1974, p. 41.

[51] See Hollis 1988, pp. 141–2 and his earlier discussion of 'objectively rational' beliefs in Hollis 1982, esp. p. 72. See also Laudan 1977 and the discussion of his position in Newton-Smith 1981, esp. pp. 245–7, 270–3.

it was not an appropriate belief for that particular agent to have espoused in that particular society at that particular time.

It might seem that this conclusion is bound to deprive the concept of rationality of any explanatory power. This is certainly the inference drawn by Richard Rorty, who assumes that once we give up the idea of rationality as a concept 'floating free of the educational and institutional patterns of the day', we shall have to admit that we cannot hope to employ the notion in the assessment or explanation of beliefs.[52] We shall find that practically everyone is capable of putting their desires and opinions together in such a way as to satisfy a pragmatist test of rationality. So the idea of asking whether it was in fact rational for them to hold their resulting beliefs becomes devoid of content and hence of explanatory force.[53]

A number of intellectual historians have recently endorsed the same viewpoint. Once we discover the inner coherence of a given system of beliefs, they maintain, we can hardly fail to count it rational for the system to have been upheld.[54] So the project of assessing the rationality of individual beliefs again drops out of sight. 'If ways of thinking are recreated sympathetically, then one never refutes but always sustains' whatever beliefs are identified.[55]

I concede that accusations of irrationality must only be hurled in the last ditch, if at all. We need to begin by recreating as sympathetically as possible a sense of what was held to connect with what, and what was held to count as a reason for what, among the peoples we are studying as historians. Otherwise we are sure to commit the characteristic sin of 'whig' intellectual history: that of imputing incoherence or irrationality where we have merely failed to identify some local canon of rational acceptability. I cannot see, however, why it should be supposed to follow that our interpretative charity must always be boundless. On the contrary, there may be many cases in which, if we are to identify what needs to be explained, it may be crucial to insist, of a given belief, that it was less than rational for a given agent to have upheld it.

As an illustration of what I have in mind, consider one of the beliefs fundamental to early-modern political philosophy, the belief that the quality of *virtù* is indispensable to military and political success. It was owing to the loss of this quality, Machiavelli particularly insists, that the Florentines of his own age became so disastrously incapable of defending themselves. In his early writings Machiavelli merely asserts this belief, but

---

[52] Rorty 1979, p. 331.   [53] See Rorty 1979, p. 174 and cf. Rorty 1983, esp. pp. 585–6.
[54] See, for example, Clark 1980, esp. p. 100.
[55] See Greenleaf 1972a, p. 28 and cf. Greenleaf 1972b, p. 140.

in the course of his *Istorie Fiorentine* he goes on to support it with some impressive examples. Describing the battle of Anghiari, for instance, he notes that in four hours of combat only a single soldier was killed.[56] Describing the even more farcical battle of Molinella, he adds that in the course of half a day's fighting there were no fatalities at all.[57] By focusing on these and similar cases, he builds up his evidence for saying that his fellow-countrymen were abjectly lacking in the kind of *virtù* they needed in order to preserve their liberty.

If we turn to Machiavelli's sources, however, we find that they hardly support these conclusions at all. What they suggest is that a total of seventy soldiers were killed and 600 wounded at Anghiari, while at Molinella there was fierce fighting and several hundred fatalities.[58] If we turn, moreover, to later sixteenth-century discussions of the *Istorie Fiorentine*, we find a number of Machiavelli's younger contemporaries complaining about his attitude towards his evidence. Scipio Ammirato, for example, insists that Machiavelli gives no adequate grounds for his conclusions; instead he changes names and alters evidence in such a way as to make his authorities say whatever he already wants us to believe.[59]

It is true that a sufficiently charitable historian could easily rescue Machiavelli at this point. Machiavelli fervently believed that the quality of *virtù* had been lost in the modern world, and he was not without strong grounds for this belief. He also believed that a willingness to behave courageously was one of the most obvious characteristics of a *virtuoso* people. But this means that he could hardly fail to conclude that his fellow-countrymen were lacking in courage. Nor could he readily interpret their military conduct except in terms of their axiomatic lack of this *virtuoso* quality.

As his own contemporaries insisted, however, Machiavelli was only able to maintain this particular article of faith at an extravagantly high cost. He was obliged to falsify the relevant authorities, and in consequence fell rather grievously short of the standards recognised by his own peers for the assessment of evidence and the justification of beliefs. As a number of them rightly observed, the outcome was a commitment which it was not appropriate for Machiavelli to uphold, or at least not in the unequivocal form in which he always upheld it. To put the point in the jargon I have been using, it was not a rational belief.

---

[56] Machiavelli 1962, V. 33, p. 383.   [57] Machiavelli 1962, VII. 20, p. 484.

[58] For these details, and for a discussion of contemporary sources (especially Biondo, Capponi and Poggio), see Villari 1892, vol. 2, pp. 452, 458–9.

[59] Ammirato 1846–9, Bk. 23, ch. 5, p. 169. For a discussion see Anglo 1969, pp. 185, 258.

I have already emphasised why it matters to be able to make such judgements. As soon as we permit ourselves such an uncharitable conclusion, we confront a new set of questions about Machiavelli's beliefs, a set of questions we had no occasion to ask or even to notice as long as we felt able to assume their rationality. Why is he so excessively insistent on the military incompetence of his fellow-countrymen? Is he nursing some private grievance? Or is he merely nostalgic for the bygone days of citizen militias? Or is he unduly influenced by the classical assumption that such forces are alone capable of displaying courage? These questions in turn suggest to the historian some wider ones. Should we be looking for a strongly emotional component in others of Machiavelli's political beliefs? Should we think of him as habitually credulous in his response to the political writings of ancient Rome? Only by enquiring into the rationality of his beliefs can we hope to recognise the range of explanatory puzzles they actually pose.

III

The above argument in response to Charles Taylor and the other Anglophone philosophers I have cited can in turn be expressed in the form of a set of maxims for historians concerned with the description and explanation of beliefs. The golden rule is that, however bizarre the beliefs we are studying may seem to be, we must begin by trying to make the agents who accepted them appear as rational as possible.[60]

This golden rule in effect embodies three precepts. The first merely states a condition *sine qua non* of the whole enterprise. We need to assume what David Lewis has called a convention of truthfulness among the peoples whose beliefs we are seeking to explain.[61] Our first task is obviously to identify what they believe. But our only evidence of their beliefs will normally be contained in whatever texts and other utterances they may happen to have left behind. It is of course likely that some of these may be pervasively marked by hidden codes such as irony. But we have no option but to assume that, in general, they can be treated as relatively straightforward expressions of belief. Unless we can assume some such convention of truthfulness, we cannot hope to make any headway with the project of explaining what they believed.

The second and closely connected precept states that we must initially be prepared to take whatever is said, however bizarre it may seem, as far

---

[60] Hollis 1970a, p. 219. See also the discussion in Skorupski 1978, pp. 88–9.
[61] Lewis 1969, pp. 148–52.

as possible at face value. If the people we are studying assert that there are witches in league with the devil, we must begin by assuming that this is exactly what they believe. This will not only serve to keep before us the precise character of our explanatory task; it will also enable us to steer clear of a familiar but condescending form of interpretative charity. It will prevent us from purportedly rescuing the rationality of the people we are studying by way of suggesting that, whenever they say something that strikes us as grossly absurd, it will be best to assume that the speech act they were performing must have been something other than that of stating or affirming a belief.

There have been two widespread applications of this principle. One of them, essentially Durkheimian in inspiration, suggests that we ought rather to assume that such statements express in symbolic form a proposition about the structure of the speaker's society and his or her commitment to upholding it. This version was until recently popular with a certain school of social anthropologists, as the writings of Beattie, Leach and others attest.[62] The second application, more Freudian in inspiration, suggests that we ought instead to assume that such statements express in a displaced or distorted form some deep and unacknowledged feelings such as frustration or anxiety. It is this version of the principle we have already encountered in Ladurie's explanation of witchcraft beliefs.

The obvious difficulty with the principle in either form is that the only criterion we are offered for distinguishing those propositions we are to take literally from those we are to take symbolically is our own cognitive discomfort. If we find it too embarrassing to take what is said literally, we are in effect instructed to take it instead as a symbolic or displaced way of saying something else. To reject this approach is not of course to deny that beliefs may perform a crucial role in expressing a society's view of itself, its unacknowledged fears, its aspirations, its sense of solidarity. Nor is it to deny that the Freudian approach in particular may be able to furnish us with indispensable insights, unavailable to the agents themselves, into why they may have held (and held on to) their particular beliefs. It is only to assert that we shall be assuming what has to be established if we take it that we can move directly to such forms of causal explanation in advance of asking whether the agents in question may not in addition have had good reasons, by their lights, for holding what they believed to be true.

---

[62] But for excellent criticisms see Hollis 1970b, esp. p. 226; Skorupski 1978, pp. 85–6; Macdonald and Pettit 1981, p. 15 and note. See also the general discussion, to which I am much indebted, in Papineau 1978, pp. 132–58.

The third precept states the positive task to which we commit ourselves as historians by virtue of this approach. We must seek to surround the particular statement of belief in which we are interested with an intellectual context that serves to lend adequate support to it. As we have seen, this commits us to something more than trying to establish that the people we are studying may have had good practical reasons for saying what they said. It commits us to trying to establish that their utterances were not merely the outcome of a rational policy, but were also consistent with their sense of epistemic rationality. The primary task must therefore be that of trying to recover a very precise context of presuppositions and other beliefs, a context that serves to exhibit the utterance in which we are interested as one that it was rational for that particular agent, in those particular circumstances, to have held to be true. As one recent commentator has proposed, the task might thus be characterised as 'archaeo-historicist' in character.[63]

We cannot know in advance what range of beliefs this may require us to excavate. So my proposal stands in contrast with one that has often been put forward in particular by historians of science. They have sometimes argued that, as Mary Hesse has put it, we ought to concentrate on studying 'the received internal tradition' of scientific discovery, and hence on deepening our knowledge of the established canon of major scientists, rather than trying to 'spell out in tedious detail every minor writing or trivial biography of forgotten figures'.[64]

In criticising this approach I am not questioning the appropriateness of concentrating on the received tradition of discovery if that is what historians of science happen to find most interesting. Rather I take it that, as I have already emphasised in chapter 2, all worthwhile forms of history are bound to be whiggish in this sense. The problems on which historians feel it worth expending their energies will be certain to reflect their own sense of intellectual priorities. It would be strange indeed if they were to conduct their researches according to a set of priorities they themselves felt to be mistaken. I am only insisting that, once we recognise that an understanding even of a received canon of major figures requires us to surround them with whatever intellectual context makes best sense of them, we cannot afford to be too quick about dismissing any feature of that context as tedious or irrelevant. To an historian of science, the details of the Anglican Church hierarchy in Sir Isaac Newton's time may very probably appear in that light. But it may well be that for Newton

---

[63] See Hume 1999, pp. 61–71 for an analysis of 'reconstructing contexts' in this way.
[64] See Hesse 1970a, p. 149 and cf. Hesse 1973.

the isomorphism between such hierarchies and those he found in the heavens gave him good reason, by his lights, for believing in the truth of his celestial mechanics. To dismiss the first as a 'religious' belief, with no relevance for Newton's scientific studies, may well be to impose such a deeply anachronistic view of how to divide up the world, and of what can count as a reason for what, as to close off the possibility of understanding Newton's most obviously 'scientific' achievements. Any impatience with what we think of as irrelevance or triviality may cheat us of just the historical understanding we seek.[65]

Philosophers sympathetic to this approach, such as Richard Rorty, are apt to insist that we can hope to state it a good deal more briskly than I have managed. What it amounts to, they assure us in Wittgensteinian style, is simply that we need to get into the swing of whatever exotic language-games are being played by the people whose beliefs we are trying to describe and explain.[66] This seems true but unhelpful. We surely need to ask about the most suitable strategy for breaking in upon such unfamiliar activities and forms of life. How in practice ought we to proceed?

As a first step, it will perhaps be best to recall that statements of belief rarely present themselves individually to the historian with evidence conveniently attached. As I have observed, the question of what it is rational to believe depends in part on what else we believe. Any particular belief in which an historian is interested will therefore be likely to present itself holistically as part of a network of beliefs, a network within which the various individual items supply each other with mutual support. As I have already implied, it follows that if an historian wishes, say, to discover whether it was rational for Jean Bodin to have believed in demonic possession, the soundest course of action will be to begin by asking whether Bodin held any other beliefs in the light of which this admittedly bizarre commitment might in some way have appeared to make good sense.[67]

Some philosophers – I am again thinking particularly of Martin Hollis – have objected that it will only be rational to hold such a belief if it was in turn rational to hold the core beliefs from which this specific item is said to follow.[68] But this image of a rational bedrock strikes me as confused. What does it mean for a purportedly core belief to be rationally held? On the one hand, it can hardly mean that we are capable of

---

[65] See Jacob 1976 and cf. Jacob and Jacob 1980.   [66] Rorty 1979, p. 267.

[67] The classic statement of this kind of holism remains the concluding sections of Quine 1961, esp. pp. 37–46. But even Quine seems to me too inclined to employ the metaphor of core and periphery.

[68] Hollis 1982, pp. 75, 83–4.

giving good reasons for holding it. For in that case it would be a derivative rather than a core belief. But on the other hand, I cannot see – as I have already conceded – what else it can mean to describe a belief as being held in a rational way. I cannot see, in short, that Hollis's proposal can be deployed in such a way as to set limits to the kind of holism I am trying to expound. Even in the most primitive perceptual cases, even in the face of the clearest observational evidence, it will always be reckless to assert that there are any beliefs we are certain to form, any judgements we are bound to make, simply as a consequence of inspecting the allegedly brute facts. The beliefs we form, the judgements we make, will always by mediated by the concepts available to us for describing what we have observed.[69] But to employ a concept is always to appraise and classify our experience from a particular perspective and in a particular way. What we experience and report will accordingly be what is brought to our attention by the range of concepts we possess and the nature of the discriminations they enable us to make. We cannot hope to find any less winding a path from experience to belief, from observational evidence to any one determinate judgement.[70]

To contentions such as these, Hollis has repeatedly retorted that, at least in the case of 'simple everyday beliefs', the historian or ethnographer 'needs to discover' that the people he or she is studying have 'common perceptions, common ways of referring to things perceived and a common notion of empirical truth'.[71] If history and ethnography are to be possible, he maintains, there must be a firm bridgehead of shared experiences which are conceptualised in an invariant way. He infers that there must be some corresponding terms in any language for the expression of these bridgehead concepts, and he roundly advises the historian or ethnographer to set about finding and translating them.[72]

Quite apart from the fact that Hollis's principle does not tell us where to look, it strikes me as a serious misconception to suppose that we can ever hope, even in 'simple perceptual situations', to isolate and describe 'what a rational man cannot fail to believe'.[73] Even the simplest action or event can be fitted into a variety of more or less complex classificatory schemes, and can in consequence be labelled in an indefinite variety

---

[69] For the claim that any disposition to think of a world of neutral materials awaiting conceptualisation amounts to a third dogma of empiricism see Rorty 1972.

[70] For an influential source of this line of argument see Hesse 1970b and Hesse 1974, esp. pp. 9–73. Hesse's arguments are invoked and developed in Barnes 1974, esp. p. 16; in Barnes and Bloor 1982, pp. 37–9; and in Papineau 1978, esp. pp. 134–8.

[71] Hollis 1970b, pp. 228, 230–1.   [72] See Hollis 1970a, p. 216 and Hollis 1970b, p. 229.

[73] Hollis 1982, p. 74.

of ways. Consider, for example, a report of the simplest possible kind of 'perceptual situation': a report, say, to the effect that it is raining.[74] When ancient Romans stated and shared this belief, they used the word *imber*, this being the only term available in classical Latin to denote a fall or shower of rain. This means that, if an ancient Roman and a modern Briton were to find themselves standing damply together, there might be many instances in which, faced with exactly the same evidence, they might arrive at conflicting statements of belief. If the Roman were to report that they were experiencing an *imber*, and if the Briton were to take this to mean a fall or shower of rain, the latter might actually dispute the judgement. The Briton might wish to insist, say, that they were enduring nothing worse than the faintest drizzle.

This is not of course to deny the obvious fact that in some sense the Roman and the Briton must be experiencing and talking about the same event. It is only to insist that, whenever we report our beliefs, we inevitably employ some particular classificatory scheme; and that, as Thomas Kuhn has especially emphasised, the fact that different schemes divide the world up in different ways means that none of them can ever be uncontentiously employed to report indisputable facts.[75] This is not to deny that there are facts to be reported. It is only to insist – *pace* Hollis's insistence that there must be 'a bridgehead of true assertions about a shared reality'[76] – that the concepts we employ to report the facts will always serve at the same time to help determine what are to count as facts. Is it or is it not raining? There will be instances in which the Roman says *yes* while the Briton says *not really*.

It follows that we cannot hope to make the distinction – which Ian Shapiro has urged me to make in his critique of my own work – between those concepts which mask and those which truly reveal 'what is actually going on' in the social world.[77] This is to presuppose that our social world contains unequivocal objects and states of affairs that any adequate system of signs can hope to pick out in such a way that no sensitive observer can fail to see what is actually going on. But it is precisely this presupposition which, it seems to me, needs to be questioned. Rather we need to recognise that any system of signs will serve to single out just those objects and states of affairs which it in turn enables us to denote,

---

[74] My example is adapted from the discussion in Papineau 1978, pp. 135–6.

[75] Kuhn 1962, esp. pp. 43–51, 110–34.

[76] See Hollis 1970a, p. 216, and cf. the even stronger stress on 'the independence of facts' in Hollis 1982, p. 83.

[77] Shapiro 1982, p. 556.

while other systems will always be capable of performing that task in different and potentially conflicting ways.

To advance these claims is to argue that our concepts are not forced upon us by the world, but represent what we bring to the world in order to understand it. To embrace this conclusion may appear to be embracing a thesis of Idealism. But this is not so. I do not mean to deny the existence of a mind-independent world that furnishes us with observational evidence as the basis of our empirical beliefs. I am only arguing that, as Hilary Putnam has put it, there can be no observational evidence which is not to some degree shaped by our concepts and thus by the vocabulary we use to express them.[78]

As I have noted, however, Hollis's principal objection – and that of many other Anglophone philosophers[79] – to this line of argument has been to say that it renders the task of the historian or ethnographer impossible.[80] Hollis's main contention is that, if we cannot 'pair' the terms used by alien peoples with 'counterparts' in our own language, then we cannot embark on the task of translating their utterances.[81] But if we cannot be sure how to translate what they say, we can never hope to identify what they believe.[82] For Hollis, as for many other philosophers of social science, translatability is thus taken to be a condition of intelligibility, with the result that the main issue is held to be that of establishing how translation is possible.[83]

Sometimes this thesis has been stated in a form that makes it seem straightforwardly false. John Gunnell, for example, contends that 'to learn a new language is only possible because one already knows a language'.[84] If this were true, no infant would ever be able to master its own mother tongue. But even in the form in which Hollis and others have defended it – as a thesis about the need to be able to pair basic terms of alien languages with equivalents in our own – the claim that intelligibility presupposes translatability is surely mistaken. Often there will be no prospect of translating terms in an alien language by means of anything approaching counterparts in our own. But this does not prevent us from learning the use of such alien terms, and in consequence finding out

[78] Putnam 1981, p. 54.

[79] See, for example, Turner 1983, esp. pp. 283–4; Keane 1988, p. 210. But for a valuable corrective see Jones 1977 and (with specific reference to my own work) Jones 1981.

[80] See Hollis 1970a, p. 216 and cf. Hollis 1970b, p. 222.   [81] Hollis 1970a, p. 215.

[82] See Hollis 1970a, p. 215 and cf. Hollis 1982, p. 74.

[83] On this assumption see also Hawthorn 1979, esp. p. 477; Dunn 1980, esp. p. 96; Macdonald and Pettit 1981, esp. p. 45.

[84] Gunnell 1979, p. 111.

what discriminations they are employed to make. If we can do this, we can eventually hope to understand the applications even of those terms which remain wholly resistant to translation. It is true that we can never hope to tell someone what those terms 'mean' by citing synonyms in our own language. The fact that translation is to this degree indeterminate seems inescapable. But the moral of this, as Quine long ago taught, is perhaps that we ought to give up the quest for 'meanings' in such an atomistic sense.[85]

It is perhaps needless to add that I am not pleading for historians to re-enact or re-create the experience of being sixteenth-century demonologists or peasants of Languedoc or any other such alien creatures.[86] I am only pleading for the historical task to be conceived as that of trying so far as possible to think as our ancestors thought and to see things their way. What this requires is that we should recover the concepts they possessed, the distinctions they drew and the chains of reasoning they followed in their attempts to make sense of their world. What I cannot see is why this should be thought to require us to map their distinctions and the terms they used for expressing them on to the very different distinctions and expressions we happen to use ourselves. Historical understanding is a product of learning to follow what Ian Hacking has called different styles of reasoning; it is not necessarily a matter of being able to translate those styles into more familiar ones.[87]

Donald Davidson has notoriously retorted that the resources of existing natural languages seem perfectly adequate for dealing with even the most dramatic cases of purported incommensurability reported by writers like Benjamin Whorf and Thomas Kuhn.[88] But Davidson's argument seems questionable in itself, relying as it does on such a strict application of the verification principle in order to rule out the idea of alternative conceptual schemes.[89] Furthermore, Davidson's scepticism is insufficient to undermine the sense in which I am defending anything resembling a thesis of incommensurability. I am merely contending that it will always be a mistake for an historian to assume that the task of explicating an alien concept can be reduced to that of finding a counterpart in his or her own language for the term that expresses it.

---

[85] Quine 1960, pp. 206–9.

[86] For an excellent account of why this aspiration is beside the point see Geertz 1983, pp. 55–70. Cf. also Inglis 2000, pp. 107–32.

[87] See the valuable remarks in Hacking 1982, pp. 59–61 and in Geertz 1983, pp. 58, 68–70.

[88] For this attempted deflation see in particular Davidson 1984.

[89] For a development of this criticism see Blackburn 1984, esp. pp. 60–2 and for a powerful critique of the argument in Davidson 1984 see Forster 1998, esp. pp. 141–6.

This still strikes me, however, as a methodological precept of considerable importance. To illustrate why this is so, let me revert to the example I have already considered from early-modern political philosophy: that of the concept of *virtù* as employed by Machiavelli and his contemporaries. Seeking a translation for this term, Anglophone historians have generally begun by observing that, even in Machiavelli's writings, persons of courage and prudence are often described as *virtuosi*. This leads to the conclusion that Machiavelli 'sometimes uses *virtù* in a traditional Christian sense'.[90] But Machiavelli also describes a number of talented but wicked leaders as *virtuosi*. This leads to the suggestion that perhaps the term has in addition 'a different meaning', signifying skill or ability in political or military affairs.[91] As further anomalous usages are uncovered, however, commentators generally come to the conclusion that the term appears to have no determinate meaning at all. Rather it bears 'a wide variety of meanings in the writings of Machiavelli', who uses it 'in a great variety of senses'.[92]

As the example indicates, such Anglophone historians have taken the task of understanding the concept of *virtù* to be that of explicating its 'meanings' by discovering their counterparts in modern English. But the example also illustrates, I hope, what is wrong with this approach. One outcome is that a different and far more promising line of enquiry is automatically closed off. The historian cannot consider the possibility that Machiavelli may have been using the term with perfect consistency to express a concept so alien to our own moral thought that we cannot nowadays hope to capture it except in the form of an extended and rather approximate periphrasis. Perhaps, for example, he used the term if and only if he wished to refer to just those qualities, whether moral or otherwise, that he took to be most conducive to military and political success. (As far as I can see, this is generally the case.) A further and consequential outcome is that a genuinely whig fallacy is almost automatically perpetrated. Such Anglophone historians begin with the assumption that, if Machiavelli's use of the term *virtù* refers to a clear concept, there must be some equivalent term in modern English for expressing it. But they quickly find themselves disappointed in their quest. As a result, it is all too easy to arrive at the completely unwarranted conclusion that Machiavelli must have been confused, since he appears (as one expert has put it) to be 'innocent of any systematic use of the word'.[93]

---

[90] Price 1973, pp. 316–17.   [91] Price 1973, p. 319.
[92] Price 1973, pp. 315, 344.   [93] Whitfield 1947, p. 105.

It would be easy to multiply examples. (Consider, for instance, the many 'confusions' that historians of philosophy have found in discussions about causation prior to Hume.) But I hope that the general point needs no further emphasis. A term such as *virtù* gains its 'meaning' from its place within an extensive network of beliefs, the filiations of which must be fully traced if the place of any one element within the structure is to be properly understood.[94] Doubtless we can only hope to embark on such a task if there is some considerable overlap between our beliefs and the beliefs of those whom we are trying to investigate. But this overlap may nevertheless be far too exiguous to allow for anything approaching term-by-term translations of the concepts involved. To suppose otherwise is not merely a philosophical error but one that leads to just the deleterious practical consequences I have tried to illustrate.

Having arrived at this position, it is possible to suggest an answer to a further and closely connected question that practising historians as well as philosophers of history have repeatedly raised.[95] As Charles Taylor puts it in the essay I began by discussing, the question is whether we are ever justified in revising the language of the peoples we are studying in such a way as to bring our descriptions into conflict with those they offered themselves.[96] Can we ascribe to past thinkers concepts they had no linguistic means to express?[97]

There is one way in which it will obviously be legitimate to go beyond, even if not to contest, the stock of descriptions available to the peoples studied by ethnographers and historians. This will be if we wish not merely to identify what they believed but to comment on the place of those beliefs within some larger historical pattern or narrative. Arthur Danto in particular has emphasised the asymmetries that are bound to result.[98] When, for example, Edward Gibbon remarked that Boethius was the last Roman who would have been recognisable as such by Cicero, he offered a comment on Boethius's beliefs to which Boethius himself could not possibly have assented. We may nevertheless wish to insist that what Gibbon says about Boethius's beliefs is true. Certainly it would be absurd to reject the description as misleading simply because Boethius himself was in no position to recognise its truth.

---

[94] Goodman 1978, p. 93 summarises this as 'meanings vanish in favour of certain relationships among terms'.

[95] See, for example, Pocock 1985, p. 13.   [96] Taylor 1988, p. 221.

[97] Here I invoke the title of Prudovsky 1997, a careful critique of my own response to this question.

[98] See Danto 1965, pp. 149–81 and cf. Dunn 1980, esp. pp. 19–20, 104–5.

There is a further point at which it will often be legitimate not merely to go beyond but to repudiate the descriptions offered by the peoples we are studying. This will be when we are confident that we have identified what they believe and wish to go on to explain why they believed it. It would be a quixotic form of self-denying ordinance to insist that our language of explanation must at this juncture match whatever language the people in question applied or could have applied to themselves. If we wish to furnish what we take to be the most powerful explanations available to us, we are bound to employ what we believe to be the best available explanatory theories and the concepts embodied in them. As a result, there will be many cases in which – to comment on a further issue raised by Taylor – we shall want to insist that, even if our resulting explanations conflict with those offered by the people we are studying, ours must be regarded as the 'superior' ones.[99] This is only to say that one of our own beliefs is that our stock of social explanations has become enriched over the course of recent centuries. If we believe, for example, that Freud's concept of the unconscious represents one of the more important of these enrichments, we shall not only want to do our best to psychoanalyse the dead, but we shall find ourselves appraising and explaining their behaviour by means of concepts that they would have found, initially at least, completely incomprehensible.

Some intellectual historians have wished to defend a third type of revision. What matters, they claim, is not the terms in which people happen to express their beliefs, but the nature of the distinctions they draw by the use of those terms. This means that, as long as we preserve their distinctions, it may be positively helpful to revise their terms. For example, we may wish to say that, although John Locke never uses the word 'image' in outlining his theory of ideas, we gain a clearer sense of what he is talking about if we speak of 'images' where he speaks of 'ideas'.[100]

Although apparently unexceptionable, this further proposal strikes me as treading on more dangerous ground. The terms we substitute may well perform the illuminating task of capturing more of the implications of a theory than its own author may have recognised. But they will almost certainly serve at the same time to import a number of irrelevant and even anachronistic resonances. As soon as this begins to happen, the intellectual historian will be failing in what I take to be his or her primary task: that of identifying and describing the beliefs to be explained. So

---

[99] Taylor 1981, esp. pp. 208–9. Cf. also Taylor 1982, pp. 87–105 for a similar stress on the cognitive superiority of the theories generated by modern scientific conceptions of rational acceptability.

[100] For a sceptical view of this proposal see Yolton 1975, pp. 507–8.

it seems to me that where an historian is trying to identify beliefs – as opposed to the logically subsequent task of explaining or commenting on them – it will generally be fatal to revise the terms in which they are expressed. The beliefs in question will only be identifiable as possessing their precise subject-matter by virtue of the particular terms in which the agents themselves chose to express them. To revise those terms will be to talk about a different set of beliefs.

As an illustration, let me conclude by reverting once more to the example of Machiavelli, and specifically to the political argument outlined in his *Discorsi*. Historians in the Anglophone tradition have often discussed Machiavelli's theory in terms of its account of the relationship between the rights and interests of individual citizens and the powers of the state.[101] But Machiavelli himself never employs the terminology of rights (*diritti*) or interests (*interessi*) at any point. The effect of revising his vocabulary in this way has been to supply him with a range of alleged beliefs about a number of topics on which he never pronounced. It is of course possible that he possessed the concept of a right even though he never talked about rights. But as I began by stressing, historians have no option but to begin by assuming that what people actually talk about provides us with the most reliable guide to their beliefs. To begin by insisting that they must really be talking about something else is to run the highest risk of supplying them with beliefs instead of identifying what they believed.

IV

The way we live now is such that anyone who defends the type of position I have outlined above is certain sooner or later to find themselves denounced (or commended) as a relativist. Sure enough, my critics have repeatedly hurled this piece of conceptual bric-à-brac at my head.[102] It is of course true that I have relativised the idea of 'holding true' a given belief. I have asserted that it may well have been rational for Jean Bodin to hold it true that there are witches in league with the devil, even if such beliefs no longer strike us as rationally acceptable. But at no point have I endorsed the thesis of conceptual relativism. I have never asserted that it *was* true that at one time there were witches in league with the devil, even though such a belief would nowadays strike us as false. To put the point generally, I have merely observed that the question of what it may

---

[101] See, for example, Cassirer 1946, pp. 133–41; Colish 1971, pp. 345–6.
[102] Graham 1981, p. 173; Shapiro 1982, p. 537; King 1983, p. 297; Hollis 1988, p. 146.

be rational for us to hold true will vary with the totality of our beliefs. I have never put forward the reckless and completely different thesis that truth itself can vary in the same way.

I have certainly claimed that, when we say of a given belief that we hold it true, what we are saying is that we find it rationally acceptable. But this is not to claim, as the conceptual relativist does, that there is nothing more to truth than acceptability. Unlike the relativist, I am not trying to offer a definition of truth. I am not in general talking about truth; I am talking about what different peoples at different times may have had good reasons by their lights for holding true, regardless of whether we ourselves believe that what they held true was in fact the truth.

I have not even suggested that the reasons people give for their beliefs need be such that an historian who recovers them need find them so much as recognisable as reasons for holding true the beliefs concerned. Historians frequently study what Martin Hollis has called ritual beliefs, cases in which the contents of the beliefs under investigation may remain unintelligible.[103] The most we can hope to do in such circumstances is to place the beliefs in question within an appropriate explanatory context of other beliefs.[104] We can certainly hope as a result to indicate why someone operating from within that context might come to assent to the propositions we ourselves find unintelligible. But we cannot hope to do more. In such cases we discharge our task as interpreters if we can explain, say, how Aquinas was able to reach and defend the belief that God is at once three persons and an indivisible Being.[105] We need not suppose that we have to be able to perform in addition what may strike us as the impossible feat of explaining what exactly it was that Aquinas believed. To paraphrase Hollis, the aim of the historian is to produce as much understanding as possible, a task not to be confused with that of producing converts.[106]

I am convinced, in short, that the importance of truth for the kind of historical enquiries I am considering has been much exaggerated. I take this to be a product of the fact that so much of the meta-historical discussion has hinged around the analysis of scientific beliefs. In such cases the question of truth may perhaps be of some interest. But in most of the cases investigated by historians of ideas, the suggestion that we need to consider the truth of the beliefs under examination is, I think, likely

---

[103] Hollis 1970b, pp. 221, 235–7. For a contrasting viewpoint see Papineau 1978, p. 150.
[104] See the valuable discussions in Skorupski 1976, pp. 225–43 and Skorupski 1978, pp. 98–102.
[105] For an account of how we can hope to do this much see Stout 1981, pp. 3, 8–9, 106–9, 173–4.
[106] Hollis 1970b, p. 237.

to strike the historian as strange. Take, for example, one of the cases I have already discussed: Machiavelli's fervently held belief that mercenary armies always jeopardise political liberty. There is of course nothing to prevent us from asking whether this is true, but the effect of doing so will be somewhat analogous to asking whether the king of France is bald. The best answer seems to be that nowadays the question does not arise.

To say this is not to adopt the position, sometimes ascribed to Wittgenstein, that we are *precluded* from asking about the truth of such beliefs on the ground that they can only be understood as part of a form of life that may be ultimately no less cognitively justifiable than our own.[107] On the contrary, that way of stating the thesis of conceptual relativism strikes me as self-refuting as it stands, embodying as it does the statement of a preferred point of view while denying that any such point of view can be attained.[108] I am merely insisting (to revert to my example) that our task as historians is to try to recover Machiavelli's point of view; and that, in order to discharge this task, what we need to employ is solely the concept of rational acceptability, not that of truth.

Some historians have admittedly sought to reintroduce the question of truth by arguing that their findings serve to underpin the thesis of conceptual relativism. Thomas Kuhn has been widely, if mistakenly, interpreted in this way, but the clearest statement of this claim has been put forward by proponents of the 'strong programme' such as Barry Barnes and David Bloor. As we have seen, they think that they have established from their historical case-studies that all our beliefs have social causes, and that all such causes operate in such a way as to distort our capacity to get in touch with the objects of our beliefs. From this they have inferred that the only possible judge of the truth of our beliefs must be whatever consensus over norms and standards may happen to prevail in what they call our local culture.[109]

I cannot see that the generalisation extracted by Barnes and Bloor from their research bears on the thesis of conceptual relativism at all. Suppose it is true that the social causation of our beliefs is such as to mask their objects from us. The obvious inference is that we have no good grounds for holding those beliefs to be true, not that we have satisfactory grounds for holding them to be true according to some relativised notion of truth.[110] By contrast with Barnes and Bloor, it seems to me that, if the practice of intellectual history serves to suggest any theoretical insights,

---

[107] On this point see Lear 1983, pp. 44–6.
[108] For this objection see Putnam 1981, pp. 119–20 and Lear 1983, p. 55.
[109] Barnes and Bloor 1982, pp. 22–9.   [110] A point excellently made in Hollis 1982, pp. 82–3.

these must be of an anti-relativist kind. I infer this from the fact that the truth of conceptual relativism and the practice of intellectual history appear to be incompatible.

The point I have in mind here is an obvious and familiar one. If we are to use our ancestors' utterances as a guide to identifying their underlying beliefs, it is indispensable that we should hold in common with them a number of assumptions at least about the process of belief formation itself. The most basic of these assumptions – to which I have already alluded – is the one stressed above all by Quine.[111] We must be able to assume, in advance of our historical enquiries, that our ancestors shared at least some of our own beliefs about the importance of consistency and coherence. We must be able, for example, to assume their acceptance of the principle that, if we affirm the truth of a given proposition, we cannot at the same time affirm the truth of the denial of that proposition.[112] Beyond this, we need to share with our ancestors some assumptions about the process of using our existing beliefs to arrive at others. This is because, even if we can identify some of their individual beliefs, we may still find our efforts at understanding defeated unless we can make some fairly strong assumptions about the character of the reasoning they must have employed in fitting their beliefs together.[113]

It can easily be made to look like pure dogmatism to insist on such anti-relativist considerations in an *a priori* style. But the need to do so can, I think, be readily vindicated if we simply recall the nature of the intellectual historian's task. The aim is to use our ancestors' utterances as a guide to the identification of their beliefs. But if they display no concern for consistency, if they employ no recognisable modes of inference, we shall have no means of marking off which of their utterances are to be classed as instances of the speech acts of stating or affirming or defending their beliefs. If they are willing, for example, both to affirm and deny the truth of some particular proposition, then we can never hope to say what belief they hold about it. As a number of philosophers have insisted, following in Quine's wake, the idea of holding rational beliefs and the idea of holding beliefs that are mainly true by our lights certainly come together at this point.[114]

---

[111] Quine 1960, p. 59.

[112] Following Quine, many philosophers have stressed this point. See, for example, Hollis 1970b, pp. 231–2; Lukes 1977, pp. 133–5.

[113] Lear 1982, pp. 389–90.

[114] Hollis 1970b, pp. 231–2; MacIntyre 1971, pp. 250, 256; Lukes 1977, pp. 133–5; Papineau 1978, p. 138; Macdonald and Pettit 1981, pp. 30–1.

This is not to assert that the idea of a 'pre-logical mentality' – an idea ritually wheeled out by philosophers in this context – is necessarily an impossibility. It is only to assert that, if an historian were really to encounter a people for whom it caused no discomfort to affirm and deny the same propositions, there would be no prospect of reporting what they believed. Nor am I denying that historians may well encounter abnormal forms of discourse in which the law of non-contradiction is deliberately flouted. I am only saying that such forms of discourse must be abnormal, and parasitic on recognisable forms, if we are to understand the linguistic community in which they take place. Nor am I even denying that agents engaged in normal discourse may turn out to have a number of beliefs about their beliefs which, strictly speaking, reveal inconsistencies.[115] I am only saying that an historian will be unable to grasp the content of any beliefs that turn out to be contradictory in and of themselves.

These conclusions can also be stated in the form of one further precept about historical method. If as historians we come upon contradictory beliefs, we should start by assuming that we must in some way have misunderstood or mistranslated some of the propositions by which they are expressed. As a simple instance of what I have in mind, let me end by considering a yet further example from Machiavelli's political works. In his *Discorsi* Machiavelli affirms that liberty is possible only under a *repubblica*.[116] But he also affirms that Rome lived *in libertà* under her early kings.[117] What then does he believe? Does he or does he not think that liberty and monarchy are incompatible?

Historians have tended to reply that he seems to be confused: he affirms but he also denies that liberty is possible only under a republic.[118] I am suggesting, however, that before we endorse such a conclusion we ought first to consider whether we may not in some way have misunderstood what he said. Sure enough, if we investigate the full range of contexts in which the term *repubblica* occurs, we discover that for Machiavelli the term can be used to denote any form of government under which the laws may be said to foster the common good. It follows that for Machiavelli the question of whether a monarchy can be a *repubblica* is not an empty paradox, as it would be for us, but a deep question of statecraft. The question is whether kings can ever be relied upon to pass only such laws as will serve the common good. This gives us an alternative reading:

---

[115] Elster 1978, p. 88.   [116] Machiavelli 1960, II. 2, p. 280.

[117] Machiavelli 1960, III. 5, pp. 388–90.

[118] See, for example, Colish 1971, p. 330 on Machiavelli's alleged 'lack of univocity' on this point.

Machiavelli is telling us that, under Romulus and his successors, the laws of Rome served the common good, so that the government, although monarchical in form, was an instance of a *repubblica*. Since this has the effect of resolving the contradiction, I am suggesting that this is also the interpretation we ought to prefer.

But what if the initial contradiction had refused to yield to any such re-interpretative efforts? I have already given my answer: at that point we should have to admit that we cannot say what Machiavelli believed. Before throwing up our hands in this way, we need to make sure that we really are in the last ditch. But if we are, we are left with no alternative. Nor should we feel that we ought to have done better. To look for complete intelligibility is to adopt an unduly optimistic view of what we can hope to bring back from the foreign lands of the past.

4

Meaning and understanding in the history of ideas

I

The task of the historian of ideas[1] is to study and interpret a canon of classic texts. The value of writing this kind of history stems from the fact that the classic texts in moral, political, religious and other such modes of thought contain a 'dateless wisdom'[2] in the form of 'universal ideas'.[3] As a result, we can hope to learn and benefit directly from investigating these 'timeless elements', since they possess a perennial relevance.[4] This in turn suggests that the best way to approach these texts must be to concentrate on what each of them *says*[5] about each of the 'fundamental concepts'[6] and 'abiding questions' of morality, politics, religion, social life.[7] We must be ready, in other words, to read each of the classic texts 'as though it were written by a contemporary'.[8] It is indeed essential to approach them in this way, focusing simply on their arguments and examining what they have to tell us about the perennial issues. If instead we become sidetracked into examining the social conditions or the intellectual contexts out of which they arose, we shall lose sight of their dateless wisdom and thereby lose contact with the value and purpose of studying them.[9]

These are the assumptions I wish to question, criticise and if possible discredit in what follows. The belief that the classic theorists can be

This chapter is a much abbreviated and extensively revised version of an article that originally appeared under the same title in *History and Theory* 8 (1969), pp. 3–53.

[1] For the confusing variety of ways in which this seemingly inescapable phrase has been used see Mandelbaum 1965.

[2] Catlin 1950, p. x.   [3] Bluhm 1965, p. 13.   [4] Merkl 1967, p. 3.

[5] Jaspers 1962; Nelson 1962, pp. 32–3. Cf. Murphy 1951, p. v on the need to concentrate on 'what Plato said'; Ryan 1965, p. 219 on the need to concentrate on 'what Locke said'.

[6] McCoy 1963, p. 7.

[7] On the 'abiding' and 'perennial' questions see Morgenthau 1958, p. 1; Sibley 1958, p. 133; Strauss and Cropsey 1963, Preface. On the perennial questions as the (sole) guarantee of the 'relevance' of the classic texts see Hacker 1954, McCloskey 1957. For a more recent exposition of a similar position see Bevir 1994.

[8] Bloom 1980, p. 128.   [9] Hacker 1954; Bluhm 1965, esp. p. 13.

expected to comment on a determinate set of 'fundamental concepts' has given rise, it seems to me, to a series of confusions and exegetical absurdities that have bedevilled the history of ideas for too long. The sense in which this belief is misleading, however, is not altogether easy to isolate. It is easy to castigate it as 'a fatal mistake',[10] but at the same time it is hard to deny that the histories of different intellectual pursuits have always been marked by the employment of relatively stable and characteristic vocabularies.[11] Even if we accept the loose-textured contention that it is only in virtue of certain family resemblances that we are able to define and distinguish such different activities, we are still committed to accepting *some* criteria and rules of usage such that certain performances can be correctly instanced, and others excluded, as examples of a given activity. Otherwise we shall eventually have no means – to say nothing of justification – for delineating and speaking of, say, the histories of ethical or political thinking as being histories of recognisable activities at all. It is in fact the truth, and not the absurdity, of the claim that all such activities must have some characteristic concepts which seems to be the main source of confusion. For if there must be at least some family resemblances connecting all the instances of any such activity, which we need first of all to apprehend in order to recognise the activity itself, it becomes impossible to consider any such activity, or any instance of it, without having some preconceptions about what we expect to find.

The relevance of this dilemma for the history of ideas – and especially for the claim that historians should concentrate on what the classic texts *say* about the canonical themes – will by now be clear. It will never be possible simply to study what any writer has *said* (especially in an alien culture) without bringing to bear our own expectations and pre-judgements about what they must be saying. This is the dilemma familiar to psychologists as the determining factor of the observer's mental *set*. By our past experience 'we are set to perceive details in a certain way', and when this frame of reference has been established, 'the process is one of being *prepared* to perceive or react in a certain way'.[12] The resulting dilemma may be stated, for my present purposes, in the form of the proposition that the models and preconceptions in terms of which we unavoidably organise and adjust our perceptions and thoughts will themselves tend to act as determinants of what we think and perceive. We must classify in order to understand, and we can only classify the unfamiliar in terms of

---

[10] MacIntyre 1966, p. 2.
[11] See Wolin 1961, pp. 11–17 on 'the vocabulary of political philosophy'.
[12] Allport 1955, esp. pp. 239–40.

the familiar.[13] The perpetual danger, in our attempts to enlarge our historical understanding, is thus that our expectations about what someone must be saying or doing will themselves determine that we understand the agent to be doing something which they would not – or even could not – have accepted as an account of what they *were* doing.

This notion of the priority of paradigms has already been fruitfully explored in the history of art,[14] where it has caused an essentially historicist story about the development of illusionism to yield place to a story content to trace changing intentions and conventions. More recently, an analogous exploration has been no less fruitfully conducted in the history of science.[15] Here I shall attempt to apply a similar set of considerations to the history of ideas. My procedure will be to try to uncover the extent to which the current historical study of ethical, political, religious, and other such modes of thought is contaminated by the unconscious application of paradigms the familiarity of which, to the historian, disguises an essential inapplicability to the past. I do not, of course, seek to deny that the methodology I criticise has sometimes yielded distinguished results. I do wish, however, to insist on the various ways in which the study of what each classic writer *says* unavoidably runs the danger of lapsing into various kinds of historical absurdity, and at the same time to anatomise the various ways in which the results may be classified not as histories but more appropriately as mythologies.

II

The most persistent mythology has been created by historians working with the expectation that each classic writer (in the history, say, of moral or political theory) will be found to enunciate some doctrine on each of the topics regarded as constitutive of the subject. It is a dangerously short step from being under the influence (however unconsciously) of such a paradigm to 'finding' a given author's doctrines on all the mandatory themes. The result is a type of discussion that might be labelled the mythology of doctrines.

---

[13] That this must result in a history conceived in terms of our own philosophical criteria and interests (whose else?) is fully brought out in Dunn 1980, pp. 13–28.

[14] See Gombrich 1962, esp. pp. 55–78, whose account of 'paradigms' I adopt. Gombrich has also coined the relevant epigram: 'only where there is a way is there also a will' (p. 75).

[15] See Kuhn 1962, esp. pp. 43–51, where he takes over the notion of 'the priority of paradigms'. Cf. the comparable insistence in Collingwood 1940, esp. pp. 11–48, that the thought of any period is organised according to 'constellations of absolute pre-suppositions'. For a valuable analysis of Kuhn's theory of science and its implications for intellectual historians see Hollinger 1985, pp. 105–29.

The mythology takes several forms. First there is the danger of converting some scattered or incidental remarks by a classic theorist into their 'doctrine' on one of the expected themes. This in turn has the effect of generating two particular kinds of historical absurdity. One is more characteristic of intellectual biographies and synoptic histories of thought, in which the focus is on the individual thinkers (or the procession of them). The other is more characteristic of 'histories of ideas' in which the focus is on the development of some 'unit idea' itself.

The special danger with intellectual biography is that of anachronism. A given writer may be 'discovered' to have held a view, on the strength of some chance similarity of terminology, about an argument to which they cannot in principle have meant to contribute. Marsilius of Padua, for example, at one point in his *Defensor Pacis* offers some typically Aristotelian remarks about the executive role of rulers by contrast with the legislative role of the people.[16] A modern commentator who comes upon this passage will be familiar with the doctrine, important in constitutional theory and practice since the American Revolution, that one condition of political freedom is the separation of executive from legislative power. The origins of this doctrine can be traced to the historiographical suggestion (first canvassed some two centuries after Marsilius's death) that the collapse of the Roman Republic into an Empire illustrates the danger to the liberty of subjects inherent in entrusting any single authority with centralised political power.[17] Marsilius knew nothing of the historiography, nor of the lessons that were to be drawn from it. (His own discussion derives from Book IV of Aristotle's *Politics*, and is not concerned with the issue of political freedom at all.) None of this, however, has been sufficient to prevent a brisk debate on the question of whether Marsilius should be said to have had a 'doctrine' of the separation of powers, and if so whether he should be 'acclaimed the founder of the doctrine'.[18] Even those who deny that Marsilius should be credited with the doctrine tend to base their conclusions on his text,[19] and not on pointing to the impropriety of supposing that he *could* have meant to contribute to a debate the terms of which were unavailable to him.

The same kind of anachronism marks the discussion centring on the *dictum* offered by Sir Edward Coke on Bonham's case to the effect that common law of England may sometimes override statute. The modern

---

[16] Marsilius of Padua 1951–6, vol. 2, pp. 61–7.　　[17] See Pocock 1965, Bailyn 1967.
[18] Marsilius of Padua 1951–6, vol. 1, p. 232.
[19] For a bibliography, see Marsilius of Padua 1951–6, vol. 1, p. 234n. For a purely textual dismissal of the claim see D'Entrèves 1939, p. 58.

(especially American) commentator brings to this remark the much later resonances of the doctrine of judicial review. Coke himself knew nothing of such a doctrine. (The context of his own suggestion is that of a party politician assuring James I that the defining characteristic of law is custom, and not, as James appeared to be claiming, the will of the sovereign.)[20] None of these historical considerations, however, has been enough to prevent the reiteration of the meaningless question of 'whether Coke actually intended to advocate judicial review',[21] or the insistence that Coke must have meant to articulate this 'new doctrine' and so to make this 'remarkable contribution to political science'.[22] Again, those experts who have denied that Coke should be credited with such clairvoyance have largely based their conclusion on the reinterpretation of Coke's text, rather than noting the prior logical oddity of the implied account of Coke's intentions.[23]

Besides the crude possibility of crediting a writer with a meaning they could not have intended to convey, there is the more insidious danger of too readily finding expected doctrines in classic texts. Consider, for example, the Aristotelian remarks that Richard Hooker offers in Book I of his *Of The Laws of Ecclesiastical Polity* about natural sociability.[24] We might well feel that Hooker's intention was merely – as with many scholastic lawyers of the time – to open up a means of discriminating the godly origins of the Church from the more mundane origins of civil associations. The modern commentator, however, who sees Hooker at the top of a 'line of descent' running 'from Hooker to Locke and from Locke to the *Philosophes*' has little difficulty in converting Hooker's remarks into nothing less than his 'theory of the social contract'.[25] Consider, similarly, the remarks on trusteeship that John Locke offers at one or two points in his *Two Treatises of Government*.[26] We might well feel that Locke is merely appealing to one of the more familiar legal analogies in the political writing of the period. Again, however, the modern commentator who sees Locke standing at the head of a tradition of 'government by consent' has little difficulty in piecing together the 'passages scattered through' the work on this topic, and emerging with Locke's 'doctrine' of 'the political trust'.[27] Consider likewise the remarks that James Harrington makes in

---

[20] Pocock 1987, esp. pp. 30–55.   [21] Gwyn 1965, p. 50n.

[22] Plucknett 1926–7, p. 68. For the claim that it was Coke's 'own intention' to articulate the doctrine 'which American courts today exercise', see also Corwin 1928–9, p. 368 and cf. Corwin 1948, p. 42.

[23] For a purely textual dismissal see Thorne 1938.   [24] Hooker 1989, I. 10. 4, pp. 89–91.

[25] Morris 1953, pp. 181–97.   [26] Locke 1988, II. 149, p. 367; II. 155, pp. 370–1.

[27] See Gough 1950, pp. 47–72 (government by consent) and pp. 136–71 (political trusteeship).

The Commonwealth of Oceana about the place of lawyers in political life. The historian who is investigating the alleged views of the English republicans of the 1650s about the separation of powers may be momentarily disconcerted to find that Harrington ('curiously') is not talking about public officers at this point. But an historian who 'knows' to expect the doctrine among this group will have little difficulty in insisting that 'this does seem to be a vague statement of the doctrine'.[28] In all such cases, where a given writer may appear to be intimating some such 'doctrine', we are left confronting the same begged question. If the writer meant to articulate the doctrine with which they are being credited, why is it that they so signally failed to do so, so that the historian is left reconstructing their alleged intentions from guesses and hints?

The mythology of doctrines can similarly be illustrated from 'histories of ideas' in the strict sense. Here the aim (in the words of Arthur Lovejoy, pioneer of this approach) is to trace the morphology of some given doctrine 'through all the provinces of history in which it appears'.[29] The characteristic point of departure is to set out an ideal type of the given doctrine – whether it is that of equality, progress, reason of state, the social contract, the great chain of being, the separation of powers, and so on. The danger with this approach is that the doctrine to be investigated so readily becomes hypostasised into an entity. As the historian duly sets out in quest of the idea thus characterised, it becomes all too easy to speak as if the developed form of the doctrine has always in some sense been immanent in history, even if various thinkers failed to 'hit upon' it,[30] even if it 'dropped from sight' at various times,[31] even if an entire era failed to 'rise to a consciousness' of it.[32] The outcome is that the story readily takes on the kind of language appropriate to the description of a growing organism. The fact that ideas presuppose agents readily disappears as the ideas get up to do battle on their own behalf. We are told, for example, that the 'birth' of the idea of progress was quite an easy one, for it 'transcended' the 'obstacles to its appearance' by the sixteenth century,[33] and so 'gained ground' through the next hundred years.[34] But the idea of the separation of powers came into the world with greater difficulty. Although it nearly managed to 'emerge' during the English civil war, it 'never quite managed fully to materialise', so that it took another century 'from the English civil war until the mid-eighteenth century for a three-fold division to emerge fully and take over'.[35]

---

[28] Gwyn 1965, p. 52.   [29] Lovejoy 1960, p. 15.   [30] Bury 1932, p. 7.
[31] Weston 1965, p. 45.   [32] Raab 1964, p. 2.   [33] Bury 1932, p. 7.
[34] Sampson 1956, p. 39.   [35] Vile 1967, p. 30.

These reifications give rise to two kinds of historical absurdity, both of which are not merely prevalent in this type of history, but seem more or less inescapable when this approach is followed.[36] The tendency to search for approximations to the ideal type yields a form of history almost entirely given over to pointing out earlier 'anticipations' of later doctrines, and hence to congratulating individual writers for the extent of their clairvoyance. Marsilius of Padua is notable for his 'remarkable anticipation' of Machiavelli.[37] Machiavelli is notable because he 'lays the foundation for Marx'.[38] John Locke's theory of signs is notable 'as an anticipation of Berkeley's metaphysics'.[39] Joseph Glanvill's theory of causation is notable for 'the extent to which he has anticipated Hume'.[40] Lord Shaftesbury's treatment of the theodicy problem is notable because it 'in a certain sense anticipated Kant'.[41] Sometimes even the pretence that this is history is laid aside, and the writers of the past are simply praised or blamed according to how far they seem to have aspired to the condition of being ourselves. Montesquieu 'anticipates the ideas of full employment and the welfare state': this shows his 'luminous, incisive' mind.[42] Machiavelli thought about politics essentially as we do: this is his 'lasting significance'. But his contemporaries did not: this makes their political views 'completely unreal'.[43] Shakespeare ('an eminently political author') was sceptical about 'the possibility of an interracial, interfaith society': this is one of the signs of his value as 'a text in moral and political education'.[44] And so on.

We encounter a connected absurdity in the endless debates as to whether a given 'unit idea' may be said to have 'really emerged' at a given time, and whether it is 'really there' in the work of some given writer. Consider again the histories of the idea of the separation of powers. Is the doctrine already 'there' in the works of George Buchanan? No, for he 'did not fully articulate' it, although 'none came closer' at the time.[45] But is it perhaps 'there' by the time we come to the constitutional proposals put forward by the royalists in the English civil war? No, for it is still 'not the pure doctrine'.[46] Or consider the histories of the doctrine of the social contract. Is the doctrine already 'there' in the pamphlets produced by the Huguenots in the French religious wars? No, for their ideas are 'incompletely developed'. But is it perhaps 'there' in the works of their Catholic

---

[36] But for an interesting defence of Lovejoy's approach see Oakley 1984, pp. 15–40.

[37] Raab 1964, p. 2.　　[38] Jones 1947, p. 50.　　[39] Armstrong 1965, p. 382.

[40] Popkin 1953, p. 300.　　[41] Cassirer 1955, p. 151.　　[42] Morris 1966, pp. 89–90.

[43] Raab 1964, pp. 1, 11. For a critique see Anglo 1966.

[44] Bloom and Jaffa 1964, pp. 1–2, 4, 36.　　[45] Gwyn 1965, p. 9.　　[46] Vile 1967, p. 46.

adversaries? No, for their statements are still 'incomplete', although they are 'decidedly more advanced'.[47]

The first form, then, of the mythology of doctrines may be said to consist, in these various ways, of mistaking some scattered or incidental remarks by one of the classic theorists for their 'doctrine' on one of the themes which the historian is *set* to expect. The second form, to which I now turn, involves the converse of this mistake. A classic theorist who fails to come up with a recognisable doctrine on one of the mandatory themes is criticised for falling short of their proper task.

The historical study of moral and political theory is currently dogged by a demonological (but highly influential) version of this mistake. These disciplines, we are first reminded, are or ought to be concerned with eternal or at least traditional 'true standards'.[48] It is thus thought appropriate to treat the history of these subjects in terms of the 'decided lowering of tone' said to be characteristic of modern reflection 'on life and its goals', and to take as the focus of this history the assessment of blame for this collapse.[49] Thomas Hobbes, or sometimes Niccolò Machiavelli, is then made to stand condemned for man's first disobedience.[50] Their contemporaries are then praised or blamed essentially according to whether they acknowledged or subverted the same 'truth'.[51] Leo Strauss, the chief proponent of this approach, accordingly 'does not hesitate to assert', when confronting Machiavelli's political works, that they deserve to be denounced as 'immoral and irreligious'.[52] He also does not hesitate to assume that such a tone of denunciation is appropriate to his stated aim of trying to 'understand' Machiavelli's works.[53] Here the paradigm determines the direction of the entire historical investigation. The history can only be reinterpreted if the paradigm itself is abandoned.

The main version, however, of this form of the mythology of doctrines consists of supplying the classic theorists with doctrines which are agreed to be proper to their subject, but which they unaccountably failed to discuss. Sometimes this takes the form of extrapolating from what these great figures said in such a way as to supply them with suitable

---

[47] Gough 1957, p. 59.   [48] Strauss 1957, p. 12.

[49] Bloom and Jaffa 1964, pp. 1–2. For a critique of this belief in political philosophy as the articulation or recovery of certain 'final truths', see Kaufman 1954. For a defence see Cropsey 1962.

[50] For this view of Hobbes see Strauss 1953; for this view of Machiavelli see Strauss 1958.

[51] See, for example, the attack on Anthony Ascham and the defence of the Earl of Clarendon in these terms in Coltman 1962, pp. 69–99, 197–242.

[52] Strauss 1958, pp. 11–12.   [53] Strauss 1958, p. 14.

beliefs. Thomas Aquinas may not have pronounced on the subject of 'foolish "civil disobedience"', but we can be sure that 'he would not have approved'.[54] Marsilius of Padua would certainly have approved of democracy, since 'the sovereignty he espoused pertained to the people'.[55] But Richard Hooker 'would not be entirely happy', since 'his own noble, religious and spacious conception of law has been desiccated into the mere fiat of popular will'.[56] Such exercises may seem merely quaint, but they could always have a more sinister undertone, as these examples may perhaps suggest: a means to fix one's own prejudices onto the most charismatic names under the guise of innocuous historical speculation. History then indeed becomes a pack of tricks we play on the dead.

The more usual strategy, however, is to seize on some doctrine that a given theorist ought to have mentioned, although they failed to do so, and then to criticise them for their incompetence. Perhaps the most remarkable evidence of the hold exercised by this approach is that it was never questioned, as a method of discussing the history of political ideas, even by that most anti-essentialist of political theorists, T. D. Weldon. The first part of his book *States and Morals* sets out the various 'definitions of the state' that all political theorists 'either formulate or take for granted'. We learn that all theories of the state fall into two main groups: 'Some define it as a kind of organism, others as a kind of machine.' Armed with this discovery, Weldon then turns 'to examine the leading theories about the state which have been put forward'. But here he finds that even 'those writers who are generally regarded as the leading theorists in the subject' let us down rather badly, for few of them manage to expound either theory without 'inconsistencies or even contradictions'. Hegel turns out to be the sole theorist 'completely faithful' to one of the two stipulated models which, we are reminded, it is the 'primary purpose' of each theorist to expound. A less confident writer might have wondered at this point whether his initial characterisation of what these theorists all took themselves to be doing can have possibly been correct. But Weldon's only comment is that it seems 'rather odd that, after more than two thousand years of concentrated thought', almost everyone has remained so confused.[57]

The exegetical literature is filled with similar instances of this mythology of doctrines. Consider, for example, the place in political theory of

54 Cranston 1964, pp. 34–5.   55 Marsilius of Padua 1951–6, vol. I, p. 312.
56 Shirley 1949, p. 256.   57 Weldon 1946, pp. 26, 63–4.

questions about voting and decision-making, and about the role of public opinion more generally. These questions have become of central importance in recent democratic political theory, although they were of little interest to theorists writing before the establishment of modern representative democracies. The historical caveat might scarcely seem worth adding, but it has not been sufficient to deter commentators from criticising Plato's *Republic* for 'omitting' the 'influence of public opinion'[58] or from criticising John Locke's *Two Treatises* for omitting 'all references to family and race' and failing to make it 'wholly clear' where he stands on the question of universal suffrage.[59] It is indeed astonishing, we are assured, that not one of 'the great writers on politics and law' devotes any space to the discussion of decision-making.[60] Consider, similarly, the question of the extent to which political power is subject to manipulation by the more socially advantaged. This too is a natural anxiety for democratic theorists, though a question of little interest to those with no commitment to popular rule. Again the historical caveat is obvious, but again it has not been sufficient to prevent commentators from offering it as a criticism of Machiavelli, of Hobbes and of Locke, that none of them offers any 'genuine insights' into this almost wholly modern debate.[61]

An even more prevalent form of the mythology consists in effect of criticising the classic writers according to the *a priori* assumption that they must have intended whatever writings they produced to constitute the most systematic contribution they were capable of making to their discipline. If it is first assumed, for example, that one of the doctrines Richard Hooker must have been trying to enunciate in the *Laws* was an account of 'the basis of political obligation', then doubtless it is a 'defect in Hooker's political views' that he failed to devote any attention to refuting the theory of absolute sovereignty.[62] Similarly, if it is first assumed that one of Machiavelli's basic concerns in *Il Principe* was to explain 'the characteristics of men in politics', then it is not difficult for a contemporary political scientist to show that Machiavelli's poor effort is 'extremely one-sided and unsystematic'.[63] Again, if it is first assumed that Locke's *Two Treatises* includes all the doctrines he might have wished to

---

[58] Sabine 1951, p. 67.   [59] Aaron 1955, pp. 284–5.   [60] Friedrich 1964, p. 178.

[61] See Plamenatz 1963, vol. 1, p. 43, on Machiavelli's 'great omission'; Russell 1946, p. 578, on Hobbes's failure to 'realise the importance of the clash between different classes'; Hacker 1961, pp. 192, 285, noting this 'great omission' in the thought of Machiavelli as well as Locke; Lerner 1950, p. xxx on Machiavelli's lack of 'any genuine insights into social organisation as the basis of politics'.

[62] Davies 1964, p. 80.   [63] Dahl 1963, p. 113.

enunciate on 'natural law and political society', then doubtless 'it might well be asked' why he fails to 'advocate a world state'.[64] And again, if it is first assumed that one of Montesquieu's aims in *De l'Esprit des lois* must have been to enunciate a sociology of knowledge, then doubtless 'it is a weakness' that he fails to explain its chief determinants, and doubtless 'we must also accuse him' of failing to apply his own theory.[65] But with all such alleged 'failures', as with the converse form of this mythology, we are still left confronting the same begged question: whether any of these writers ever intended, or could have intended, to do what they are castigated for not having done.

III

I now want to consider a second type of mythology that tends to be created by the fact that historians will unavoidably be *set* in approaching the ideas of the past. It may turn out that some of the classic writers are not altogether consistent, or even fail to give any systematic account of their beliefs. Suppose, however, that the paradigm for the conduct of the investigation has again been taken to be that of elaborating each classic writer's doctrines on each of the themes most characteristic of the subject. It will then become dangerously easy for the historian to treat it as his or her task to supply these texts with the coherence they may appear to lack. Such a danger is exacerbated by the notorious difficulty of preserving the proper emphasis and tone of a work when paraphrasing it, and by the consequent temptation to find a 'message' which can be abstracted and more readily communicated.[66]

The writing of the history of moral and political philosophy is pervaded by this mythology of coherence.[67] If 'current scholarly opinion' can see no coherence in Richard Hooker's *Laws*, the moral is to look harder, for coherence must surely be present.[68] If there is doubt about the 'most central themes' of Hobbes's political philosophy, it becomes the duty of the exegete to discover the 'inner coherence of his doctrine' by reading such texts as *Leviathan* over and over until – in a revealing phrase – the argument has 'assumed some coherence'.[69] If there is no coherent system 'readily accessible' to the student of Hume's political writings, the

---

[64] Cox 1960, pp. xv, 189.   [65] Stark 1960, pp. 144, 153.

[66] For a recent discussion of some related issues see Lemon 1995, pp. 225–37.

[67] A similar point about the problem of accommodating different 'levels of abstraction' has been made in Pocock 1962. For a critique of Pocock's and my views about myths of coherence see Bevir 1997.

[68] McGrade 1963, p. 163.   [69] Warrender 1957, p. vii.

exegete's duty is 'to rummage through one work after another' until the 'high degree of consistency in the whole corpus' is duly displayed (again in a revealing phrase) 'at all costs'.[70] If Herder's political ideas are 'rarely worked out systematically', and are 'scattered throughout his writings, sometimes within the most unexpected contexts', the duty of the exegete becomes that of trying 'to present these ideas in some coherent form'.[71] The most revealing fact about such reiterations of the scholar's task is that the metaphors habitually used are those of effort and quest. The ambition is always to 'arrive' at 'a unified interpretation', to 'gain' a 'coherent view of an author's system'.[72]

This procedure gives the thoughts of the major philosophers a coherence, and an air generally of a closed system, which they may never have attained or even aspired to attain. If it is first assumed, for example, that the business of interpreting Rousseau's philosophy must centre on the discovery of his most 'fundamental thought', it will readily cease to seem a matter of importance that he contributed over several decades to several different fields of enquiry.[73] If it is first assumed that every aspect of Hobbes's thought was designed as a contribution to an overarching 'Christian' system, it will cease to seem peculiar to suggest that we may turn to his autobiography to elucidate so crucial a point as the relations between ethics and political life.[74] If it is first assumed in the case of Edmund Burke that a 'coherent moral philosophy' underlies everything he wrote, then it will cease to seem problematic to treat 'the corpus of his published writings' as 'a single body of thought'.[75] Some measure of the lengths to which such procedures can be carried is provided by an influential study of Marx's social and political thought, in which it is felt to be necessary, to justify the exclusion of Engels's contributions, to point out that Marx and Engels were 'two distinct human beings'.[76]

It does sometimes happen, of course, that the aims and successes of a given writer remain so various as to defy even the efforts of such exegetes to extract a coherent system from their thoughts. Frequently, however, this merely generates a converse form of historical absurdity: such lack of system then becomes a matter for reproach. It is felt, for example, to be a point of some ideological urgency as well as exegetical convenience that Marx's various pronouncements should be available under some systematic headings. Despite the efforts of his critics, however, such a system

---

[70] Stewart 1963, pp. v–vi. [71] Barnard 1965, pp. xix, 139.
[72] Watkins 1965, p. 10. [73] Cassirer 1954, pp. 46, 62.
[74] Hood 1964, p. 28. [75] Parkin 1956, pp. 2, 4. [76] Avineri 1968, p. 3.

remains hard to find. We might ascribe this fact to Marx's concern at different times with a wide range of different social and economic issues. But it has instead become a standard criticism that he never managed to work out what is supposed to be 'his' basic theory in anything but a 'fragmentary manner'.[77] Such criticisms occur even more readily when writers are first classified according to a model to which they are then expected to aspire. If it is first assumed that all conservative thinkers must hold some 'organic' conception of the state, then doubtless Lord Bolingbroke 'should have had' such a conception, and doubtless it is strange that he did not organise his thoughts in that way.[78] If it is first assumed that any philosopher who writes about the theory of justice can be expected to 'contribute' to one of three 'basic' views on the subject, then doubtless the fact that neither Plato nor Hegel did so can be taken to show that they 'seem to resist taking a definite position' on the subject.[79] In all such cases, the coherence or lack of it which is discovered readily ceases to be an historical account of any thoughts that anyone ever thought.

The objection is an obvious one, but it has not in practice proved sufficient to forestall the development of the mythology of coherence in two directions that can only be called metaphysical in the most pejorative sense. First there is the assumption that it may be quite proper, in the interests of extracting a message of maximum coherence, to discount statements of intention that authors themselves make about what they are doing, or even to discount whole works that may seem to impair the coherence of their systems of thought. The exegetical literature on Hobbes and Locke may be used to illustrate both tendencies. It is now known that, in his earliest writings on political theory, Locke was concerned to set out and defend a markedly conservative and even authoritarian stance.[80] Yet it is still apparently possible in the face of this knowledge to treat Locke's politics as a body of views that can simply be labelled the work of a 'liberal' political theorist, without further consideration of the fact that these were the views that Locke held in his fifties, and which he would himself have repudiated in his thirties.[81] Locke at thirty is evidently not yet 'Locke' – a degree of patriarchalism to which even Sir Robert Filmer did not aspire.

---

[77] Sabine 1951, p. 642.   [78] Hearnshaw 1928, p. 243.

[79] Adler 1967, p. xi; Bird 1967, p. 22. Adler 1967, pp. ix–xi holds out the promise (in his Foreword to Bird 1967) that the Institute for Philosophical Research will continue to 'transform' the 'chaos of differing opinions' on other subjects 'into an orderly set of clearly defined points'. The topics to be rendered orderly will include progress, happiness and love.

[80] Abrams 1967, pp. 7–10, 63–83.   [81] Seliger 1968, pp. 209–10.

As for Hobbes, it is known from his own explicit statements what character he intended his political theory to bear. His *Leviathan*, as he informs us in the Review and Conclusion, was written 'without other design' than to show that the 'Civill Right of Soveraigns, and both the Duty and Liberty of Subjects' can be grounded 'upon the known naturall Inclinations of Mankind', and that a theory so grounded must centre on 'the mutuall Relation between Protection and Obedience'.[82] Yet it has still seemed possible to insist that this 'scientific part' of Hobbes's thought is nothing more than a rather ineptly detached aspect of a transcendent 'religious whole'. The fact, moreover, that Hobbes himself appeared unaware of this higher order of coherence provokes not retraction but counter-assertion. Hobbes merely 'fails to make clear' that his discussion of human nature 'in fact' subserves a religious purpose. It 'would have been clearer' if Hobbes had 'written in terms of moral and civil obligations' and thus brought out the 'real unity' and the basically religious character of his whole 'system'.[83]

I turn to the other metaphysical tendency to which the mythology of coherence gives rise. Since the classic texts can be expected to exhibit an 'inner coherence' which it is the duty of the interpreter to reveal, any apparent barriers to this revelation, constituted by any apparent contradictions, cannot be real barriers because they cannot be real contradictions. The assumption, in other words, is that the correct question to ask in such a doubtful case is not whether the given writer was inconsistent, but rather 'how are his contradictions (or apparent contradictions) to be accounted for?'[84] The explanation dictated by the principle of Ockham's razor (that an apparent contradiction may *be* a contradiction) is explicitly set aside. Such incompatibilities, we are told, should not be left in this unresolved state, but should be made to help towards 'a full understanding of the whole theory'[85] – of which the contradictions, evidently, form only an unsublimated part. The very idea that the 'contradictions and divergences' of a given writer may be 'supposed to prove that his thought had changed' has been dismissed by an influential authority as just another delusion of nineteenth-century scholarship.[86]

To think in these terms is to direct the historian of ideas down the scholastic path of 'resolving antinomies'. We are told, for example, that our aim in studying the politics of Machiavelli need not be restricted to anything so straightforward as an attempt to trace the developments that

---

[82] Hobbes 1996, pp. 489, 491.   [83] Hood 1964, pp. 64, 116–17, 136–7.   [84] Harrison 1955.
[85] Macpherson 1962, p. viii.   [86] Strauss 1952, pp. 30–1.

took place in his thinking between the completion of *Il Principe* in 1513 and of the *Discorsi* in 1519. The appropriate task is instead held to be that of constructing for Machiavelli a scheme of beliefs sufficiently generalised for the doctrines of *Il Principe* to be capable of being *aufgehoben* into the *Discorsi* with any apparent contradictions resolved.[87] The historiography of Marx's social and political thought reveals a similar trend. Marx is not allowed to have developed and changed his mind from the humanistic strains of the *Economic-Philosophical Manuscripts* to the apparently more mechanistic system outlined over twenty years later in volume 1 of *Das Kapital*. Sometimes we are instead assured that the appropriate task must be to construct 'a structural analysis of the whole of Marx's thought', so that these apparent divergences can be viewed as part of 'one corpus'.[88] Sometimes we are instead informed that the existence of the earlier material shows that Marx was always 'obsessed with a moral vision of reality', and that this can be used to discredit his later scientific pretensions, since he 'appears not as the scientist of society that he claimed to be, but rather as a moralist or religious kind of thinker'.[89]

This belief in the desirability of resolving antinomies has even received an explicit defence. This has come from the pen of Leo Strauss, who maintains that the clue to understanding any apparent 'blunders' committed by any 'master of the art of writing' lies in reflecting on the threat of persecution and its likely effects on the voicing of our thoughts.[90] During any 'era of persecution' it becomes necessary to hide one's less orthodox beliefs 'between the lines' of one's published work. ('The expression', one learns with relief, 'is clearly metaphoric.') It follows that, if 'an able writer' in such a situation appears to contradict himself in setting out his ostensible views, then 'we may reasonably suspect' that the apparent contradictions have been deliberately planted as a signal to his 'trustworthy and intelligent' readers that he is really opposed to the orthodox views he may appear to hold.

The difficulty with this defence is that it depends on two *a priori* assumptions which, although implausible, are not merely left unargued

---

[87] For a survey of this approach see Cochrane 1961. The assumption appears in Federico Chabod's as well as (especially) in Friedrich Meinecke's work. For a critical survey of such assumptions see Baron 1961.

[88] Avineri 1968, p. 2.

[89] Tucker 1961, pp. 7, 11, 21. This allows the useful conclusion that the 'relevance' usually accorded to the classic texts stops short at Marx, for his religious obsession means that he 'has very little to say to us' about capitalism (p. 233), and 'not only made no positive contribution but performed a very great disservice' in what he had to say about freedom (p. 243).

[90] Strauss 1952, pp. 24–5, 30, 32.

but are treated as 'facts'. First, the enquiry gains its direction from the assumption that to be original *is* to be subversive. For this is the means by which we know in which texts to look for doctrines between the lines. Secondly, any interpretation based on reading between the lines is virtually insulated from criticism by the further 'fact' that 'thoughtless men are careless readers'. It follows that to fail to 'see' the message between the lines *is* to be thoughtless, while to 'see' it *is* to be trustworthy and intelligent. But suppose we ask for some means of testing whether or not we are dealing with one of the relevant 'eras of persecution', and whether in consequence we should or should not be trying to read between the lines. We are answered with two obviously circular arguments. How are we to recognise eras of persecution? They are those in which heterodox writers will be forced to cultivate this 'peculiar technique of writing'. Should we assume that the technique is invariably in play? We should not assume its presence 'when it would be less exact than not doing so'. Despite this explicit defence, therefore, it remains hard to see how the insistence that we must look for the 'inner coherence' of a given writer's thoughts can give rise to anything more than mythological accounts of what they actually thought.

IV

Both the mythologies I have been discussing arise from the fact that historians of ideas will unavoidably be *set*, in approaching any given writer, by some pre-judgements about the defining characteristics of the discipline to which the writer is supposed to have contributed. It may well seem, however, that even if such mythologies proliferate at this level of abstraction, they will scarcely arise – or will be much easier to detect and discount – when the historian operates simply at the level of describing the internal economy and argument of some individual work. It is indeed usual to insist that there can be nothing very problematic about the business of anatomising the contents and arguments of the classic texts. It is therefore all the more necessary to insist that even at this level we are still confronted with further dilemmas generated by the priority of paradigms, and still confronted in consequence with a further set of ways in which historical exegesis can lapse into mythology.

When considering what significance some particular text may be said to have for us, it is rather easy in the first place to describe the work and its alleged relevance in such a way that no place is left for the analysis of what its author may have intended or meant. The characteristic result of this confusion is a type of discussion that might be labelled the mythology of prolepsis, the type of mythology we are prone to generate when we are more interested in the retrospective significance of a given episode than in its meaning for the agent at the time. For example, it has often been suggested that, with Petrarch's ascent of Mount Ventoux, the age of the Renaissance dawned. Now this might, in a romantic sort of way, be said to give us a true account of the significance of Petrarch's action and its interest for us. But no account under this description could ever be a true account of any action Petrarch intended, or hence of the meaning of his act.[91] The characteristic, in short, of the mythology of prolepsis is the conflation of the asymmetry between the significance an observer may justifiably claim to find in a given historical episode and the meaning of that episode itself.

One such prolepsis which has constantly been exposed, but has constantly recurred, has been the attempt to stigmatise Plato's political views in *The Republic* as those of a 'totalitarian party-politician'.[92] Another has been the attempt to insist that Rousseau's political views not only 'provided the philosophical justification for the totalitarian as well as the democratic national state',[93] but that the force of this 'provision' was such that Rousseau should be 'given special *responsibility* for the emergence of totalitarianism'.[94] In both cases an account that might be true of the historical significance of a work becomes conflated with an account of what its author was doing that could not in principle be true.

Such crude versions of the mythology can be (and have been) very readily exposed. But this has not been sufficient to prevent the same type of prolepsis from recurring, in a less noticeable fashion, in discussions of other admittedly influential political theorists. By way of example, consider the cases of Machiavelli and Locke. Machiavelli, we are often told, 'was the founder of the modern political orientation'.[95] With Machiavelli 'we stand at the gateway of the modern world'.[96] Now this may well provide a true account of Machiavelli's historical significance (though it seems to presuppose a somewhat naive view of historical causation). But the claim is frequently used to preface a discussion of the characteristically 'modern' elements in Machiavelli's thought, and has

---

[91] For these considerations, and for other examples of a similar kind, see the discussion in Danto 1965, pp. 149–81.

[92] Popper 1962, vol. 1, p. 169.　　[93] Bronowski and Mazlish 1960, p. 303.

[94] Chapman 1956, p. vii. My italics. For the judgements there discussed, see for example Cobban 1941, p. 67 and especially Talmon 1952 where it is claimed (p. 43) that Rousseau 'gave rise to totalitarian democracy'.

[95] Winiarski 1963, p. 247.　　[96] Cassirer 1946, p. 140.

even been offered as an account of 'the *intention* of Machiavelli's political teaching'.[97] The danger here is not merely that of too readily 'seeing' the 'modern' elements that the commentator is now programmed to find. There is also the danger that such interpretations may part company with anything that could in principle be a plausible account of what Machiavelli's political writings were meant to achieve.

A similar problem has bedevilled the discussion of Locke's political philosophy. We are frequently told (no doubt correctly) that Locke was one of the founders of the modern empirical and liberal school of political thought. But all too often this characterisation is elided into the claim that Locke was himself a 'liberal' political theorist.[98] The effect has been to turn a claim about Locke's significance which might be true into a claim about the content of his works which could not be true. For Locke can scarcely have intended to contribute to a school of political philosophy which, so this interpretation suggests, it was his great achievement to have made possible.[99] The surest sign, in short, that we are in the presence of the mythology of prolepsis is that the discussion will be open to the crudest type of criticism that can be levelled against teleological forms of explanation: the episode has to await the future to learn its meaning.

Even when these cautions have been given their due weight, the apparently simple aim of describing the contents of a given classic text may still be capable of giving rise to comparable difficulties. For there is still the possibility that the observer may misdescribe, by a process of historical foreshortening, the intended meaning of the text. This danger can hardly fail to arise in any attempt to understand an alien culture or an unfamiliar conceptual scheme. If there is to be any prospect of the observer's successfully communicating such an understanding within their own culture, it is obviously dangerous, but it is equally inescapable, that they should apply their own familiar criteria of classification and discrimination. The attendant danger is that the observer may 'see' something apparently familiar in the course of studying an unfamiliar argument, and may in consequence provide a misleadingly recognisable description of it.

The writing of the history of ideas is marked by two particular forms of such parochialism. First there is the danger that the historian may misuse his or her vantage-point in describing the apparent *reference* of

97 Winiarski 1963, p. 273. My italics.
98 As is assumed in Gough 1950, Gough 1957, Plamenatz 1963 and Seliger 1968.
99 For an analysis of this confusion and a corrective to it see Dunn 1969, pp. 29–31, 204–6. See also Tully 1993, esp. pp. 2, 6, 73–9.

some statement in a classic text. An argument in one work may happen to remind the historian of a similar argument in another and earlier work, or may appear to contradict it. In either case the historian may mistakenly come to suppose that it was the intention of the later writer to refer to the earlier, and so may come to speak misleadingly of the 'influence' of the earlier work.

This is not to suggest that the concept of influence is devoid of explanatory force. The danger is, however, that it is easy to use the concept in an apparently explanatory way without considering whether the conditions sufficient or at least necessary for the application of the concept have been met. The frequent result is a narrative that reads like the opening chapters of the First Book of Chronicles, although without the genetic justification. Consider, for example, the alleged genealogy of Edmund Burke's political views. His aim in his *Thoughts on the Causes of the Present Discontents* was 'to counteract the influence of Bolingbroke'.[100] Bolingbroke himself is said to have written under the influence of Locke.[101] Locke in turn is said either to have been influenced by Hobbes, whom he must 'really' have had in mind in the *Two Treatises*,[102] or else to be concerned to counter Hobbes's influence.[103] And Hobbes in turn is said to have been influenced by Machiavelli,[104] by whom everyone was apparently influenced.[105]

Most of these explanations are purely mythological, as can readily be seen if we consider what the necessary conditions would have to be for helping to explain the appearance in a given writer B of any doctrine by invoking the 'influence' of an earlier writer A.[106] Such a set of conditions would have to include at least the following: (i) that B is known to have studied A's works; (ii) that B could not have found the relevant

---

[100] See Mansfield 1965, p. 86 and cf. also pp. 41, 66, 80. For the corresponding claim that Bolingbroke 'anticipates' Burke, see Hart 1965, pp. 95, 149 *et passim*.

[101] Mansfield 1965, p. 49 *et passim*. Textbooks on eighteenth-century thought find 'the tradition of Locke' indispensable as a means of accounting for some of the most salient features of the period. See, for example, Laski 1961, pp. 47–53, 131.

[102] For this assumption see Strauss 1953 and Cox 1960.

[103] This is the theory in general circulation. Even Wolin 1961, p. 26 insists that 'a careful reader cannot fail to see' that Locke was aiming to refute Hobbes. The assumption figures in most textbooks of early-modern political thought. See, for example, Martin 1962, p. 120.

[104] See, for example, Strauss 1957, p. 48 for the claim that Hobbes 'accepted' Machiavelli's 'critique of traditional political philosophy'.

[105] See Raab 1964, and cf. Cherel 1935 and Prezzolini 1968.

[106] For a fuller analysis of problems about 'influence' see Skinner 1966. For the claim that my argument here is unduly sceptical, even disabling, see Oakley 1999, pp. 138–87. But I do not deny that the concept is capable of being fruitfully used. (I sometimes use it myself.) I only assert that we must have some confidence that our invocations of the concept do something to pass the tests I have proposed.

doctrines in any writer other than A; and (iii) that B could not have arrived at the relevant doctrines independently. Now consider my above example in terms of this model. It is arguable that the alleged influence of Machiavelli on Hobbes, and of Hobbes on Locke, fails even to pass test (i). Certainly Hobbes never explicitly discusses Machiavelli, and Locke never explicitly discusses Hobbes. It is demonstrable that the alleged influence of Hobbes on Locke, and of Bolingbroke on Burke, fails to pass test (ii). Burke could equally well have found the doctrines of Bolingbroke by which he is said to have been influenced in a range of early eighteenth-century political pamphleteers hostile to the government of Walpole.[107] Locke could similarly have found the doctrines said to be characteristic of Hobbes in a range of *de facto* political writings of the 1650s – which Locke is at least known to have read, while it is not clear how closely he read Hobbes.[108] Finally, it is evident that none of the examples cited passes test (iii). (It might even be said that it is not clear how test (iii) could ever be passed.)

The other prevalent form of parochialism stems from the fact that commentators unconsciously misuse their vantage point in describing the *sense* of a given work. There is always the danger that the historian may conceptualise an argument in such a way that its alien elements dissolve into a misleading familiarity. Two obvious instances must suffice to illustrate the point. Consider first the case of an historian who decides (perhaps quite rightly) that a fundamental feature of the radical political thinking of the English Revolution during the mid-seventeenth century was a concern with the extension of the right to vote. Such an historian may then be led to conceptualise this characteristically Leveller demand in terms of an argument for democracy. The danger arises when the concept of a 'philosophy of liberal democracy'[109] is then used as a paradigm for the description and understanding of the Leveller movement. The paradigm makes it unnecessarily difficult to account for some of the most characteristic features of Leveller ideology. If we are programmed, for example, to think in terms of the 'republican secularism' of the Leveller leadership, then it is not surprising that their agonisings over the monarchy and their appeals to religious sentiment begin to look baffling.[110] The

---

[107] For the large number and general drift of these see Foord 1964, esp. pp. 57–109, 113–59.

[108] For the *de facto* theorists of the early 1650s and their relationship to Hobbes see below, vol. 3 chs. 9 and 10. On Locke's reading see Laslett 1965.

[109] See Brailsford 1961, p. 118 and cf. Wootton 1986, pp. 38–58 on the emergence of 'democracy' in seventeenth-century England.

[110] Brailsford 1961, pp. 118, 457.

paradigm of 'democracy' will also tend to lead the historical investigation in inappropriate directions. Some anachronistic concept of 'the welfare state' has to be found in Leveller thought, as well as a belief in universal suffrage which they never held.[111]

Consider, in a similar vein, an historian who decides (again perhaps quite rightly) that the argument in Locke's *Two Treatises* about the right to resist tyrannical governments is related to his argument about the place of consent in any lawful political community. Such an historian may then be led to use the notion of 'government by consent' as a paradigm for the description of Locke's argument.[112] The same danger arises. When we speak about government by consent, we generally have in mind a theory about the conditions that must be met if the legal arrangements of a civil association are to count as legitimate. It is thus natural to turn with this conceptualisation in mind to Locke's text, and duly to find some such theory rather bunglingly set out. But when Locke speaks of government by consent, this does not seem to have been what he had in mind at all. Locke's concern with the concept of consent arises in connection with his account of the *origins* of legitimate political societies.[113] This is hardly what we should regard as an argument for consent. But it seems to have been Locke's argument, and the only result of failing to start from this point will be to misdescribe his theory, and so to accuse him of having bungled an account which he was not, in fact, trying to write.

The difficulty with which I have been concerned throughout is thus that, while it is inescapable, it is also dangerous for historians of ideas to approach their materials with preconceived paradigms. It will by now be evident that the point at which such dangers arise is the point at which the historian in effect begins to ignore certain general considerations applicable to the enterprise of making and understanding statements. A consideration of these issues will enable me to summarise the methodological lessons on which I have so far sought to insist.

One such consideration is that no agent can be said to have meant or achieved something which they could never be brought to accept as a correct description of what they had meant or achieved. This special authority of agents over their intentions does not exclude the possibility that an observer might be in a position to give a fuller or more convincing account of the agent's actions than they could give themselves.

[111] Brailsford 1961, p. 233; cf. Woodhouse 1938, p. 83.
[112] As, for example, in Gough 1950, pp. 47–72.   [113] For this claim see Dunn 1980, pp. 29–52.

(Psychoanalysis is founded on this possibility.) But it does exclude that an acceptable account of an agent's behaviour could ever survive the demonstration that it was dependent on the use of criteria of description and classification not available to the agent. For if an utterance or other action has been performed by an agent at will, and has a meaning for the agent, any plausible account of what the agent meant must necessarily fall under, and make use of, the range of descriptions that the agent could in principle have applied to describe and classify what he or she was saying or doing. Otherwise the resulting account, however compelling, will not be an account of the agent's utterance or action.[114]

It will be evident that it is precisely this consideration which is so readily ignored whenever the classic theorists are criticised by historians of ideas for failing to enunciate their doctrines in a coherent fashion, or for failing to enunciate a doctrine on one of the allegedly perennial issues. For it cannot be a correct appraisal of any agent's action to say that they have failed to do something unless it is first clear that they could have had, and did in fact have, the intention to perform that particular action. To apply this test is to recognise that many of the questions I have considered (questions such as whether Marsilius enunciated a doctrine of the separation of powers and so on) are, strictly speaking, void for lack of reference. There is no means of formulating such questions in terms that could in principle have made sense to the agents concerned. The same test makes it clear that the claims about 'anticipations' I have been examining – claims of the form that 'we may regard Locke's theory' of signs 'as an anticipation of Berkeley's metaphysics' – are likewise meaningless.[115] There is no point in so regarding Locke's theory if our aim is to say anything about Locke. (It can scarcely have been Locke's intention to anticipate Berkeley's metaphysics.) We can tell such stories if we like, but the writing of history (notwithstanding a fashionable attitude among philosophers) cannot simply consist of stories: a further feature of historical stories is that they are supposed to track the truth.[116]

One final consideration worth highlighting relates to the activity of thinking itself. We need to reckon with the fact that thinking is an effortful activity, not simply a manipulation of a kaleidoscope of mental images.[117] The attempt to think out problems, as a matter of common introspection

---

[114] Hampshire 1959, esp. pp. 135–6, 153–5, 213–16. Some kindred issues are developed in Taylor 1964, esp. pp. 54–71.

[115] Armstrong 1965, p. 382.   [116] For an elaboration see Mandelbaum 1967.

[117] Dunn 1980, pp. 13–28 includes a fuller statement of this point.

and observation, does not seem to take the form of, or be reducible to, a patterned or even a uniformly purposive activity. Rather we engage in an often intolerable wrestle with words and meanings, we spill over the limits of our intelligence and become confused, and we often find that our attempts to synthesise our views reveal conceptual disorders at least as much as coherent doctrines. But it is precisely this consideration which is ignored whenever an interpreter insists on collecting the regrettably 'scattered' thoughts of some classic writer and presenting them systematically, or on discovering some level of coherence at which the efforts and confusions that ordinarily mark the activity of thinking are made to disappear, all passion spent.

V

By now it may seem that there is an obvious objection to the line of argument I have been laying out. I have been anatomising the dangers that arise if one approaches the classic texts in the history of ideas by treating them as self-sufficient objects of enquiry, concentrating on what each writer *says* about each of the canonical doctrines and thereby seeking to recover the meaning and significance of their works. One might retort, however, that with sufficient care and scholarship such dangers can surely be avoided. But if they can be avoided, what becomes of my initial claim that there is something inherently misguided about this approach?

By way of answer, I wish to advance a thesis complementary to, but stronger than, the one I have so far defended. The approach I have been discussing, I shall argue, cannot in principle enable us to arrive at an adequate understanding of the texts we study in the history of thought. The fundamental reason is that, if we wish to understand any such text, we must be able to give an account not merely of the meaning of what was said, but also of what the writer in question may have meant by saying what was said. A study that focuses exclusively on what a writer *said* about some given doctrine will not only be inadequate, but may in some cases be positively misleading as a guide to what the writer in question may have intended or meant.

Consider first the obvious point that the meanings of the terms we use to express our concepts sometimes change over time, so that an account of what a writer says about a given concept may yield a potentially misleading guide to the meaning of their text. Take, for example, the reception of Bishop Berkeley's doctrine of immaterialism at the hands of his contemporary critics. Both Andrew Baxter and Thomas Reid remark on the 'egoism' of Berkeley's outlook, and it was under this heading that his work was discussed in the *Encyclopédie*.[118] It is thus of some consequence to know that, if Berkeley's contemporaries had intended to accuse him of what we should mean by egoism, they would have been much more likely to refer to his 'Hobbism'. When they spoke of his egoism, what they meant was something much more like what we should mean by solipsism.[119]

A second and more important reason for thinking that what a writer says about a given doctrine may prove a misleading guide to what they may have meant is that writers often deliberately employ a range of what might be called oblique rhetorical strategies. Of these the most obvious is irony, the deployment of which has the effect of prising apart what is said from what is meant. I examine some of the problems raised by this strategy in chapter 6, but the essential point can perhaps be briefly introduced here. Take, for example, the doctrine of religious toleration as it presented itself to English intellectuals at the time of the Toleration Act of 1689. There are good reasons for saying that the various contributions to the debate largely reflected a common outlook. But it would only be as the result of a most sophisticated historical investigation that we could come to recognise, say, that Daniel Defoe's *Shortest-Way* of dealing with the dissenters, Benjamin Hoadly's *Letter* to the Pope about the powers of the Church and John Locke's *Letter Concerning Toleration* all aim to convey a similar message about the value of tolerating religious dissent. A study of what each writer *says* about the issue would guarantee blank misunderstanding in the case of Defoe and considerable confusion in the case of Hoadly. Only Locke seems to say anything resembling what he means, and even here we might wish (remembering Swift) to find some means of reassuring ourselves that no irony is involved. It is hard, in short, to see how any amount of reading such texts 'over and over', as we are exhorted to do,[120] will enable us to move in such cases from what was said to an understanding of what was meant.

A further and more intractable problem about oblique strategies can readily arise. There may be some reason to doubt whether, as one expert has put it, it is 'historically more credible' to say of a given writer that he 'believed what he wrote' than to suppose that he must have been insincere. Consider, for example, the way in which this problem arises in the interpretation of such philosophers as Thomas Hobbes or Pierre Bayle. When Hobbes discusses the laws of nature, the doctrine he enunciates

---

[118] Baxter 1745, vol. 2, p. 280; Reid 1941, p. 120.   [119] Bracken 1965, pp. 1–25, 59–81.
[120] Plamenatz 1963, vol. 1, p. x.

includes the claim that the laws of nature are the laws of God, and that we are obliged to obey the laws of nature. These overt sentiments have traditionally been dismissed as the work of a sceptic pressing a familiar vocabulary into heterodox use. But a number of revisionist commentators have sought to insist (the form of words is revealing) that Hobbes must after all have 'meant quite seriously what he so often says, that the "Natural Law" is the command of God, and to be obeyed because it is God's command'.[121] Hobbes's scepticism is thus treated as a disguise; when the mask is torn off, he emerges as the exponent of a Christian deontology. So too with Bayle, whose *Dictionnaire* contains most of the doctrines appropriate to a Calvinist theology of the most rigorous and unforgiving kind. Again it has been usual to dismiss this overt message by insisting that Bayle cannot possibly have been sincere. But again a number of revisionist commentators have sought to argue that, far from being the prototype of a sneering *philosophe*, Bayle was a man of faith, a religious thinker whose pronouncements need to be taken at face value if his arguments are to be understood.[122]

I am not concerned to ask directly which of these lines of interpretation is to be preferred in the case of either Hobbes or Bayle. But I do wish to point to the inadequacy of the methodology by which these revisionist interpretations have been guided. We are told that 'a close study of the texts', a concentration on the texts 'for themselves' will be sufficient in each instance to establish the revisionist case.'[123] It does not seem to have been recognised that an acceptance of these interpretations entails the acceptance of some very peculiar assumptions about Hobbes, Bayle and the age in which they lived. Both thinkers were accepted by the *philosophes* as their great predecessors in scepticism, and were understood in the same way by contemporary critics as well as sympathisers, none of whom ever doubted that they had intended to speak destructively of prevailing religious orthodoxies. It is, of course, possible to dismiss this objection by insisting that all of Hobbes's and Bayle's contemporary critics were equally mistaken, and in exactly the same way, about the nature of the intentions underlying their texts. But to accept this improbable hypothesis is merely to raise further difficulties about the attitudes of Hobbes and Bayle themselves. Both had good reason to recognise that

---

[121] Taylor 1938, p. 418. Warrender 1957 takes up a comparable position, while Hood 1964 offers a more extreme statement. For a more incisive version of the argument see Martinich 1992, pp. 71–135.

[122] See Dibon 1959, p. xv and cf. Labrousse 1964, pp. 346–86, discussing Bayle's articles on David and on Manicheanism.

[123] Hood 1964, p. vii; Labrousse 1964, p. x.

religious heterodoxy was a dangerous commitment. Hobbes (according to John Aubrey) lived for a time in dread lest the bishops bring in 'a motion to have the good old gentleman burn't for a heretique'.[124] Bayle was dismissed from his professorship at Sedan for being anti-Catholic, and later dismissed from his professorship at Rotterdam for not being anti-Catholic enough. If both writers intended their works to propagate orthodox religious sentiment, it becomes impossible to understand why neither of them removed from later editions of their works – as both could have done, and as Bayle was urged to do – those portions which had apparently been so grievously misunderstood, and why neither of them attempted to correct the apparent misconceptions which arose about the underlying intentions of their works.[125]

Hobbes's and Bayle's texts, in short, raise questions that we can never hope to resolve by reading them 'over and over' until we come to believe that we have understood them. If we now decide – as a result of reflecting on the implications I have emphasised – that it is doubtful whether their texts mean what they say, this will be because of information beyond the texts themselves. If, by contrast, we still feel able to insist that the texts say what they mean, we are left with the problem of accounting for the peculiar implications of this commitment. Whichever interpretation we accept, we cannot hope to defend it simply by referring to the apparent meanings of the texts.

Far more important, however, than any of these considerations is the fact that, in the case of *any* serious utterance, the study of what someone says can never be a sufficient guide to understanding what was meant. To understand any serious utterance, we need to grasp not merely the meaning of what is said, but at the same time the intended force with which the utterance is issued. We need, that is, to grasp not merely what people are saying but also what they are *doing in* saying it. To study what past thinkers have *said* about the canonical topics in the history of ideas is, in short, to perform only the first of two hermeneutic tasks, each of which is indispensable if our goal is that of attaining an historical understanding of what they wrote. As well as grasping the meaning of what they said, we need at the same time to understand what they meant by saying it.

To insist on this claim is to draw on Wittgenstein's arguments about what is involved in the recovery of meaning and on J. L. Austin's development of Wittgenstein's arguments about meaning and use. I offer a fuller account of these theories and their relevance for the activity of

---

[124] Aubrey 1898, vol. I, p. 339.
[125] For these details about Hobbes see Mintz 1962 and about Bayle see Robinson 1931.

textual interpretation in chapters 5 and 6. Here I content myself with illustrating the difference it makes to the study of individual texts and 'unit ideas' if we take seriously the fact that there is always a question to be asked about what writers are *doing* as well as what they are saying if our aim is to understand their texts.

By way of illustrating this claim, consider first the case of an individual text. Descartes in his *Meditations* thinks it vital to be able to vindicate the idea of indubitable knowledge. But why was this an issue for him at all? Traditional historians of philosophy have scarcely acknowledged the question; they have generally taken it for granted that, since Descartes was an epistemologist, and since the problem of certainty is one of the central problems of epistemology, there is no special puzzle here at all. They have accordingly felt able to concentrate on what they have taken to be their basic interpretative task, that of critically examining what Descartes *says* about how we can come to know anything with certainty.

My dissatisfaction with this approach – to express it in R. G. Collingwood's helpful terms – stems from the fact that it leaves us without any sense of the specific question to which Descartes may have intended his doctrine of certainty as a solution.[126] It leaves us in consequence without any understanding of what he may have been doing in presenting his doctrine in the precise form in which he chose to present it. This being so, it has I think been a major advance in Descartes scholarship of recent years that a number of scholars – Richard Popkin, E. M. Curley and others – have begun to ask themselves precisely these questions about the *Meditations*.[127] By way of answer, they have suggested that part of what Descartes was doing was responding to a new and especially corrosive form of scepticism arising from the recovery and propagation of the ancient Pyrrhonian texts in the later sixteenth century. They have thereby provided us not merely with a new way of characterising the *Meditations*, but at the same time with a key to interpreting many of its detailed effects. They have enabled us to think anew about why the text is organised in a certain way, why a certain vocabulary is deployed, why certain arguments are particularly singled out and emphasised, why in general the text possesses its distinctive identity and shape.

A similar set of considerations applies to Lovejoy's project of concentrating on 'unit ideas'[128] and 'tracking a grand but elusive theme' through

---

126 Collingwood 1939, pp. 34–5.   127 See Popkin 1969, 1979 and Curley 1978.
128 On 'unit ideas' as objects of study see Lovejoy 1960, esp. pp. 15–17.

a given period or even 'over many centuries'.[129] Consider, for example, the project of trying to write the history of the idea of *nobilitas* in early-modern Europe. The historian might begin, quite properly, by pointing out that the meaning of the term was given by the fact that it was used to refer to a particularly prized moral quality. Or the historian might, equally properly, point out that the same term was used to denote membership of a particular social class. It might not in practice be clear which meaning should be understood in a given case. When Francis Bacon remarks that nobility adds majesty to a monarch, but diminishes power, we might (remembering his admiration for Machiavelli) think of the first meaning as readily as we might (remembering his official position) think of the second. A further problem arises from the fact that this ambiguity is often used by moralists in a studied way. Sometimes the aim is to insist that one can have noble qualities even if one lacks noble birth. The possibility that someone might rightly be called noble 'more for remembrance of their virtue than for discrepance of estates' was a frequent paradox in Renaissance moral thought.[130] But sometimes the aim is to insist that, while nobility is a matter of attainment, it happens to be connected with nobility of birth. This fortunate coincidence was even more commonly pointed out.[131] It was always open to the moralist, moreover, to turn the basic ambiguity against the concept of *nobilitas* itself, contrasting nobility of birth with accompanying baseness of behaviour. When Sir Thomas More in *Utopia* describes the noble behaviour of the military aristocracy, he may well have been aiming to bring the prevailing concept of *nobilitas* into disrepute.[132]

My example is obviously oversimplified, but it is still sufficient, I believe, to bring out two weaknesses inherent in the project of writing histories of 'unit ideas'. First, if we wish to understand a given idea, even within a given culture at a given time, we cannot simply concentrate à la Lovejoy on studying the terms in which it was expressed. For they are likely to have been used, as my example suggests, with varying and incompatible intentions. We cannot even hope that a sense of the context of utterance will necessarily resolve the difficulty, for the context itself may be ambiguous. Rather we shall have to study all the various contexts in which the words were used – all the functions they served, all the various things that could be done with them. Lovejoy's mistake lies not merely in looking for the 'essential meaning' of the 'idea' as something that must

---

[129] Lakoff 1964, p. vii.   [130] Elyot 1962, p. 104.
[131] See, for example, Humphrey 1563, Sig. K, 4[r] and 5[v].
[132] Hexter 1964 includes a subtle exploration of this possibility.

necessarily 'remain the same', but even in supposing that there need be any such 'essential' meaning (to which individual writers 'contribute') at all.[133]

A second problem is that, in writing such histories, our narratives almost instantly lose contact with statement-making agents. When they figure in such histories, they generally do so only because the relevant unit idea – the social contract, the idea of progress, the great chain of being and so forth – makes some appearance in their works, so that they can be said to have contributed to its development. What we cannot learn from such histories is what role – trivial or important – the given idea may have played in the thought of any individual thinker. Nor can we learn what place – central or peripheral – it may have occupied in the intellectual climate of any given period in which it appeared. We may perhaps learn that the expression was used at different times to answer a variety of questions. But we cannot hope to learn (to recur to R. G. Collingwood's point) *what* questions the use of the expression was thought to answer, and so what reasons there were for continuing to employ it.

The criticism to be made of such histories is not merely that they seem perpetually liable to lose their point. It is rather that, as soon as we see that there *is* no determinate idea to which various writers contributed, but only a variety of statements made by a variety of different agents with a variety of different intentions, what we are seeing is that there is no history of the idea to be written. There is only a history of its various uses, and of the varying intentions with which it was used. Such a history can hardly be expected even to retain the form of the history of a 'unit idea'. For the persistence of particular expressions tells us nothing reliable about the persistence of the questions that the expressions may have been used to answer, nor of what the different writers who used the expressions may have meant by using them.

To summarise. Once we see that there is always a question to be answered about what writers are *doing* in saying what they say, it seems to me that we shall no longer want to organise our histories around tracing 'unit ideas' or focusing on what individual writers say about 'perennial issues'. To say this is not to deny that there have been long continuities in Western moral, social and political philosophy, and that these have been reflected in the stable employment of a number of key concepts and modes of argument.[134] It is only to say that there are good reasons for not

---

[133] For these assumptions see Bateson 1953.   [134] On this point see MacIntyre 1966, pp. 1–2.

continuing to organise our histories around the study of such continuities, so that we end up with yet more studies of the kind in which, say, the views of Plato, Augustine, Hobbes and Marx on 'the nature of the just state' are laid out and compared.[135]

One reason for my scepticism about such histories, as I have tried to stress in the first part of my argument, is not merely that each thinker – to take the example I have just given – appears to answer the question about justice in his own way. It is also that the terms employed in phrasing the question – in this case the terms 'state', 'justice' and 'nature' – feature in their different theories, if at all, only in such divergent ways that it seems an obvious confusion to suppose that any stable concepts are being picked out. The mistake, in short, lies in supposing that there is any one set of questions to which the different thinkers are all addressing themselves.

A deeper reason for my scepticism is the one I have been seeking to illustrate in the present section of my argument. The approach I have been criticising involves abstracting particular arguments from the context of their occurrence in order to relocate them as 'contributions' to allegedly perennial debates. But this approach prevents us from asking what any given writer may have been *doing* in presenting their particular 'contribution', and thereby cuts us off from one of the dimensions of meaning we need to investigate if the writer in question is to be understood. This is why, in spite of the long continuities that have undoubtedly marked our inherited patterns of thought, I remain sceptical about the value of writing histories of concepts or 'unit ideas'. The only histories of ideas to be written are histories of their uses in argument.

VI

If my argument so far makes sense, two positive conclusions may be said to follow from it. The first concerns the appropriate method to adopt in studying the history of ideas. The understanding of texts, I have suggested, presupposes the grasp of what they were intended to mean and of how that meaning was intended to be taken. To understand a text must at least be to understand both the intention to be understood, and the intention that this intention be understood, which the text as an intended act of communication must have embodied. The question we accordingly need to confront in studying such texts is what their

---

[135] See Lockyer 1979 and cf. Collingwood 1939, pp. 61–3.

authors – writing at the time when they wrote for the specific audience they had in mind – could in practice have intended to communicate by issuing their given utterances. It seems to me, therefore, that the most illuminating way of proceeding must be to begin by trying to delineate the full range of communications that could have been conventionally performed on the given occasion by the issuing of the given utterance. After this, the next step must be to trace the relations between the given utterance and this wider linguistic context as a means of decoding the intentions of the given writer.[136] Once the appropriate focus of study is seen in this way to be essentially linguistic, and the appropriate methodology is seen in consequence to be concerned with the recovery of intentions, the study of all the facts about the social context of the given text can then take their place as a part of this linguistic enterprise. The social context figures as the ultimate framework for helping to decide what conventionally recognisable meanings it might in principle have been possible for someone to have intended to communicate. As I have sought to show in the case of Hobbes and Bayle, the context itself can thus be used as a sort of court of appeal for assessing the relative plausibility of incompatible ascriptions of intentionality. I do not suggest, of course, that this conclusion is in itself particularly novel.[137] What I do claim is that the critical survey I have conducted goes some way towards establishing a case for this methodology – towards establishing it not as an aesthetic preference or a piece of academic imperialism, but as a matter of grasping the necessary conditions for the understanding of utterances.

My second general conclusion concerns the value of studying the history of ideas. The most exciting possibility here is that of a dialogue between philosophical analysis and historical evidence. The study of statements uttered in the past raises special issues, and might yield insights of corresponding philosophical interest. Among the topics that might be more brightly illuminated if we were to adopt a strongly diachronic approach, one thinks in particular of the phenomenon of conceptual innovation and the study of the relationship between linguistic and ideological change. I begin to try to pursue some of these implications myself in chapters 8, 9 and 10 of this volume.

---

[136] For critical discussions of this suggestion about the primacy of context, especially linguistic context, see Turner 1983; Boucher 1985; Gunn 1988–9; Zuckert 1985; Spitz 1989; Arnold 1993, pp. 15–21; King 1995; Bevir 2001.

[137] For a brief statement of a similar commitment see Greene 1957–8. Cf. also Collingwood 1939 and Dunn 1980, pp. 13–28, two discussions to which I am deeply indebted. See also Dunn 1996, pp. 11–38. For a discussion of Collingwood's influence on those who began to write about the history of political philosophy in the 1960s see the valuable survey in Tuck 1993.

My main conclusion, however, is that the critique I have mounted suggests a more obvious point about the philosophical value of studying the history of ideas. On the one hand, it seems to me a lost cause to try to justify the subject in terms of the answers it can provide to the 'perennial problems' allegedly addressed in the classic texts. To approach the subject in these terms, I have sought to show, is to render it gratuitously naive. Any statement is inescapably the embodiment of a particular intention on a particular occasion, addressed to the solution of a particular problem, and is thus specific to its context in a way that it can only be naive to try to transcend. The implication is not merely that the classic texts are concerned with their own questions and not with ours; it is also that – to revive R. G. Collingwood's way of putting the point[138] – there are no perennial problems in philosophy. There are only individual answers to individual questions, and potentially as many different questions as there are questioners. Rather than looking for directly applicable 'lessons' in the history of philosophy, we shall do better to learn to do our own thinking for ourselves.

It by no means follows, however, that the study of the history of ideas has no philosophical value at all. The very fact, it seems to me, that the classic texts are concerned with their own problems, and not necessarily with ours, is what gives them their 'relevance' and current philosophical significance. The classic texts, especially in moral, social and political theory, can help us to reveal – if we will let them – not the essential sameness but rather the variety of viable moral assumptions and political commitments. It is here that their philosophical, even moral, value may be said to lie. There is a tendency (sometimes explicitly urged, as by Hegel, as a mode of proceeding) to suppose that the best, and not merely the inescapable, vantage point from which to survey the ideas of the past must be that of our present situation, because it is by definition the most highly evolved. Such a claim cannot survive a recognition of the fact that historical differences over fundamental issues may reflect differences of intention and convention rather than anything like a competition over a community of values, let alone anything like an evolving perception of the Absolute.

To recognise, moreover, that our own society is no different from any other in having its own local beliefs and arrangements of social and political life is already to reach a quite different and, I should wish to argue, a much more salutary point of vantage. A knowledge of the

---

[138] Collingwood 1939, p. 70.

history of such ideas can show the extent to which those features of our own arrangements which we may be disposed to accept as 'timeless' truths[139] may be little more than contingencies of our local history and social structure. To discover from the history of thought that there are in fact no such timeless concepts, but only the various different concepts which have gone with various different societies, is to discover a general truth not merely about the past but about ourselves.

It is a commonplace – we are all Marxists to this extent – that our own society places unrecognised constraints upon our imagination. It deserves, then, to become a commonplace that the historical study of the beliefs of other societies should be undertaken as one of the indispensable and irreplaceable means of placing limits on those constraints. The allegation that the history of ideas consists of nothing more than 'outworn metaphysical notions' – frequently advanced at the moment, with terrifying parochialism, as a reason for dispensing with this kind of history – would then become the very reason for regarding such histories as indispensably 'relevant', not because crude 'lessons' can be picked out of them, but because the history itself can provide a lesson in self-knowledge. To demand from the history of thought a solution to our own immediate problems is to commit not merely a methodological fallacy but something like a moral error. But to learn from the past – and we cannot otherwise learn at all – the distinction between what is necessary and what is contingently the product of our own local arrangements is to learn one of the keys to self-awareness itself.

[139] For the claim that 'the central problems of politics are timeless' see Hacker 1961, p. 20.

5

Motives, intentions and interpretation

I

We live in post-modern times (I am not the first to notice this) and one of
the more challenging features of post-modern culture has been a deep-
ened scepticism about the traditional humanist project of interpreting
texts. Given this development, it seems well worth asking anew how far
it remains defensible to speak – as I have done with some confidence
in chapter 4 – of recovering the motives and intentions of authors, of
ascribing particular meanings to their utterances, and of distinguishing
acceptable from unacceptable readings of literary or philosophical texts.
This is the far from modest task on which I shall now attempt to make
a modest start.

II

It is not difficult in retrospect to pick out a number of different schools of
thought that converged on the conclusion that questions about authors,
intentions and the meanings of texts ought no longer to be asked. The
exponents of the New Criticism spearheaded an influential attack on the
idea of recovering authorial intentionality when they declared that any
such project will inescapably involve us in a fallacious form of reasoning. As Wimsatt and Beardsley proclaimed in their classic article on the
alleged intentional fallacy, 'the design or intention of the author is neither
available nor desirable' as a guide to recovering the meaning of a literary
text.[1] Soon afterwards a yet more lethal attack was launched by Roland
Barthes and Michel Foucault when they jointly announced the death of

---

This chapter is partly based on my article 'Motives, Intentions and the Interpretation of Texts'
in *New Literary History* 3 (1972), pp. 393–408 and partly on my article 'From Hume's Intentions to
Deconstruction and Back' in *The Journal of Political Philosophy* 4 (1996), pp. 142–54.

[1] Wimsatt and Beardsley 1976, p. 1. This classic article, often republished, originally appeared in
the *Sewanee Review* in 1946. Cf. also Wimsatt 1954, Beardsley 1958 and Beardsley 1970.

the author, thereby burying the time-honoured dwelling-place of motives and intentionality.[2] But by far the most damaging campaign was opened in the late 1960s and early 1970s by Jacques Derrida when he began to argue that the very idea of textual interpretation is a mistake, since there are no such readings to be gained. There are only misreadings, since it is an error to suppose that we can ever arrive unambiguously at anything recognisable as the meaning of a text.[3]

A number of different senses of 'meaning' were frequently run together in the course of these sceptical attacks. At least three discriminable senses of the term appear to be in play, and we need to begin by trying if possible to prise them apart. The first is that to ask about meaning in this context may be equivalent to asking: what do the words mean, or what do certain specific words or sentences mean, in a given text? (I shall call this meaning$_1$.) It seems to be meaning$_1$ that Wimsatt and Beardsley principally have in mind in their essay on the intentional fallacy. They speak of explicating 'the meaning of a poem' by way of 'our habitual knowledge of the language, through grammars, dictionaries' and so on, and when they turn to discuss a poem by T. S. Eliot they concentrate on the need to decode 'the meaning of phrases in the poem'.[4] More recently, Beardsley has reiterated that the proper task of literary critics is to concentrate on examining 'textual meaning', the meaning of the words in front of us, not the supposed intentions of those who originally wrote them.[5]

When Derrida speaks about the irrecoverability of meaning, he likewise seems in general to be talking about meaning$_1$. He associates the attempted recovery of meaning with what he calls logocentrism, the belief that meanings originate in the world and are conveyed to us by the capacity of words to refer to things. This belief is said to give rise, in his Heideggerian phrase, to a metaphysics of presence; to the illusion that the truth about the world can be made present to the mind through the medium of a denotative language. The unavailability of such meanings stems from the fact that the terms we employ to signify things not only fail to do so univocally but float apart from what is purportedly signified until they come to exist in a state of free play. The alleged meanings of such signifiers are deferred until they ultimately disappear and are replaced by a state of pure intertextuality.[6] Here it seems moderately clear that we are talking about meaning$_1$. As one of Derrida's Anglophone

---

[2] Barthes 1979, pp. 73–8; Foucault 1979, pp. 141–60.   [3] Derrida 1976, pp. 6–100.
[4] Wimsatt and Beardsley 1976, pp. 6, 11.   [5] Beardsley 1992, p. 33.
[6] See Derrida 1976, pp. 6–73 and cf. Derrida 1978, pp. 278–82.

admirers has more crudely put it, the crucial contention is that the words we employ to refer to things lack 'fixed meanings'.[7]

By contrast with meaning$_1$, we may instead be asking: what does this text mean to me? (I shall call this meaning$_2$.) This is the sense that exponents of the New Criticism usually seem to have in mind when they speak about 'structures of effects' and the need to concentrate on assessing their impact on the reader. The same preoccupation with meaning$_2$ appears to underlie the phenomenological approach to literary criticism. When Wolfgang Iser, for example, speaks of the reading process as a 'realisation' of the text 'accomplished by the reader', he seems to be mainly preoccupied with meaning$_2$, especially when he argues that 'one must take into account not only the actual text but also, and in equal measure, the actions involved in responding to that text'.[8]

The theorists who have made it most evident that they are primarily interested in meaning$_2$ are those who have developed the insights of the phenomenologists into what has come to be called a reader-response approach to interpretation. One eminent exponent has been Paul Ricoeur, especially in his *Hermeneutics and the Human Sciences*. Ricoeur concedes that texts may well have pristine intended meanings, but he stresses that over the course of time, as well as because of the polysemic and metaphorical features of language, any text will acquire 'an autonomous space of meaning which is no longer animated by the intention of its author'.[9] Ricoeur's principal suggestion is that interpreters should concentrate on these changing public meanings of texts, rather than on the meanings that their original authors may have intended to assign to them. 'What the text says now matters more than what the author meant to say',[10] so that the act of interpretation should be viewed as equivalent to asking what the text now means for us, and hence as equivalent to appropriating it for our own purposes.[11]

An even more enthusiastic exponent of the reader-response approach has been Stanley Fish, especially in his collection of essays entitled *Is There a Text in this Class?* Fish makes it very clear that he is basically concerned with what I am calling meaning$_2$, especially when he announces at the outset that 'the reader's response is not *to* the meaning; it *is* the meaning' of a literary text.[12] Developing this insight, Fish thinks of readers so entirely as the sources of meaning that he writes of them as creators of all the information normally assumed by traditional theories

---

[7] Harlan 1989, p. 582.   [8] Iser 1972, p. 279.   [9] Ricoeur 1981, p. 174.
[10] Ricoeur 1981, p. 201.   [11] On interpretation as appropriation see Ricoeur 1981, pp. 145–64.
[12] Fish 1980, p. 3.

of interpretation to be embodied in texts. The act of interpretation is seen in consequence as 'the source of texts, facts, authors and intentions'; the only meanings we can hope to recover are the meanings we create.[13]

Rather than asking about meaning$_1$ or meaning$_2$, we may instead be asking: what does a writer mean by what he or she says in a given text? (I shall call this meaning$_3$.) Sometimes it appears to be this sense of meaning that Wimsatt and Beardsley have in mind in their purported exposure of the intentional fallacy. When they speak about 'the pursuit of full meanings' in the course of discussing the problem of allusiveness, they maintain that the question to be answered is 'what a poet means' by what he or she has said.[14] And when they bring their article to a close by contrasting 'the true and objective way of criticism' with 'the way of genetic and biographical inquiry', the question they leave us to ponder is which method is to be preferred if our aim in studying a poet is to understand 'what he meant'.[15]

Sometimes it is similarly clear that meaning$_3$ is what Derrida has in mind when he writes about the impossibility of recovering the meanings of texts. This certainly seems to be the case in the much-discussed example he offers of a fragment, found among Nietzsche's papers, which reads 'I have forgotten my umbrella.'[16] Even Derrida is willing to concede that in this instance there seems no difficulty about recovering what I am calling meaning$_1$, the meaning of the sentence itself. As Derrida remarks, 'Everyone knows what "I have forgotten my umbrella" means.'[17] Derrida's objection is that we are still left without any means of recovering what I am calling meaning$_3$, that is, of recovering what Nietzsche may have meant by writing just those words.[18] Perhaps, as Derrida concludes, he may have meant nothing at all. Derrida's point is that we have no means of knowing, since we have no means of recovering meaning$_3$, and hence no prospect of understanding what (if anything) Nietzsche may have meant.

III

My aim in this ground-clearing chapter is to assess how much attention, if any, we should pay to the motives and intentions of writers in seeking

---

[13] Fish 1980, p. 16.　　[14] Wimsatt and Beardsley 1976, p. 10.

[15] Wimsatt and Beardsley 1976, p. 13.

[16] Derrida 1979, pp. 122, 123. For a valuable discussion see Hoy 1985, pp. 54–8.

[17] Derrida 1979, p. 128: 'Chacun comprend ce que veut dire "j'ai oublié mon parapluie".'

[18] Derrida 1979, pp. 123, 125, 131.

to interpret the meaning of what they write. So far I have focused on a number of confusions attending the discussion of 'meaning' in these debates. I now turn to the other side of the coin, examining the various arguments that have been put forward in defence of the claim that we should pay no attention to motives or intentions in arriving at our readings of texts.

Two main types of argument can be distinguished. One is concerned with the need for purity in critical procedures, and thus with the claim that, even if it may be possible to discover such essentially biographical information about a writer, we must never allow such information to condition and so contaminate our response to their work. Hence it is that Wimsatt and Beardsley stigmatise the desire to consider anything other than the information provided by the text itself as a 'romantic fallacy'.[19] The claim, as one commentator on their theory has expressed it, is that all works of art must be 'self-explicatory'. We are merely registering 'a failure of art and criticism' if we make use of extraneous information of an historical or biographical kind.[20] As Wimsatt and Beardsley themselves declare, what we must deal with is simply 'the text itself'.[21]

The other and more prominent argument, however, derives from two contrasting (indeed incompatible) claims often made about the concepts of motive and intention themselves. One claim has been that the reason why critics should pay no attention to such factors is that the motives and intentions of writers are to be found 'inside' their texts, not separate from them, and accordingly stand in need of no separate consideration. This is one of the main grounds on which Wimsatt and Beardsley argue for the irrelevance of intentionality. They ask how a critic can 'find out what the poet tried to do' and answer that 'if the poet succeeded in doing it, then the poem itself shows what he was trying to do'.[22] The same view has been adopted by a number of more recent commentators on the so-called intentional fallacy. T. M. Gang, for example, insists that 'whenever something is plainly and unambiguously said, it hardly makes sense to ask the speaker what he intended his words to signify'.[23] Graham Hough agrees that 'with a completely successful poem all is achievement, and the question of a separately conceivable intention does not arise'.[24]

The other (and incompatible) claim has been that, on the contrary, it is because motives and intentions stand 'outside' a writer's works, and accordingly form no part of their structure, that critics should pay no

---

[19] Wimsatt and Beardsley 1976, pp. 3, 12.　　[20] Morris Jones 1964, p. 140.
[21] Wimsatt and Beardsley 1976, p. 9.　　[22] Wimsatt and Beardsley 1976, p. 2.
[23] Gang 1957, p. 178.　　[24] Hough 1966, p. 60.

attention to them in attempting to elucidate the meanings of texts. This second argument, however, has often been mounted in a somewhat confused way. At least three different reasons have been given for supposing that it follows from the way in which a writer's motives and intentions stand 'outside' their works that they must be irrelevant to the activity of interpretation. We need to begin by trying to disentangle them.

One contention has been that motives and intentions are simply impossible to recover. They are 'private entities to which no one can gain access'.[25] This is the first argument advanced by Wimsatt and Beardsley, who rhetorically ask 'how a critic expects to get an answer to the question about intention', and respond that such an awareness of 'design or intention' is simply not available.[26] The same commitment underlies a number of more recent contributions to the debate. We are told that 'intention is really unknowable'[27] and thus that literary critics and intellectual historians find themselves confronting an 'inevitable uncertainty about mental processes'.[28] They will be deceiving themselves if they suppose that they can ever 'project themselves into the minds of their authors' in such a way as to recover the intentions with which they wrote.[29]

A second contention has been that, while it may be possible to recover such motives and intentions, to pay attention to such information will be to furnish an undesirable standard for measuring the value of a literary or philosophical work. Wimsatt and Beardsley shift somewhat inconsistently to this ground at the outset of their discussion, arguing that a knowledge of a writer's intentions is not 'desirable as a standard for judging the success of a work of literary art'.[30] The same commitment recurs in a number of more recent presentations of the anti-intentionalist case. We are told, for example, that 'the problem is how far the author's intention in writing a work is relevant to the critic's judgement on it'[31] and we are warned that a concern about intention may affect the response of a reader in an undesirable way.[32]

A third contention has been that, while it may be possible to recover a writer's motives and intentions, it will never be *relevant* to pay attention to this type of information if the aim is to establish the meaning of a text. Wimsatt and Beardsley eventually shift to this further position, declaring that their sole concern is with 'the meaning of a poem' and that the

[25] See Aiken 1955, p. 752 for a discussion (but not an endorsement) of this argument.
[26] Wimsatt and Beardsley 1976, pp. 1–2.   [27] Smith 1948, p. 625.   [28] Gang 1957, p. 179.
[29] Harlan 1989, p. 587.   [30] Wimsatt and Beardsley 1976, pp. 1–2.   [31] Gang 1957, p. 175.
[32] Smith 1948, p. 625.

poet's state of mind is a wholly separate matter.[33] A similar commitment has sometimes underpinned the phenomenological and, more generally, the reader-response approach to the interpretation of texts. As we have seen, a theorist like Ricoeur does not doubt that texts have 'pristine' and intended meanings; he merely regards their recovery as a matter of secondary importance by contrast with the primary and more interesting task of investigating the 'public meanings' they subsequently come to acquire.

IV

I am now in a position to ask whether any of the above arguments succeeds in establishing, for any of the senses of 'meaning' I have discriminated, that the motives and intentions of writers can and ought to be ignored in attempting to recover the meanings of their texts. The first argument I considered – stemming from the desire to maintain purity in our critical procedures – appears to rest on a confusion. It may be that a knowledge of a writer's motives and intentions is irrelevant to elucidating 'the meaning' of their works in every sense of 'meaning' I have discriminated. But it does not follow that critics ought – or can hope – to ensure that this knowledge plays no role in helping to determine their response to that writer's work. To know about motives and intentions is to know the relationship in which a writer stands to what he or she has written. To know about intentions is to know such facts as whether the writer was joking or serious or ironic, or in general what speech acts they may have been performing in writing what they wrote. To know about motives is to know what prompted those particular speech acts, quite apart from their character and truth-status as utterances. Now it may well be that to know, say, that a certain writer was largely motivated by envy and resentment tells us nothing about 'the meaning' of their works. But once a critic possesses such knowledge it can hardly fail to condition their response to the work. The discovery, say, that a work was written not out of envy or resentment, but out of a simple desire to enlighten and amuse, seems virtually certain to engender a new and different response to it. This may or may not be desirable, but it seems to some degree inevitable.[34]

I now turn to the various arguments derived from analysing the concepts of motive and intention themselves. The first – to the effect that it is impossible to recover such mental acts – gains its plausibility from

---

[33] Wimsatt and Beardsley 1976, pp. 6–9.   [34] A point well brought out in Cioffi 1976, pp. 70–3.

ignoring the extent to which the intentions embodied in any successful act of communication must, *ex hypothesi*, be publicly legible. Suppose that (to adapt an example from Wittgenstein) I come to understand that the man waving his arms in the next field is not trying to chase away a fly, as I had initially supposed, but is warning me that the bull is about to charge. To come to recognise that he is warning me is to come to understand the intentions with which he is acting. But to recover these intentions is not a matter of identifying the ideas inside his head at the moment when he first begins to wave his arms. It is a matter of grasping that arm-waving can count as warning, and that this is the convention being exploited in this particular case. This makes it seriously misleading to characterise such intentions as 'private entities to which no one can gain access'.[35] To the extent that the meanings of such episodes can be intersubjectively understood, the intentions underlying such performances must be entities with an essentially public character. As Clifford Geertz has finely remarked, ideas are 'envehicled meanings'; they 'are not, and have not been for some time, unobservable mental stuff'.[36]

I turn to the second argument, which seems to embody a misstatement. It would clearly be a mistake to suppose that a knowledge of a writer's motives or intentions could ever supply a standard for judging the merit or success of their work. As Frank Cioffi has remarked in a similar context, it certainly will not do for a writer to assure a critic that he intended to produce a masterpiece.[37] The third argument, by contrast, seems at least partly correct. I shall concede, that is, that even if it may not be true in the case of a writer's intentions, it may well be true in the case of his or her motives, that they may be said to stand 'outside' their works in such a way that the recovery of such motives will be irrelevant – for all the senses of 'meaning' I have discriminated – to an understanding of the meaning of their works.

This last claim rests, however, on a distinction between motives and intentions which has not usually been made explicit in the debate about the so-called intentional fallacy, but which my argument now requires me to spell out. It has certainly been a striking and unsatisfactory feature of the debate that, although most commentators have focused on intentionality, they have generally taken it for granted that everything they say about intentions will hold good for motives as well.[38] It seems to me, however, that it is indispensable to distinguish motives from intentions

---

[35] Aiken 1955, p. 752.   [36] Geertz 1980, p. 135.   [37] Cioffi 1976, p. 57.
[38] A point well made in Morris Jones 1964, p. 143.

in relation to questions about interpretation, and I shall next attempt to suggest how this distinction might most fruitfully be understood.[39]

To speak of a writer's motives seems invariably to speak of a condition antecedent to, and contingently connected with, the appearance of their works. But to speak of a writer's intentions may either be to refer to a plan or design to create a certain type of work (an intention to do x) or else to refer to an actual work in a certain way (as embodying a particular intention in x-ing). In the former case we seem (as in talking about motives) to be alluding to a contingent antecedent condition of the appearance of the work. But in the latter we seem to be alluding to a feature of the work itself. Specifically, we seem to be characterising it in terms of its embodiment of a particular aim or intention, and thus in terms of its having a particular purpose or point.

We can conveniently corroborate this claim by borrowing the jargon invented by philosophers of language to discuss the logical relations between the concepts of intention and meaning. They have concentrated on the fact (following J. L. Austin's classic analysis) that to issue any serious utterance is always to speak not only with a certain meaning but also with what Austin dubbed a certain illocutionary force.[40] When we issue a meaningful utterance, we may succeed at the same time in performing such illocutionary acts as promising, warning, entreating, informing and so on. Austin's usual way of putting the point was to say that gaining 'uptake' of the illocutionary force of an utterance will be equivalent to understanding what the speaker was *doing in* issuing it.[41] But another way of putting the point – crucial to my present argument – would be to say that an understanding of the illocutionary act performed by a speaker will be equivalent to understanding their primary intentions in issuing their utterance.

I turn to the significance for my present argument of these distinctions between motives and intentions, with the resulting isolation of the idea of an intention *in* speaking or writing with a certain force. These distinctions, it seems to me, lend strong support to the suggestion that the recovery of motives is indeed irrelevant to the activity of interpreting the meanings of texts. When we speak, that is, about a writer's motives *for* writing (although not their intentions *in* writing) we do indeed appear to be speaking of factors standing 'outside' their work, and in a contingent

---

[39] I am indebted to Anscombe 1957 and Kenny 1963, two classic discussions in which the concepts of motive and intention are distinguished along similar lines. For a (partial) endorsement of my deployment of these distinctions see Hancher 1972, esp. pp. 836n. and 842–3n.

[40] Austin 1980, pp. 98–108. [41] Austin 1980, p. 94 *et passim*.

relationship to it, in such a way that they can hardly be said to affect the meaning of the work itself.

If, however, we recall the other (and incompatible) claim usually made by literary theorists about the concepts of motive and intention, it might appear that I have already committed myself to saying that this conclusion holds good for the concept of intention as well. I have argued that we may speak of a writer's intentions *in* writing, and of these intentions as being in some sense 'inside' their texts, rather than 'outside' and contingently connected with their appearance. According to the first argument I cited, however, it is precisely because a writer's intentions are 'inside' their texts that, we are told, the critic need pay no special attention to their recovery in the attempt to interpret the meaning of their work.

This contention, however, rests on conflating two different sorts of question we might wish to ask about a writer's intentions. It will be convenient to revert to the jargon of the philosophers of language by way of making the point. On the one hand, we may wish to ask about the perlocutionary intentions embodied in a work.[42] We may wish, that is, to consider whether it may have been intended to achieve a certain effect or response such as (to take a well-worn example) that of inducing in the reader a feeling of sadness.[43] But on the other hand we may wish, as I have suggested, to ask about a writer's illocutionary intentions as a means of characterising their work. We may wish, that is, to ask not whether they achieved what they intended to achieve, but rather what their exact intentions were *in* writing what they wrote.

This brings me to my central contention about the relations between a writer's intentions and the meaning of a text. On the one hand, I shall concede that a writer's perlocutionary intentions (what they may have intended *by* writing in a certain way) do not need to be further considered. They do not seem to need any separate study, since the question of whether a work was intended by its author, say, to induce a feeling of sadness in the reader does seem to be capable of being settled (if at all) only by considering the work itself and such clues about its intended effects as may be contained within it. On the other hand, I now wish to argue that in the case of a writer's illocutionary intentions (what they may have intended *in* writing in a certain way) their recovery does require a separate form of study, which it will be essential to undertake if the critic's aim is to understand the meaning of what they wrote.

<hr>

[42] For the introduction of the concept of perlocutionary effects see Austin 1980, pp. 99, 101–2.

[43] Gang 1957, p. 177. Richards 1929, esp. pp. 180–3 appears to have been influential in directing attention towards these types of intentional effects.

If this contention is to be made good, however, I now need to revert to the three senses of 'meaning' I began by discriminating in order to determine how the sense of intentionality I have now isolated may be relevant to understanding 'the meaning' of a text.

If we turn first to meaning$_1$, it must be conceded that an understanding of a writer's illocutionary intentions scarcely seems relevant to understanding the meanings of texts in this sense. To say this is not to take sides on the immense and immensely difficult question of whether our statements about the meanings of words and sentences may not ultimately be reducible to statements about *someone's* intentions. It is only to assert the truism that questions about the meanings of the words and sentences I use cannot be equivalent to questions about my intentions in using them.[44]

If we turn next to meaning$_2$, it must again be conceded that an understanding of a writer's intentions in writing scarcely seems relevant to this sense of the meaning of a text. It seems clear, that is, that the question of what a literary or philosophical work may mean to a given reader can be settled quite independently of any considerations about what its creator may have intended.

If we turn to meaning$_3$, however, it seems possible to establish the closest possible connection between the intentions of writers and the meanings of their texts. For it seems that a knowledge of a writer's intentions in writing, in the sense I have sought to isolate, is not merely relevant to, but equivalent to, a knowledge of the meaning$_3$ of what they write. The stages by which I arrive at this conclusion will by now be clear. To gain 'uptake' of these intentions is equivalent to understanding the nature and range of the illocutionary acts that the writer may have been performing in writing in a particular way. As I have suggested, to recover such intentions is to be in a position to characterise what the writer was doing – is to be able to say that he or she must have been intending, for example, to attack or defend a particular line of argument, to criticise or contribute to a particular tradition of discourse, and so on. But to be able to characterise a work in such a way, in terms of its intended illocutionary force, is equivalent to understanding what the writer may have *meant by* writing in that particular way. It is equivalent, that is, to being able to say that he or she must have *meant* the work *as* an attack on, or a defence of, as a criticism of, or as a contribution to, some particular attitude or line of argument, and so on. And so the equivalence between these intentions

---

[44] For a survey of these issues see Strawson 1971, pp. 170–89.

in writing, and the meaning$_3$ of what is written, is established. For as I have already indicated, to know what a writer meant by a particular work *is* to know what his or her primary intentions were in writing it.

I wish finally to protect my thesis from two possible misinterpretations. My argument must first be distinguished from the much stronger claim often advanced to the effect that the recovery of these intentions, and the decoding of the 'original meaning' intended by the writer, must form the whole of the interpreter's task.[45] It has often been suggested that 'the final criterion of correctness' in interpretation can only be provided by studying the original context in which the work was written.[46] I have not been concerned, however, to lend support to this very strong version of what F. W. Bateson called the discipline of contextual reading. I see no impropriety in speaking of a work having a meaning which its author could not have intended. Nor does my thesis conflict with this possibility. I have been concerned only with the converse point: that whatever an author was *doing in* writing what he or she wrote must be relevant to interpretation, and thus that *among* the interpreter's tasks must be the recovery of the author's intentions *in* writing what he or she wrote.

This thesis must also be distinguished from the claim that, if we are concerned with the intentions of authors in this way, we must be prepared to accept whatever statements they make about their own intentions as a kind of final authority on what they were doing in a particular work. It is true that any agent is obviously in a privileged position when characterising their own intentions and actions. But I see no difficulty about reconciling the claim that we need to be able to characterise a writer's intentions if we are to interpret the meaning$_3$ of their works with the claim that it may sometimes be appropriate to discount their own accounts of what they were doing. This is not to say that we have lost interest in understanding such intentions as a guide to interpreting their works. It is only to say that a writer may not fully understand his or her intentions, or may be self-deceiving about recognising them, or may be incompetent at stating them. These are failures to which all flesh is perpetually heir.

But how are such illocutionary intentions to be recovered? I shall turn to this further question in the course of chapter 6, but it may be worth ending by gesturing at what I take to be the most crucial point. We need to focus not merely on the particular text in which we are interested but on the prevailing conventions governing the treatment of the issues or

---

[45] See, for example, Close 1972, pp. 36–8.   [46] Bateson 1953, p. 16.

themes with which the text is concerned. This injunction gains its force
from the consideration that any writer will normally be engaged in an
intended act of communication. It follows that whatever intentions a
writer may have, they must be conventional in the strong sense that they
must be recognisable as intentions to uphold some particular position
in argument, to contribute to the treatment of some particular topic,
and so on. It follows in turn that to understand what a writer may have
been doing in using some particular concept or argument, we need first
of all to grasp the nature and range of things that could recognisably
have been done by using that particular concept, in the treatment of that
particular theme, at that particular time. We need, in short, to be ready
to take as our province nothing less than the whole of what Cornelius
Castoriadis has described as the social imaginary, the complete range of
the inherited symbols and representations that constitute the subjectivity
of an age.[47]

[47] Castoriadis 1987, esp. pp. 353–73.

6

Interpretation and the understanding of speech acts

I

One of the most important of the many injunctions contained in Wittgenstein's *Philosophical Investigations* is that we ought not to think in isolation about 'the meanings of words'. We ought rather to focus on their use in specific language-games and, more generally, within particular forms of life.[1] Less than a decade after Wittgenstein threw down this epoch-making challenge, J. L. Austin picked it up by asking, in *How to Do Things with Words*, what exactly might be meant by investigating the use of words as opposed to their meanings,[2] and what might consequently be meant by saying that words are also deeds.[3] As I have already intimated in chapter 4, it has always seemed to me that, taken together, Wittgenstein's and Austin's insights offer a hermeneutic of exceptional value for intellectual historians and, more generally, for students of the cultural disciplines.[4] I have already spoken in chapter 5 of one particular way in which their approach seems to me of value in helping us to think about the project of understanding utterances and interpreting texts. I should now like to enlarge on these earlier discussions, to respond to criticisms of them, and thereby to present my argument in a more systematic and wide-ranging style.

II

Wittgenstein and Austin alike remind us that, if we wish to understand any serious utterance, we need to grasp something over and above the

<hr>

This chapter has been adapted and developed from the final section of my 'Reply to my Critics' in *Meaning and Context: Quentin Skinner and his Critics*, ed. James Tully (Cambridge, 1988), pp. 259–88.

[1] Wittgenstein 1958, paras. 138–9, 197–9, 241, pp. 53–4, 80–1, 88.   [2] Austin 1980.
[3] As is also claimed in Wittgenstein 1958, para. 546, p. 146.
[4] For an account of the applicability of Wittgenstein's insights to ethnography see Geertz 2000, pp. xi–xiii.

sense and reference of the terms used to express it. To cite Austin's formula, we need in addition to find the means to recover what the agent may have been *doing in* saying what was said, and hence of understanding what the agent may have meant by issuing an utterance with just that sense and reference.[5] Wittgenstein had already gestured at the two distinct dimensions of language that appear to be involved,[6] but the abiding value of Austin's formulation stems from the fact that he furnished a means of separating them out. He conceded that we first need to turn to the dimension conventionally described by speaking about the meanings of words and sentences. But he placed his main emphasis on the fact that we need in addition to grasp the particular *force* with which any given utterance (with a given meaning) may have been issued on a particular occasion.[7]

Austin tried further to clarify this fundamental point by introducing a neologism to distinguish the precise sense of 'the use of language' in which he was principally interested. He stressed that, in speaking about the force of an utterance, he was mainly pointing to what an agent may have been doing *in* saying what was said. He sought to distinguish this dimension from another whole range of things we may be doing in using words. This further range incorporates the things we may succeed in bringing about (whether intentionally or otherwise) as a result of speaking with a certain force. To separate the question of what we may be doing *in* saying something from what we may happen to bring about *by* saying something, Austin proposed that we speak of the illocutionary as opposed to the perlocutionary force of utterances.[8]

To illustrate the refinements that Austin was thus able to introduce into Wittgenstein's suggested analysis of 'meaning' in terms of 'the use of words', it may be helpful to keep in mind a single example. In the discussion that follows, as well as in my attempt to explore some further implications of it in chapter 7, I adapt an example originally put forward by P. F. Strawson in his analysis of the role of intentions and conventions in the understanding of speech acts.[9] A policeman sees a skater on a pond and says 'The ice over there is very thin.' The policeman says something and the words mean something. To understand the episode, we obviously need to know the meaning of the words. But we also need to know what the policeman was *doing in* saying what he said. For example, the

---

[5] Austin 1980, pp. 94, 98.

[6] On the force of utterances as an abstractable dimension of language see Holdcroft 1978, pp. 143–55.

[7] Austin 1980, p. 99.   [8] Austin 1980, pp. 109–20.   [9] Strawson 1971, p. 153.

policeman may have been *warning* the skater; the utterance may have been issued on the given occasion with the (illocutionary) force of warning. Finally, the policeman may at the same time have succeeded in bringing about some further (perlocutionary) consequences *by* saying what was said. For example, the policeman may have succeeded in persuading or frightening or perhaps merely irritating or amusing the skater.

Austin's chief aim was to clarify the idea of 'the use of language' in communication. So he placed his main emphasis on the fact that speakers are able to exploit the dimension of illocutionary force in order – as the title of his book puts it – to do things with words. As a result, he had rather little to say about the nature of the relationship between the linguistic dimension of illocutionary force and the capacity of speakers to exploit that dimension in order to perform the range of speech acts – and especially illocutionary acts – in the classification of which he was principally interested.

I take it, however, that the right way to think about this relationship is to focus on the fact that, as Austin always stressed, to speak with a certain illocutionary force is normally to perform an *act* of a certain kind, to engage in a piece of deliberate and voluntary behaviour. As this suggests, what serves to connect the illocutionary dimension of language with the performance of illocutionary acts must be – as with all voluntary acts – the intentions of the agent concerned. By way of clarifying this point, consider again the speech act of warning someone. To perform that particular act, we must not only issue a particular utterance with the form and force of a warning. We must at the same time mean or intend the utterance as a warning and mean it to be taken as a warning by way of its being recognised as an instance of just that intentional act. As Austin put it with his customary exactitude, to recover the intended illocutionary force of a given utterance, and thus the nature of the illocutionary act performed by the agent in saying what was said, what we need to understand is the way in which the given utterance, on the given occasion, 'ought to have been taken'.[10]

It is true that Austin wavered at this point. When he first introduced the concept of an illocution, he suggested that the question of whether someone has performed the act, say, of warning is essentially a question about how they meant their utterance to be understood.[11] But he assumed (in Wittgensteinian vein) that the 'uptake' of illocutionary acts requires the presence of such strong linguistic conventions that he later

[10] Austin 1980, p. 99.   [11] Austin 1980, p. 98.

appeared to suggest that such conventions, rather than the intentions of speakers, must be definitive of illocutionary acts.[12] Nevertheless, I still think it correct to expand Austin's analysis in the direction subsequently taken by P. F. Strawson[13] and John Searle,[14] and later by Stephen Schiffer and David Holdcroft.[15] It seems to me that if we wish to furnish the definition of illocutionary acts which Austin failed to provide, we need to take seriously their status as acts and think about the kinds of intentions that need to go into their successful performance.[16]

Although my remarks so far have been expository, it is I think vital to add that we run the risk of missing their significance if we think of them as an exposition of something called 'the theory of speech acts'. It seems to me seriously misleading to describe Wittgenstein or Austin as proposing a theory in the sense of putting forward an hypothesis about language. Their achievement is better described as that of finding a way of describing, and hence of calling to our attention, a dimension and hence a resource of language that every speaker and writer exploits all the time, and which we need to identify whenever we wish to understand any serious utterance.

To express their claim in this style is not just to insist on a preferred *façon de parler*. It is rather to insist that we shall miss the relevance of speech act analysis if we think of it as just another piece of philosophical jargon that we can brush aside if we happen not to like the sound of it. The terminology I have been describing points to a fact about language.[17] We may of course wish to deny that it performs that task adequately. But we can hardly deny the fact itself – that anyone issuing a serious utterance will always be doing something as well as saying something, and doing it in virtue of saying what is said. We make use of numerous verbs the precise function of which is to enable us to make explicit, in order to avoid misunderstanding, what exactly we see ourselves as doing in saying what we say. We subjoin comments like: I am warning you; I am ordering you (or else: I am not issuing orders, I am only advising/suggesting/telling you something). The problem of interpretation

---

[12] Austin 1980, p. 128.

[13] Strawson's expansion in Strawson 1971, pp. 149–69 takes the form of questioning the prominence Austin assigns to conventions (as opposed to speakers' intentions) in his analysis of 'uptake'.

[14] For the place of reflexive intentions in Searle's analysis of illocutionary acts see Searle 1969, pp. 60–1.

[15] Schiffer 1972, pp. 88–117 deploys a version of Grice's intentionalist theory of meaning to analyse the relationship between meaning and speech acts. Cf. also the centrality assigned to the recognition of communicative intentions in Bach and Harnish 1979.

[16] As I originally argued in Skinner 1970.

[17] This point is well brought out in Petrey 1990, p. 22.

arises in part because we do not generally trouble, even in such everyday cases, to make explicit exactly what we see ourselves as doing, still less in the case of such enormously complex acts of communication as those which normally attract the attention of literary critics and intellectual historians. It may indeed be impossible to recover anything more than a small fraction of the things that Plato, say, was doing in *The Republic*. My point is only that the extent to which we can hope to understand *The Republic* depends in part on the extent to which we can recover them.

III

I should next like to draw on, and at the same time to elaborate, some of my own studies about meaning and speech acts with a view to examining the bearing of these topics on the interpretation of texts.[18] Before I can do so, however, I need to meet one serious objection that a number of critics have levelled against my statement of the case. I cannot hope, they claim, to draw from the theory of linguistic action the implications for textual interpretation I claim to find in it, since my account of these implications embodies a misunderstanding of the theory itself.

My critics claim to find two contrasting mistakes in my exposition of the connections between the intentions of speakers and the force of utterances. One is that, as Keith Graham has put it, I fail to recognise that illocutionary intentions may be present in the absence of any corresponding illocutionary acts. For example, even if I succeed in speaking or writing with the intended force of a warning, I may still fail to perform the corresponding illocutionary act of bringing it about that someone is warned.[19]

This criticism can be traced back to Austin's original account of speech acts, and even more clearly to Strawson's elaboration of it. Austin admittedly thought it essential to the successful performance of an act, say, of warning that the agent should secure 'uptake' of the act *as* an act of warning.[20] Austin makes it clear, moreover, and Strawson makes it even clearer, that this notion of 'uptake' depends upon a particular analysis of the descriptive element in the concept of action, an analysis that Graham's criticism in turn assumes to be correct. The analysis in question is Aristotelian in provenance. The basic idea is that any voluntary action must be capable of being represented by the formula 'bringing

---

[18] I shall be drawing in particular on Skinner 1970, Skinner 1971, Skinner 1975, Skinner 1978a and Skinner 1996.

[19] Graham 1988, p. 151.   [20] Austin 1980, p. 116.

it about that p', where the value assigned to 'p' must be such as to indicate the new state of affairs brought about as a result of the action.[21] To perform an action is thus to produce some discernibly new end-state, one that can be represented not merely as a consequence of, but as an indication of, the successful performance of the action. As Austin himself put it, 'I cannot be said to have warned an audience unless it hears what I say and takes what I say in a certain sense.'[22] Something must be newly true of my audience for my act to have been performed. I must at least have succeeded in altering its state of understanding, even if I do not succeed in affecting its will.

It is this familiar analysis, however, that seems to me defective.[23] It is of course true that I cannot be said to warn you unless I bring it about that p (that you are warned). But this is only to put the description through a passive transformation; it remains to assign a value to 'p'. And here it seems to me (*pace* Austin as well as Graham) that there are very many locutions describing actions in which the only value we can hope to assign to 'p' – the state of affairs brought about by the action – is that it *is* the state of affairs brought about by the action. To put the point more elegantly, as Donald Davidson has done, there are many cases in which 'p' merely designates an event, not a newly true state of affairs which can be represented as the consequence of the successful performance of the act.[24] This certainly seems to me to apply to the case of warning. To warn someone is to advert to the fact that they are in danger. To succeed in performing the illocutionary act of warning is thus to succeed in adverting to that fact.[25] So too with such paradigm cases of illocutionary acts as complimenting, informing and so on. To bring it about that someone is complimented is merely to address them in an appropriately admiring style; to bring it about that they are informed is merely to issue an instruction of an appropriate kind. It is necessary in none of these cases to the successful performance of the illocutionary act that there should be some end state 'newly true' of the person to whom the words are addressed. All this being so, it makes no sense to suggest, as Austin and Graham both do, that someone might succeed in speaking with the intended illocutionary force of a warning and yet fail to perform the corresponding illocutionary act of bringing it about that someone is warned. For to bring it about that someone is warned is simply to succeed in adverting to the fact that they are in danger.

---

[21] For an elaboration of this proposal see Kenny 1963, pp. 171–86.   [22] Austin 1980, p. 116.
[23] As I tried to show in Skinner 1971, pp. 3–12.   [24] Davidson 1967, p. 86.
[25] On the semantics of 'warn' see also Vanderveken 1990, vol. I, p. 174.

I now turn to the contrasting mistake that Graham and others[26] have claimed to detect in my analysis of the relations between intentions and illocutionary acts. They have argued that, just as there can be illocutionary intentions without corresponding acts, so 'I may perform an illocutionary act in the absence of an appropriate intention.'[27] What I am said to overlook is thus the class of what Graham has described as 'unintentional illocutionary acts'.[28]

It is not the case, however, that I overlook this class; it is rather that I disbelieve in its existence. To say this, however, is by no means to fall into the absurdity – as Graham assumes – of believing that it is impossible to warn someone unintentionally. It is only to insist that, if I warn someone unintentionally, this will not be because I have performed the illocutionary act of warning, but unintentionally. To perform the illocutionary act of warning, as I have argued above, is always to speak with the form and intended force of a warning; the act is constituted as the act of warning by the complex intentions that go into its performance. The reason why it is nevertheless possible to warn someone unintentionally is that there may be circumstances in which the issuing of a certain utterance will inevitably be taken to be a case of adverting to danger. In such circumstances the agent will be understood to have spoken, and will in fact have spoken, with the illocutionary force of a warning. This will remain the case even if the agent spoke without any intention to warn, and in consequence failed to perform the corresponding illocutionary act.

My critics fail to grasp what I take to be the essence of Austin's original distinction between illocutionary forces and illocutionary acts. The former term points to a resource of language; the latter to the capacity of agents to exploit it in communication. The illocutionary acts we perform are identified, like all voluntary acts, by our intentions; but the illocutionary forces carried by our utterances are mainly determined by their meaning and context. It is for these reasons that it can readily happen that, in performing an illocutionary act, my utterance may at the same time carry, without my intending it, a much wider range of illocutionary force.[29] (For example, although I may intend only to warn you, my utterance may at the same time have, as it happens, the illocutionary

---

[26] For a careful discussion see McCullagh 1998, pp. 150–5. For further criticisms see Bevir 1999, pp. 40–2.

[27] Graham 1988, p. 152. For the same criticism see Shapiro 1982, p. 563 and Boucher 1985, pp. 220, 230.

[28] Graham 1988, pp. 153, 163.   [29] Holdcroft 1978, pp. 149–50, 154.

force of informing you of something.) But this is only to say that, due to the richness of any natural language, many and perhaps most of our utterances will carry some element of unintended illocutionary force.[30] It is not in the least to point to a class of unintentional illocutionary acts.

With these attempted clarifications, I am now in a position to return to the question I posed at the outset. What can the theory of speech acts hope to tell us about the interpretation of texts? Here I need to begin by making a negative point with as much emphasis as possible. The theory does *not* tell us, nor do I believe, that the intentions of speakers and writers constitute the sole or even the best guide to understanding their texts or other utterances.

There has of course been a school of criticism which has aimed to ground interpretation on just such an account of authorial intentionality. E. D. Hirsch, Peter Juhl and others have maintained that, in Hirsch's words, if we wish to understand 'the meaning of a text' we need to understand 'what the text says', which in turn requires us to recover 'the saying of the author'.[31] Hirsch's thesis, like that of Juhl, is thus that the 'verbal meaning' of a text 'requires the determining will' of an author, and that this is what the interpreter must concentrate on trying to recover if the aim is to understand aright the meaning of the text.[32]

According to many of my critics, this is the thesis I endorse.[33] But in fact I have scarcely engaged with this argument,[34] and insofar as I have ever done so I have largely endorsed the anti-intentionalist case. I agree that, where a text says something other than what its author intended to say, we are bound to concede that this is nevertheless what the text *says*, and thus that it bears a meaning other than the one intended by its author.[35] This is not perhaps a very subtle point on which to insist with as much vehemence as has become fashionable. But if the question is seen, in a sufficiently myopic style, as one about the understanding of

---

[30] As Holdcroft notes, it is not clear that this is recognised in Schiffer's account. See also the 'generative' account of illocutionary forces given in Travis 1975, which operates without the distinction between the illocutionary force of utterances and the intended illocutionary force with which speakers may issue them, and accordingly concludes (p. 49) that, in general, 'each utterance will have exactly one illocutionary force'.

[31] Hirsch 1967, pp. 12, 13. Cf. Hirsch 1976 and Juhl 1976, pp. 133–56.

[32] Hirsch 1967, p. 27. For Juhl's comments on Hirsch, see Juhl 1980, pp. 16–44.

[33] LaCapra 1980, p. 254; Baumgold 1981, p. 935; Gunnell 1982, p. 318; Seidman 1983, pp. 83, 88; Femia 1988, p. 157; Keane 1988, p. 207; Harlan 1989. I have responded to Harlan's criticisms in Skinner 1996.

[34] As is rightly pointed out in Jenssen 1985. Cf. also Vossenkuhl 1982; Viroli 1987.

[35] A point excellently made in Dunn 1980, p. 84.

texts, then of course the claim must stand. It would certainly be amazing if all the meanings, implications, connotations and resonances that an ingenious interpreter might legitimately claim to find in a text could in turn be shown to reflect its author's intentions at every point. And it would be a straightforward mistake to infer that, if we came upon some such obviously unintended element, we should have to exclude it from an account of the meaning of the *text*.

I have only wished, however, to say as much about this issue as will enable me to distinguish it from a second and different question that arises about authorial intentionality. This is the question of what an author may have meant or intended by an utterance (whatever may be the meaning of the utterance itself). To put the point in the jargon I have been using, my principal concern has not been with meaning but rather with the performance of illocutionary acts.

As I have already argued, the question of what a speaker or writer may have meant by saying something arises in the case of any serious utterance. But it poses the most acute problems for interpretation in two main types of case. One is when we are confronted with hidden rhetorical codes such as that of irony. As I have already intimated in chapter 4, it seems indisputable in this case that our understanding must depend on our capacity to recover what the author intended or meant by what was said. But it seems worth underlining the way in which this is so. For it seems to me that the argument has been misstated by those, like Peter Juhl, who have wished to uphold the thesis about authorial intentionality which I have just considered and set aside.

Juhl and others have argued that the phenomenon of irony provides the clearest evidence in favour of the claim that we need to recover an author's intentions if we wish to understand 'the meaning of a work', the meaning of what was said.[36] But when someone speaks or writes ironically, it may well be that there is no difficulty at all about understanding the meaning of what was said. It may well be that everything was said in virtue of its ordinary meaning. Where there is a difficulty about understanding such utterances, it generally arises not because of any doubts about meaning, but rather because of some doubt as to whether the speaker really meant what was said.

The problem of detecting irony arises, in other words, as a problem not about meaning but about illocutionary acts. The ironic speaker issues an utterance with a certain meaning. At the same time, the speaker

---

[36] Juhl 1980, pp. 62, 64. See also Stern 1980, pp. 122–4.

appears to perform an illocutionary act of a kind that falls within the range conventionally performed by such utterances. To develop an example mentioned in chapter 4, the form and apparent force of Daniel Defoe's argument in *The Shortest-Way with the Dissenters* is that of suggesting, recommending or calling for a particular course of action. (That religious dissenters be suppressed and preferably executed.) Reading Defoe's simple proposal, however, we begin to doubt whether the standard way in which the meaning of an utterance helps us to decode its intended illocutionary force applies in this particular case. We come to see that Defoe is making a comment about the very idea of issuing such an utterance with the intended force that a mere inspection of its meaning might tempt us to assign to it. The utterance has the undoubted form and apparent force of a recommendation, even of a demand. But Defoe is not performing the corresponding illocutionary act. On the contrary, his illocutionary intention is that of ridiculing the intolerance that would be embodied in performing it.

This, then, is one type of case in which it is, I think, indispensable to recover the intentions of authors if we wish to understand their utterances. But the reason is not, *pace* Juhl, that we shall otherwise fail to understand the meaning of what was said. The meaning of what Defoe said was at no point unclear. What he said was that religious dissent should be ranked among capital offences.[37] What this means is that religious dissent should be ranked among capital offences. The reason we need to recover Defoe's intentions is rather that we shall otherwise fail to understand what he was *doing in* issuing this particular utterance. The intentions we need to recover are the illocutionary intentions that went into his act of ridiculing and thereby questioning contemporary religious intolerance. They are the intentions we may be said to have recovered when we come to appreciate that this is how he meant his utterance (with its given meaning) to be understood.

I turn to the other and enormously broader range of cases in which the recovery of this form of intentionality raises special difficulties. This is where the speaker or writer issues a serious utterance but fails to make clear how exactly the utterance is to be taken or understood. This may of course happen because (as in the case of irony) the speaker lacks the standard motive we normally possess for making fully explicit the intended force of our utterances. But the usual reason will rather be

---

[37] Defoe 1965, p. 96. Stern 1980 mentions the example (p. 124) but in my view draws the wrong moral from it. But cf. the helpful discussion in Bevir 1999, pp. 81–2.

that the meaning of the utterance itself, together with the context of its occurrence, are such that the speaker feels no doubt about the capacity of his or her audience to secure 'uptake' of the intended illocutionary act.

Such confidence is generally well-founded in the case of everyday communications. So we usually regard it as over-emphatic to employ what Austin called explicit performative formulae for making manifest how exactly we intend our utterances to be taken.[38] Even here, however, we may sometimes feel the need to reassure our intended audience. This is what prompts us to say things like 'When I said that the ice over there is very thin, I wasn't criticising you, I was only issuing a warning.' As soon as we turn to more complex cases, especially historical utterances where we are no longer the intended audience, such problems of 'uptake' readily become acute. In these instances it may be impossibly hard to recover what the writer was doing in saying what was said. But the point on which I have been insisting all along is that, unless we can somehow perform this act of recovery, we shall remain cut off from an entire dimension of understanding.

To summarise: I have distinguished two questions about the meaning and understanding of texts. One is the question of what the text means, the other the question of what its author may have meant. I have argued that, if we are to understand a text, both questions must be answered. It is true, however, that while these questions are separable, they are not in the end separate. If I am to understand what someone meant or intended by what they said, I must first be sure that the meaning of what they said was itself intended. For otherwise there will be nothing that they meant by it. As I have tried to insist, however, this must at all costs be distinguished from the thesis that the meaning of a text can be identified with what its author intended. Any text will normally include an intended meaning, and the recovery of that meaning certainly constitutes a precondition of understanding what its author may have meant. But any text of any complexity will always contain far more in the way of meaning than even the most vigilant and imaginative author could possibly have intended to put into it. Paul Ricoeur has spoken in this connection of surplus meaning, and with this formulation I am in complete agreement.[39] So I am far from supposing that the meanings

<hr>

[38] Austin 1980, pp. 56ff; cf. also p. 116n.

[39] For the centrality of this theme in Paul Ricoeur's hermeneutics see Leeuwen 1981. For a discussion of my own approach by contrast with Ricoeur's see Thompson 1993.

of texts can be identified with the intentions of their authors; what must be identified with such intentions is only what their authors meant by them.

IV

I now turn to the methodological – and hence the practical – implications of what I have so far argued. I have been claiming (to revert to Austin's way of formulating the point) that the understanding or 'uptake' of the intended illocutionary force of any utterance will always constitute a necessary condition of understanding the utterance itself. But how is this process of 'uptake' to be achieved in practice in the case of the vastly complex linguistic acts in which literary critics and intellectual historians are characteristically interested?[40]

The philosophers of language are not much help at this stage, but it seems to me that, in outline, we can distinguish two main ingredients in the concept of 'uptake'. The most obvious determinant of the intended force of any utterance must be the meaning of the utterance itself. Consider only the most obvious fact: that meaning is affected by grammatical mood. When the policeman issues the utterance 'The ice over there is very thin', the intended illocutionary force cannot, for example, be that of questioning the skater.[41] This is not to say – with Jonathan Cohen, Stephen Schiffer and others – that the concept of illocutionary force simply describes an aspect of the meaning of utterances.[42] It has been my whole purpose to insist that it points to a separable dimension of language.[43] But there can be no doubt that the meaning of utterances helps to limit the range of illocutionary forces they can bear, and thereby serves to exclude the possibility that certain illocutionary acts are being performed.

The second determinant I have tried to emphasise is the context and occasion of utterances.[44] The relevant notion of context here is one of great complexity,[45] but we can readily single out the most crucial

---

[40] Graham 1980, pp. 147–8. Shapiro 1982, p. 548 repeats the criticism. See also Boucher 1985, p. 212; Levine 1986, pp. 38, 44–5.

[41] On interrogatives and performatives see Holdcroft 1978, pp. 102–6.

[42] I have tried to rebut Cohen's scepticism in Skinner 1970, pp. 120–1, 128–9. Cf. also Graham 1977.

[43] For a discussion of this point see Bevir 1999, pp. 134–7.

[44] For a critique of this conception of the context of utterances see Oakley 1999, pp. 8–24.

[45] On the philosophical complexities see Holdcroft 1978, pp. 151–70. On the practical difficulties attendant on reconstructing the historical contexts of texts see Hume 1999.

element in it. This is the fact, which I have already sought to emphasise in chapter 4, that all serious utterances are characteristically intended as acts of communication. So they characteristically occur, as Austin always insisted, either as acts of a conventionally recognisable character, or else more broadly in the form of recognisable interventions in what Austin called a total speech act situation.[46] This second point can be extended, and brought into line with my present concerns, by emphasising that the types of utterance I am considering can never be viewed simply as strings of propositions; they must always be viewed at the same time as arguments. But to argue is always to argue for or against a certain assumption or point of view or course of action. It follows that, if we wish to understand such utterances, we shall have to find some means of identifying the precise nature of the intervention constituted by the act of uttering them. This I consider the most important step we need to take in any attempt to grasp what someone may have meant by saying something.[47] If we fail to take it we shall find ourselves, as David Wootton has remarked, in a position comparable to that of someone listening to the prosecution or the defence in a criminal trial without having heard the other side. We shall find it impossible to understand 'why apparently promising lines of argument are never pursued, while at other times what seem to be trivial distinctions and secondary issues are subjected to lengthy examination'.[48] To put the point in another way, there is a sense in which we need to understand why a certain proposition has been put forward if we wish to understand the proposition itself.[49] We need to see it not simply as a proposition but as a move in an argument. So we need to grasp why it seemed worth making that precise move by way of recapturing the presuppositions and purposes that went into the making of it.

Here I am generalising R. G. Collingwood's dictum to the effect that the understanding of any proposition requires us to identify the question to which the proposition may be viewed as an answer.[50] I am claiming, that is, that any act of communication will always constitute the taking up of some determinate position in relation to some pre-existing conversation or argument. It follows that, if we wish to understand what has been said, we shall have to identify what exact position has been taken up. So far I have expressed this contention in terms of Austin's claim that

---

[46] Austin 1980, pp. 116–20.   [47] Tully 1988, pp. 8–10.   [48] Wootton 1986, p. 10.
[49] For this formulation see Ayers 1978, p. 44 and Hylton 1984, p. 392.
[50] Collingwood 1939, p. 39.

we need to be able to understand what the speaker or writer may have been doing in saying what was said. But it is, I think, a fascinating though unnoticed feature of Austin's analysis that it can in turn be viewed as an exemplification of what Collingwood called the logic of question and answer.[51]

One final observation about this notion of intervening in a context. There is no implication that the relevant context need be an immediate one.[52] As J. G. A. Pocock has especially emphasised, the problems to which writers see themselves as responding may have been posed in a remote period, even in a wholly different culture.[53] The appropriate context for understanding the point of such writers' utterances will always be whatever context enables us to appreciate the nature of the intervention constituted by their utterances. To recover that context in any particular case, we may need to engage in extremely wide-ranging as well as detailed historical research.

I have already gestured at these commitments in chapters 4 and 5, but now is the moment to summarise my case. My contention, in essence, is that we should start by elucidating the meaning, and hence the subject matter, of the utterances in which we are interested and then turn to the argumentative context of their occurrence to determine how exactly they connect with, or relate to, other utterances concerned with the same subject matter. If we succeed in identifying this context with sufficient accuracy, we can eventually hope to read off what it was that the speaker or writer in whom we are interested was doing in saying what he or she said.

By way of illustration, consider the most straightforward type of case, that of a simple declarative statement. For example, consider again one of the statements I discussed in chapter 3: Machiavelli's claim that mercenary armies always undermine liberty. There is little difficulty about understanding the meaning of the utterance itself. But we wish in addition to understand what Machiavelli meant by it. So we turn to the general context in which it occurred. Suppose we find that the sentiment expressed by the utterance was frequently expressed in the political literature of the time. Then we are already justified in saying that Machiavelli is repeating, upholding or agreeing with an accepted attitude or viewpoint. Looking more closely at the intervention constituted

---

[51] Collingwood 1939, pp. 29–43. On the pragmatics of explanation see also Garfinkel 1981, pp. 7–14.
[52] Here I attempt to meet a criticism made in Turner 1983, pp. 283–6.
[53] See Pocock 1980, esp. pp. 147–8, and cf. also Pocock 1973.

by his utterance, we may feel able to go further. We may feel justified in adding that he is endorsing, confirming or concurring with an accepted truth; or alternatively, that he is only conceding, admitting or allowing it to be true. On the other hand, we may find that he is saying something no longer generally accepted, even though it may at one time have been widely agreed. Then perhaps what he is doing is restating, reaffirming or recalling his audience to the truth of what he is saying; perhaps, more specifically, he is at the same time emphasising, underlining or insisting on its truth. Or again, we may find that what he says is not generally accepted at all. Then perhaps what he is doing is denying and repudiating, or perhaps correcting and revising, a generally accepted belief. Or he may be enlarging, developing or adding to an established argument by drawing out its implications in an unexplored way. At the same time, he may be pressing or urging a recognition of this new viewpoint, or advising, recommending or even warning his audience of the need to adopt it. By paying as close attention as possible to the context of utterance, we can hope gradually to refine our sense of the precise nature of the intervention constituted by the utterance itself. We can hope, that is, to recapture with an increasing sense of nuance what exactly Machiavelli may have intended or meant.

The upshot of employing this approach, it is perhaps worth underlining, is to challenge any categorical distinction between texts and contexts.[54] Critics such as John Keane have accused me of adopting a traditional 'author-subject' approach, the implication being that I have yet to hear about the death of the author announced a long time ago by Roland Barthes and Michel Foucault.[55] It is true that their announcement has always struck me as exaggerated. I accept of course that we are all limited by the concepts available to us if we wish to communicate. But it is no less true that language constitutes a resource as well as a constraint – a point I shall go on to explore in chapters 8 and 9.[56] This means that, if we wish to do justice to those moments when a convention is challenged or a commonplace effectively subverted, we cannot simply dispense with the category of the author. The point takes on an added significance when we reflect that, to the extent that our social world is

---

[54] Jenssen 1985, p. 129 valuably emphasises this point. On genres and the expectations they arouse see also Jauss 1970, pp. 11–14.

[55] See Keane 1988, p. 205 and cf. also Kjellström 1995. On the death of the author see Barthes 1979, pp. 73–81.

[56] For a sympathetic appraisal of the view I am taking here about the relations of structure and agency see Edling and Mörkenstam 1995, pp. 120–4.

constituted by our concepts, any successful alteration in the use of a concept will at the same time constitute a change in our social world. As James Tully has observed, the pen can be a mighty sword.[57]

Nevertheless, it ought to be obvious that the approach I am sketching leaves the traditional figure of the author in extremely poor health. Reiterating, underpinning and defending commonplace insights as they generally do, individual authors can readily come to seem the mere precipitates of their contexts, as Barthes and Foucault originally emphasised. It is certainly an implication of my approach that our main attention should fall not on individual authors but on the more general discourse of their times.[58] The type of historian I am describing is someone who principally studies what J. G. A. Pocock calls 'languages' of debate, and only secondarily the relationship between individual contributions to such languages and the range of discourse as a whole.[59]

A number of my critics – most notably Martin Hollis and James Tully – have objected that the method I am sketching still falls short of establishing what individual writers may have intended or meant. We may be able to say of a contribution to a pre-existing discourse that it constitutes an attack on one position, a defence of another, a revision of a third, and so forth. We may be able, that is, to establish what its author was doing. But as Hollis has remarked, this is only to show that the cap fits, not that the author was wearing it.[60] To express the objection in the idiom I have been using, we can hope by these means to identify illocutionary forces, but not necessarily any illocutionary acts.

There seem two possible retorts. The more radical would be to turn the objection back and ask whether we need concern ourselves with the states of mind of individual authors at all. We are speaking about texts, and the performativity in which I am interested can validly be treated as a property of texts in themselves. We can perfectly well rest content with observing that a text constitutes an attack on one position, a defence of another, a revision of a third, and so forth. We can limit ourselves to arguing about the defensibility of such claims, and to pursuing the kinds of historical research that will enable us to enrich and refine them. We can thereby limit our study entirely to texts, their characteristics and behaviour, and forget about authors altogether.

---

[57] Tully 1988, p. 7.

[58] For some especially perceptive remarks on Foucault's conception of discourse see Hollinger 1985, pp. 149–51.

[59] Pocock 1985, pp. 7–8, 23.   [60] See Hollis 1988, pp. 139–40 and cf. Tully 1988, p. 10.

There is much to be said in favour of this proposal that we should limit ourselves to studying what Foucault characterised as discursive regimes, and thus to a pure archaeology of utterances. But an alternative reply would be to acknowledge that texts do, after all, have authors, and that authors have intentions in writing them. Perhaps the right aspiration is to try to close the gap between claiming that a text is doing something and claiming that its author is doing it. To express the point as a reply to Hollis and Tully, it sometimes seems a matter of no great difficulty to move from the claim, say, that an utterance constituted a retort to an established line of argument to the further claim that this is to be explained by the fact that its author intended the utterance to constitute just such a retort.

By way of illustration, consider again the example I have been taking of Machiavelli's views about mercenary armies. We already know a list of the things he was undoubtedly doing in saying what he said about them. But we also know that, if he was engaged in an intended act of communication, there must have been something that he was intentionally doing in saying what he said. Perhaps the best hypothesis to adopt is that, whatever he was doing, he was doing it intentionally, and thus that we have in fact identified the range of intended illocutionary forces with which his utterance was produced.

Once this stage is reached, we can hope to close the gap still further by testing our hypothesis in various ways. Since intentions depend on beliefs, we can perform one obvious test by making sure that Machiavelli possessed the beliefs appropriate to the formation of the kinds of intentions we are ascribing to him. We can perform a yet further test by taking advantage of the fact that the intentions with which we act are always closely connected with our motives. This provides a vital means of corroborating any hypothesis to the effect that a speaker or writer may have intended a certain utterance to bear a particular illocutionary force. For the suspicion that someone may have performed a certain action will always be greatly strengthened (as every reader of detective stories knows) by the discovery that they had a motive for performing it. Finally, ascriptions of intentionality can be further corroborated by examining the coherence of a speaker's or writer's beliefs. Suppose that, in issuing the utterance we have been considering, Machiavelli upheld one position in argument, rejected another, denounced one course of action, recommended another, and so on. Assuming that he held minimally coherent beliefs, we can safely assume – in a sense we can predict – that he will also adopt a number of related attitudes. If he upholds position (a) we can expect him to reject the negation of (a); if he recommends alternative (x) we can expect him to criticise the contrary of (x); and so on. If upon further investigation we find these expectations defeated, we shall begin to feel at a loss. But if we succeed in recovering just such a network of attitudes, we shall feel increasingly justified in our initial hypothesis: that, in issuing an utterance with the force of upholding and commending a certain position, he must have intended his utterance to bear exactly that force.

I need to end by underlining the Wittgensteinian character of these commitments. Nothing I am saying presupposes the discredited hermeneutic ambition of stepping empathetically into other people's shoes and attempting (in R. G. Collingwood's unfortunate phrase) to think their thoughts after them. The reason why no such conjuring trick is required is that, as Wittgenstein established long ago in criticising the concept of a private language, the intentions with which anyone performs a successful act of communication must, *ex hypothesi*, be publicly legible. Consider again the imaginary example I offered in chapter 5 of the man waving his arms by way of warning me that the bull is about to charge.[61] To recognise that he is warning me is to understand the intentions with which he is acting. As I observed, however, to recover these intentions is not a matter of identifying the ideas inside his head at the moment when he first begins to wave his arms. It is a matter of grasping the fact that arm-waving can count as warning, and that this is evidently the convention being exploited in this particular case. Nothing in the way of 'empathy' is required, since the meaning of the episode is public and intersubjective.[62] As a result, as I have now sought to argue, the intentions with which the man is acting can be inferred from an understanding of the conventional significance of the act itself.

I have been arguing that texts are acts, so that the process of understanding them requires us, as in the case of all voluntary acts, to recover the intentions embodied in their performance. But this is not the mysterious empathetic process that old-fashioned hermeneutics may have led us to believe. For acts are in turn texts: they embody intersubjective meanings that we can hope to read off.[63]

It has been fashionable of late to object that this line of argument concedes in effect that intentionality is irrecoverable after all. This is

---

[61] But for a critique of my interpretation of this example see Rosebury 1997.

[62] Cf. the discussion in Geertz 1980, pp. 134–6. On the fallacy of supposing that historians must be able to 'commune with the dead' see also Strout 1992.

[63] On social actions as texts see Ricoeur 1973 and Geertz 1983, pp. 30–3. For a discussion of texts/actions see also Makkreel 1990.

the moral drawn by Jacques Derrida from his consideration of an example I have already mentioned in chapter 5: that of the fragment, found among Nietzsche's manuscripts, which reads 'I have forgotten my umbrella.'[64] Derrida concedes that in this instance there is no difficulty about understanding the meaning of the sentence. 'Everyone knows what "I have forgotten my umbrella" means.'[65] His objection is that this still leaves us without any 'infallible way' of recovering what Nietzsche may have intended or meant.[66] 'We shall never know *for sure* what Nietzsche wanted to do or say in noting these words.'[67] To phrase the objection in the jargon of speech act theory (to which Derrida appears to be alluding) we have no means of recognising what Nietzsche was doing, no means of recovering what speech act he intended to perform. Was he merely informing someone that he had forgotten his umbrella? Or was he perhaps warning them, or reassuring them? Or was he instead explaining something, or apologising, or criticising himself, or simply lamenting a lapse of memory? Perhaps, as Derrida suggests, he meant nothing at all. Derrida's point is that we shall never know.

It will be clear by now that I have no wish to dispute such obvious truths. Some utterances are completely lacking in the sorts of context from which we can hope to infer the intentions with which they were uttered. We may well be obliged to concede in such cases that we can never hope to arrive at even a plausible hypothesis about how the utterance in question should be understood. The example of the umbrella seems, indeed, to be just such a case. As usual, Derrida's example is excellently chosen to make his point.

To this we must add that, even when an utterance can be assigned to a highly determinate context, Derrida remains right to insist that we can never hope to know 'for sure' or by any 'infallible means' what may have been meant. The outcome of the hermeneutic enterprise, I fully agree, can never be anything resembling the attainment of a final, self-evident or indubitable set of truths about any text or other utterance whatsoever. Even our most confident ascriptions of intentionality are nothing more than inferences from the best evidence available to us, and as such are defeasible at any time.

---

[64] Derrida 1979, pp. 122, 123.

[65] Derrida 1979, p. 128: 'Chacun comprend ce que veut dire "j'ai oublié mon parapluie".'

[66] Derrida 1979, pp. 123, 125, 131. Nehamas 1985, pp. 17, 240 interestingly discusses the lack of any defence by Derrida of 'his assumption that infallibility and certainty are necessary if interpretation is to be possible'.

[67] Derrida 1979, p. 122: 'Nous ne serons jamais *assurés* de savoir ce que Nietzsche a voulu faire ou dire en notant ces mots.'

It scarcely follows, however, that we can never hope to construct and corroborate plausible hypotheses about the intentions with which an utterance may have been issued. We can frequently do so in just the manner I have been trying in this section to set out. We can of course stipulate, if we like, that the result will not be a valid interpretation, since it will fall far short of certitude. If we insist, as Derrida does, on such an equation between establishing that something is the case and being able to demonstrate it 'for sure', then admittedly it follows that we can never hope to establish the intentions with which a text may have been written, and thus what its author may have meant. But equally it follows that we can never hope to establish that life is not a dream. The moral of this, however, is not that we have no reason to believe that life is not a dream. The moral is rather that the sceptic is insisting on too stringent an account of what it means to have reasons for our beliefs. Haunted as Derrida appears to be by the ghost of Descartes, he has concentrated on attacking a position that no theorist of intentionality need defend.

V

My friendliest critics have raised no objections to the general line of argument I have now tried to lay out. They have merely wondered whether it is of much importance. They concede that we can certainly hope to recover the intended force of texts and other utterances. But they insist that, as Hough puts it, we can hardly expect that the outcome will be to supply us with anything more than 'meagre platitudes' about the works concerned.[68]

The best way of showing that this doubt is misplaced will be to consider some specific examples. Consider, for instance, the nature of the satire we encounter in Cervantes's *Don Quixote*. One tradition of interpretation has always maintained that, since the Don's aspirations include the righting of wrongs and the succouring of the oppressed, we are to think of the satire as directed only at his sadly outdated approach to life, not at his values in themselves. We are asked, that is, to think of the Don as having 'a noble half and a comic half' to his character.[69] As a number of scholars have observed, however, such a reading becomes harder to sustain once we begin to examine Cervantes's comedy in relation to the genre of chivalric romances so popular at the time, and thereby begin to acquire

---

[68] Hough 1976, p. 227. Cf. also Seidman 1983, p. 91.
[69] See Close 1972 for a discussion of the historiography.

a sense of what Cervantes was doing in so continually alluding to them.[70] We begin to see, as Close in particular has argued, that Don Quixote's values and aspirations, no less than his actual conduct, constitute 'a madly literal mimicry of the stereotype behaviour of the heroes of chivalric romance'.[71] We begin to see, in other words, that what Cervantes is doing is seeking to discredit not merely the possibility of living a chivalric life but the values associated with that life as well. But to see this much is to come away with far more than a meagre characterisation of Cervantes's masterpiece. It is to come away with a new sense of how to appraise the character of the protagonist, with a new view of the reach and direction of the satire, and hence with a different understanding of the underlying morality of the work. These are hardly meagre results.

Nor is the approach I have been sketching limited to providing general characterisations of this kind. I have perhaps encouraged this misconception by the way in which I have often spoken, grammatically in the singular, about the recovery of intended illocutionary force.[72] But it ought to be obvious that an immense range of illocutionary acts will normally be embedded within the types of texts I have been discussing, and that even the smallest individual fragments of such texts may carry a heavy freight of intended illocutionary force.

As an illustration of this further claim, consider the end of E. M. Forster's novel *A Passage to India*. The novel closes with the words: 'Weybridge, 1924'.[73] The meaning is clear enough: Forster is stating that he completed the book while living in a London suburb in the year 1924. At the same time he is following a convention, more common at the time than nowadays, of informing his readers about the circumstances in which he wrote the book. It may seem that there is nothing more to be said. Indeed, it may seem almost absurd to go on to ask the type of question in which I am interested – but what is Forster *doing* in stating such facts? Surely he is simply stating them.

But is this so clear? We may find ourselves reflecting that the convention of signing-off novels in this way was sometimes used to draw attention to the romantically nomadic life of the author. James Joyce's *Ulysses*, for example, published only two years before, is signed

[70] Close 1972 offers a pioneering reading along these lines.
[71] See Close 1972, p. 37 and for a more general consideration of the issues involved see Kiremidjian 1969–70, esp. pp. 231–2.
[72] For example, Parekh and Berki 1973, p. 169 complain that I am only interested in 'a definite "intention" in performing a single action to bring about a definite result'.
[73] Forster 1924, p. 325. The signing-off has unfortunately been omitted, without explanation, from the Abinger Edition of *A Passage to India* (1978).

'Trieste-Zürich-Paris'.[74] By locating himself firmly in Weybridge – the classic instance of a prosaic English suburb – Forster introduces an audible note of mockery as well as self-ridicule. At the same time, we may find ourselves reflecting that the convention of signing-off was sometimes used in addition to underline the fact that literary labour can be an impressively protracted affair. The dates at the end of *Ulysses*, for example, read '1914–1921'. By confining himself to a single year, Forster allows himself a touch of hauteur, even of scorn, at the expense of those who preferred to emphasise their creative agonies. Once we see this much, we may well begin to suspect that Forster is satirising the entire convention of signing-off fictional works by indicating the posturing to which the convention gave rise.

I end with this example as a way of underlining the fact that the proposal I have been putting forward about the dimension of illocutionary acts is neither so jejune nor so restricted in scope as many of my critics have maintained. It is certainly a mistake to suppose that the recovery of this dimension will be of no interest except in the case of certain restricted genres of texts. The dimension is present in the case of all serious utterances, whether in verse or in prose, whether in philosophy or in literature.[75] It is a further mistake to suppose that the recovery of this dimension will merely provide us with general characterisations of the works involved. Any text of any complexity will contain a myriad of illocutionary acts, and any individual phrase in any such text – as I have just indicated – may even contain more acts than words. This is one of the most obvious reasons why we can never expect our debates about interpretation to have a stop. As I have tried to indicate, the reason is not that there is nothing determinate to be said. It is rather that, in the case of a work of any complexity, there will always be room for legitimate and fruitful but potentially endless debate about – to end with Austin's phrase – how exactly the work may have been meant to be taken.

VI

The chief aspiration underlying the method I have been describing is that of enabling us to recover the historical identity of individual texts in

---

[74] Joyce 1969, p. 704.

[75] This point is well brought out in Pratt 1977, in which the main target is the idea that literary discourse represents a special type of language rather than a particular use of language.

the history of thought. The aim is to see such texts as contributions to particular discourses, and thereby to recognise the ways in which they followed or challenged or subverted the conventional terms of those discourses themselves. More generally, the aim is to return the specific texts we study to the precise cultural contexts in which they were originally formed.

Critics have repeatedly complained that this reduces the study of the history of thought to nothing more edifying than a conducted tour of a graveyard.[76] But this objection seems to me to embody a depressingly philistine failure to appreciate what we can hope to learn about ourselves from a serious study of unfamiliar modes of thought. As I have already suggested at the end of chapter 4, the 'relevance' of such studies lies in their capacity to help us stand back from our own assumptions and systems of belief, and thereby to situate ourselves in relation to other and very different forms of life. To put the point in the way that Hans-Georg Gadamer and Richard Rorty have more recently done, such investigations enable us to question the appropriateness of any strong distinction between matters of 'merely historical' and of 'genuinely philosophical' interest, since they enable us to recognise that our own descriptions and conceptualisations are in no way uniquely privileged.[77]

But what is the value, it is often asked, of seeing ourselves in this way as one tribe among others? There are many cogent answers, although it is hard to avoid sounding sententious in mentioning them. We can hope to attain a certain kind of objectivity in appraising rival systems of thought. We can hope to attain a greater degree of understanding, and thereby a larger tolerance, for elements of cultural diversity. Above all, we can hope to acquire a perspective from which to view our own form of life in a more self-critical way, enlarging our present horizons instead of fortifying local prejudices.[78]

It would be good to be able to refer at once to a long list of scholarly works from which it is possible to improve one's education in just these ways. But one cannot in the nature of things hope for so much. For a fine attempt, however, to deliver on all these promises, it is certainly possible

[76] Leslie 1970, p. 433; Tarlton 1973, p. 314; Warrender 1979, p. 939; Gunnell 1982, p. 327; Femia 1988, pp. 158–9, 163; Mandell 2000, pp. 119–20. For a still more radical doubt see Rée 1991, pp. 978–80.

[77] See Gadamer 1975, pp. 235–74 on 'the historicality of understanding' and cf. Rorty 1979, pp. 362–5, 371 and references to Gadamer there.

[78] For these and other considerations about the value of diversity see Geertz 1983, pp. 3–16.

to turn, for example, to James Tully's recent work, and especially to his critique of modern constitutionalism from the perspective of an earlier tradition swept aside by the onrush of the imperialist phase of modern European history.[79] The buried treasure he has excavated has the power to enrich our political arguments here and now.

I do not mean to confine myself, moreover, to the suggestion that our historical and ethnographic studies can help us only by such indirect means to become less parochial in our attachment to our inherited beliefs. We may also find, as a result of engaging in such excavations, that some of what we currently believe about, say, our moral or political arrangements turns out to be directly questionable. We are prone, for example, to think that the concept of individual responsibility is indispensable to any satisfactory moral code. But A. W. H. Adkins's analysis of ancient Greek values casts considerable doubt on that article of faith.[80] We are prone to think that there can be no concept of the state in the absence of centralised systems of power. But Clifford Geertz's study of classical Bali shows us how the one can flourish in the absence of the other.[81] We are prone to think that there can be no theory of individual liberty in the absence of a theory of rights. But as I try to indicate in volume 2 of the present work, one value of investigating the pre-modern history of political philosophy is to show that there need be no necessary connection between the two. The alien character of the beliefs we uncover constitutes their 'relevance'. Reflecting on such alternative possibilities, we provide ourselves with one of the best means of preventing our current moral and political theories from degenerating too easily into uncritically accepted ideologies.[82] At the same time, we equip ourselves with a new means of looking critically at our own beliefs in the light of the enlarged sense of possibility we acquire.

Ours is a reactionary age, filled with noisy pundits eager to assure us that the kind of argument I am here sketching is merely another way of proclaiming the relativity of all values, and thus of leaving us bereft of any values at all.[83] This seems to me as far as possible from the truth. The kind of enquiry I am describing offers us an additional means of reflecting on what we believe, and thus of strengthening our present

---

[79] Tully 1995, esp. pp. 99–182. For an appraisal see Owen 1999.

[80] Adkins 1960, pp. 348–51.

[81] Geertz 1980, pp. 121–36. For an excellent discussion see Inglis 2000, pp. 156–80.

[82] Here I am much influenced by MacIntyre 1971, esp. pp. viii–ix.

[83] See, for example, the arguments cited and criticised in Geertz 2000, pp. 42–67.

beliefs by way of testing them against alternative possibilities, or else of improving them if we come to recognise that the alternatives are both possible and desirable. A willingness to engage in this kind of reflection seems to me a distinguishing feature of all rational agents. To denounce such studies is not a defence of reason but an assault on the open society itself.

7

'Social meaning' and the explanation of social action

I

A social action may be said to have a meaning for the agent performing it. The acceptance of this rather vague claim represents the one major point of agreement in the continuing debate between those philosophers who assert and those who deny the naturalist thesis[1] to the effect that social actions can sufficiently be accounted for by the ordinary processes of causal explanation. The significance of the fact that actions have a 'meaning' has been emphasised in each of the three main traditions of anti-naturalist opposition to the idea of a social science. The followers of Wilhelm Dilthey, and of the wider tradition concerned with the importance of *Verstehen*, stress that the distinctive feature of 'the human studies' is their concern 'with a world which has meaning for the actors involved'.[2] The phenomenologists likewise stress that the aim of the social sciences must be to gain 'insight into the meaning which social acts have for those who act'.[3] And the followers of Wittgenstein argue that the 'forms of activity' studied in the social sciences will characteristically be those 'of which we can sensibly say that they have a *meaning*'.[4]

This emphasis has been scarcely less marked in the various strands of thought that have converged on accepting the theoretical possibility of establishing a causal and predictive science of human behaviour. Those who have sought to vindicate this approach continue to recognise the need to take account of 'the meaning of people's movements'.[5] Similarly, those who maintain that even an agent's reasons may be the causes of their actions still allow for the fact that such agents will characteristically

This chapter is an abbreviated and much revised version of an essay that originally appeared under the same title in *Philosophy, Politics and Society*, 4th series, ed. Peter Laslett, W. G. Runciman and Quentin Skinner (Oxford, 1972), pp. 136–57.

[1] Here and throughout I adopt the terminology proposed in Morgenbesser 1966, p. 255.
[2] Rickman 1967, p. 23.   [3] Schutz 1960, p. 203.
[4] Winch 1958, p. 45.   [5] Gibson 1960, p. 52.

see 'a point or meaning' in their behaviour.[6] Even those who uphold the strictest thesis of positivism – that actions must always be explained by deducing their occurrence from some known empirical law covering such movements – have continued to acknowledge that 'what distinguishes a mere bodily movement from an action' is 'the *meaning* of that movement'.[7]

It is in fact possible, I shall next seek to show, to view the entire debate between the social science naturalists and their adversaries in terms of the different conclusions that the two sides have drawn from their common stress on the fact that acting individuals (as Max Weber put it) normally attach a 'subjective meaning' to their social behaviour.[8]

The anti-naturalists trace a logical connection between the meaning of a social action and the agent's motives for performing it. They accordingly see the recovery of the agent's motives as a matter of placing their action within a context of social rules. This view of social meaning has issued in two general conclusions about the explanation of social action. One is that to decode the meaning of an action is equivalent to giving a motive-explanation for the performance of it (thesis A). The other is taken to be an implication of the fact that the recovery of an agent's motives is a matter of placing their action in a context of rules rather than causes. It follows, we are told, that to cite the meaning and motives of an action will be to provide a form of explanation that stands in contrast with – and is in fact incompatible with – a causal explanation of the same action (thesis B).

These anti-naturalist conclusions have in part derived, and have gained considerable strength, from the powerful impact of Wittgenstein's later philosophy on recent philosophical psychology. This is perhaps most evident in a work such as A. I. Melden's *Free Action*. Melden lays his main emphasis on the idea of 'making sense' of actions, and argues that this is essentially a matter of recovering motives by way of understanding the 'background' against which the agent acted. His principal conclusion is that this process makes causal explanation 'wholly irrelevant to the understanding' of social behaviour.[9]

There is a longer tradition of analysis lying behind this anti-naturalist commitment. In the philosophy of history it is best represented by R. G. Collingwood and the view of explanation he summarised in his *Idea of History*. To explain an action, Collingwood maintains, is always a matter of attempting 'to discern the thoughts' of the agent who performed it.

---

[6] Ayer 1967, p. 23.   [7] Brodbeck 1963, p. 309.   [8] Weber 1968, vol. 1, pp. 4, 8.
[9] Melden 1961, pp. 87–8, 102, 104, 184.

This in turn requires the historian to focus on questions of individual motivation, and means that any historian who instead seeks to 'emulate the scientist in searching for causes or laws' is simply 'ceasing to be an historian'.[10] The same contrast between understanding actions in terms of motives and explaining events in terms of causes looks back to Benedetto Croce as well as to Wilhelm Dilthey,[11] and forward to the development of their arguments by William Dray, Alan Donagan and others.[12]

In the philosophy of social science a similar commitment has always informed the Weberian tradition of analysis. Max Weber himself never implied that the concepts of *Verstehen* and causal explanation are incompatible. But he opens his *Wirtschaft und Gesellschaft* by discussing motive-explanations, and at that juncture he equates the 'understanding of motivation' with the business of 'placing the act in an intelligible and more inclusive context of meaning'.[13] Since that time, a more strongly anti-naturalist case has been developed by at least two schools of thought that have acknowledged Weber's influence. The phenomenologists (such as Alfred Schutz, at least in certain moods) have gone on to insist that understanding 'the meaning which social phenomena have for us' is a matter of recovering 'typical motives of typical actors', and that this is a form of understanding 'peculiar to social things'.[14] So too the disciples of Wittgenstein such as Peter Winch. They have insisted that 'the notion of meaningful behaviour is closely connected with notions like *motive* and *reason*'. And they have inferred that the explanation of such behaviour, by way of relating the agent's motives to a context of social rules, requires 'a scheme of concepts which is logically incompatible with the kinds of explanation offered in the natural sciences'.[15]

The naturalists, by contrast, have given an account of social meaning from which they have derived two conclusions strongly opposed to those I have now set out. They first of all maintain that the decoding of the meaning of a social action merely provides a way of redescribing it. But since redescriptions cannot in themselves be explanatory, it must be a mistake to suppose that the placing of a social action in its context, or the decoding of its social meaning, can ever serve as an explanation of the action concerned (thesis C). The second naturalist thesis is that, if

---

[10] Collingwood 1946, pp. 214–15.
[11] For convenient extracts from Croce's and Dilthey's writings on these issues see Gardiner 1959, pp. 213–25 and pp. 226–41.
[12] See Dray 1957, pp. 122–6 and cf. Donagan 1957.
[13] Weber 1968, vol. 1, p. 8.   [14] Schutz 1960, pp. 206, 211, 214.   [15] Winch 1958, pp. 45, 72.

the idea of decoding the meaning of an action is so much extended that
it becomes equivalent to recovering the agent's motives, then there is no
incompatibility between social meaning and causality. This is because the
provision of an explanation by way of citing motives, or even intentions, is
itself a form of causal explanation. The naturalists accordingly conclude
that there is nothing in the fact that social actions may be said to have a
meaning or to consist in the following of rules from which it follows that
such episodes may not be entirely explicable by the ordinary processes
of causal explanation (thesis D).

These naturalist conclusions, like those of their opponents, have in
part derived from a recent movement in philosophical psychology. This
has taken the form of a reaction against the Wittgensteinian assumption
that motives and intentions cannot function as causes. The critique of
this position has been sustained by some powerful arguments (best stated
by Donald Davidson)[16] and has prompted several philosophers (notably
Alasdair MacIntyre) to recant their earlier anti-naturalist views about the
explanation of action. The implications of the critique have been brought
out with particular clarity by A. J. Ayer in his essay 'Man as a Subject for
Science'. On the one hand, Ayer insists that to redescribe a phenomenon
cannot be 'in any way to account for it'. On the other hand, he argues that
to cite a motive or an intention to explain an action, as we do 'in the normal way', must ultimately be to point to 'lawlike connections' of a causal
form. Ayer concludes that, even if we can 'estimate an action in terms of
its conforming to a rule', and even if we need to understand such actions
'in terms of their social contexts', these factors affect the agent only as
'part of his motivation'. They give us no grounds for doubting that the
action can be sufficiently explained 'by means of a causal law'. So there is
'nothing about human conduct that would entitle us to conclude *a priori*
that it was in any way less lawlike than any other sort of natural process'.[17]

As with the anti-naturalists, there is a considerable tradition of analysis lying behind this line of thought. In the philosophy of history the
Idealism associated with Dilthey and Collingwood was always confronted
by a positivist tradition stemming from the philosophy of science. The
latter outlook is perhaps best summarised by Carl Hempel in his classic
essay 'The Function of General Laws in History'. The attempt, Hempel
there claims, to explain the actions of historical individuals in an *ad hoc*

[16] Davidson 1963.
[17] Ayer 1967, pp. 16, 17, 21, 22–3. See also Mulligan, Richards and Graham 1979, p. 97 for the
claim that, because all explanations must take the form of assigning causes, redescriptions cannot
be explanatory.

manner, in terms of 'the circumstances under which they acted, and the motives which influenced their actions', does not 'in itself constitute an explanation'. The fact that historians may concern themselves with 'the "*meanings*" of given historical events', as well as with motives and actions, does nothing to vitiate the claim that any satisfactory explanation of an historical phenomenon must consist of 'subsuming it under general empirical laws'.[18]

If we turn to the philosophy of social science we encounter an analogous point of view. The followers of Max Weber have always found themselves confronted by the more strongly naturalist approach associated with Emile Durkheim and his disciples. Durkheim's most powerful statement of his own commitment can be found in his *Rules of Sociological Method*, in which we find him dismissing any need to study individual intentions and motives in our efforts to explain social phenomena. Durkheim always insists that 'the determining cause of a social fact' – under which heading he includes social action – 'should be sought among the social facts preceding it, and not among the states of individual consciousness'.[19]

My aim in what follows will be to reconsider these two opposed theoretical traditions by seeking to do three things. I shall first attempt (section II) to make a new start on analysing what might be involved in speaking about the 'meanings' of actions. I shall then try (section III) to show that, if my analysis is sound, there would seem to be grounds for doubting each of the four theses I have now set out. Finally, I shall go on to suggest (section IV) some methodological implications of my argument for historians and social scientists, at least in so far as they are concerned with the explanation of action.

II

There is a tendency, particularly among anti-naturalists, to apply the concept of social meaning in an over-extended way. (This is perhaps evident from several of the quotations I have already given.) I shall begin, therefore, by restricting myself to considering the way in which the concept is used in the discussion of a single class of social actions. Later I shall try tentatively to extend the application of this analysis. But I shall first concentrate on the class in which the idea of meaning something

[18] Hempel 1942, pp. 44–5.   [19] Durkheim 1964, p. 110.

in or by doing something has its clearest and most obvious application, namely in the class of linguistic actions.

I have already spoken in chapter 6 about the concept of linguistic action and J. L. Austin's classic exposition of it in *How to Do Things with Words*. Here I need only recall Austin's central contention to the effect that anyone issuing a serious utterance will always be doing something as well as saying something, and will be doing something *in* saying what he or she says, not merely as a consequence of what is said. As we have seen, Austin reached this conclusion by way of claiming that to issue any serious utterance is always to speak not only with a certain meaning but also with what he called a certain illocutionary force. Austin's pivotal contention was that to understand this element of illocutionary force co-ordinate with the ordinary meaning of a locution is equivalent to understanding what the speaker was *doing in* issuing their utterance.

Expounding this analysis in chapter 6, I offered a simple example as an aid to clarifying the sense in which the issuing of a serious utterance may be said to constitute the performance of a social action. A policeman sees a skater on a pond and calls out: 'The ice over there is very thin.'[20] The policeman says something and the words mean something. But Austin's further point is that the utterance also has a certain intended illocutionary force, corresponding to the fact that the policeman will also have been doing something in issuing his utterance. He may, for example, have been performing the illocutionary act of *warning the skater*.

I now wish to suggest that this account of linguistic action may be used to establish two crucial points about the sense of 'meaning' with which we are concerned in examining the meaning of social actions. The first is that the decoding of the meaning of an action seems equivalent, in the case of linguistic action, to understanding the nature of the illocutionary act performed by the speaker. To understand, for example, that the policeman was performing the act of warning seems equivalent to understanding the meaning of the act of issuing his utterance. To invoke H. P. Grice's helpful formula, it is to understand what the policeman (non-naturally) meant by acting in this way.[21]

Grice introduced the concept of non-natural meaning in order to draw a contrast with the natural meaning of signs, and thus with the contrasting

---

[20] As noted in chapter 6, I am here adapting an example originally put forward in Strawson 1971, p. 153. Here I need to add that I also follow Strawson in extending J. L. Austin's concept of a convention and in relating H. P. Grice's theory of meaning to Austin's account of illocutionary acts. For a defence of these commitments see Skinner 1970.

[21] See Grice 1957 and the revisions in Grice 1969.

sense of 'meaning' that seems to be in play when we say things like 'those spots mean measles'.[22] My second point is that to ask about this non-natural sense of meaning, at least in the case of linguistic actions, seems equivalent to asking about the agent's intentions in performing their action. It is perhaps necessary to be more precise, and to stress that to ask this question is to ask about their *primary* intention. It is arguable that Austin's way of stating his theory encouraged the belief that for every action there must be a single intention underlying it. But we often have several different intentions in performing a single action. Some may be less important than others from the point of view of characterising what we are doing, but all of them may nevertheless form part of the complex of intentions realised in the act. It remains true, however, that to understand that what the policeman meant to do, in issuing his utterance, was *to warn the skater* is equivalent to understanding the primary intention with which the policeman acted.

It might be doubted whether this analysis of 'social meaning' can usefully be extended to non-linguistic cases. My response is to appeal to authority – or rather, to a series of relevant authorities. Suppose we endorse Austin's own claim – which seems to me unquestionable – that certain illocutionary acts are invariably performed non-verbally.[23] Then there is good reason to suppose that my analysis can at least be used to decode the meaning of the 'ritual and ceremonial' acts in which Austin was chiefly interested. Suppose in addition we accept P. F. Strawson's contention – for which he offered strong arguments[24] – that the account given by Austin of the conventions of illocutionary force was unduly narrow in scope. Then there is good reason to believe that the analysis can also be used to decode the meaning of a whole range of non-ritual as well as non-linguistic actions. Finally, it is relevant to recall that the main aim of H. P. Grice's original discussion of non-natural meaning was 'to show that the criteria for judging linguistic intentions are very like the criteria for judging non-linguistic intentions', and thus to show 'that linguistic intentions are very like non-linguistic intentions'.[25]

These suggestions may be corroborated by considering some examples of non-linguistic action. Consider first a case of a ritual but non-linguistic action. (Martin Hollis has popularised the following example.) Certain Yoruba tribesmen 'carry about with them boxes covered with cowrie

---

[22] Grice 1957, p. 377.   [23] Austin 1980, pp. 19, 119.
[24] See Strawson 1971, pp. 149–69 and my own attempt to extend and apply his analysis in Skinner 1970.
[25] Grice 1957, p. 388.

shells, which they treat with special regard'.[26] My interest lies in the meaning of the action and the questions we need to answer in order to decode it. The crucial question certainly seems to be about what the tribesmen are *doing in* performing this action. The answer (Hollis tells us) is that they believe 'that the boxes are their heads or souls' and that what they are doing in treating the boxes with reverence is protecting their souls against witchcraft. This in turn suggests that to ask and answer this question about the illocutionary force of the tribesmen's behaviour is, as I have suggested, equivalent to asking about their intentions in acting in this way. Notice that we do not learn the motive that prompted (and perhaps caused) them to treat their boxes with special regard, although we may now infer that it is likely to have been respect or fear for the power of unknown forces. What we learn is their primary intention in acting, their intention being to protect their souls.

Consider next a case of a non-ritual, non-linguistic action. (I derive the example from one of the case-histories reported by R. D. Laing and A. Esterson in *Sanity, Madness and the Family*.)[27] An adolescent girl becomes an apparently compulsive reader, 'burying herself in her books' and refusing to stop or allow herself to be interrupted. Laing and Esterson's interest in the case lies primarily in their suggestion that the behaviour can be seen as a strategy, a deliberate action rather than a symptom of illness. My related interest is in the meaning of the behaviour, and in the appropriate question to ask in order to determine whether it has any meaning, and if so how it should be decoded. The crucial question again seems to be about what the girl is *doing in* performing this action. Laing and Esterson's answer is that she is 'taking refuge' and preventing what she takes to be intrusions by an overdemanding family. As before, moreover, it seems that to ask and answer this question about the illocutionary force of the action is equivalent to asking about the girl's intentions in acting in this way. Notice again that this does not tell us the motives that prompted (and perhaps caused) the girl's behaviour. Laing and Esterson suggest that her motive may have been a desire for what they call 'autonomy' but one might infer other motives as well – perhaps a kind of pride, perhaps an element of resentment. What we learn is the girl's primary intention in acting, the intention to register a protest against, and to protect herself from, an excessively demanding situation.

It may still seem, however, that to extend the discussion to include such non-linguistic actions is to give an illegitimate application to Austin's

---

[26] Hollis 1996, p. 199.   [27] Laing and Esterson 1970, pp. 34–5, 46.

and Grice's theories. Consider finally, therefore, a further case of a (non-ritual) linguistic action, and one of some historical importance. Niccolò Machiavelli, in chapter 15 of *Il Principe*, enunciates the following rule: 'it is necessary for a prince to learn how not to be good'.[28] A large number of commentators have asked what exactly he may have meant by offering this advice. Here it cannot I think be doubted that the crucial question to raise is what Machiavelli was *doing in* counselling rulers in this way. One widely accepted answer (originally put forward by Felix Gilbert) has been that Machiavelli was 'consciously refuting his predecessors' within the highly conventionalised genre of advice-books to princes.[29] Again it seems unquestionable that to ask and answer this question about the illocutionary force of Machiavelli's utterance is equivalent to asking about his intentions in saying what he said. Notice once more that this does not tell us the motives which prompted (and perhaps caused) him to offer his advice. Gilbert suggests that the most likely motives may have been a mixture of frustration at the prevailing 'idealist interpretation of politics', combined with a simple desire to shock and a belief in the importance of saying something genuinely useful.[30] The point once more is that what we learn is Machiavelli's primary intention in writing what he wrote. I do not wish to imply here, of course, that what we learn is the intention lying behind the writing of the particular sentence I have quoted, nor do I wish to imply that Machiavelli need have had any isolable intention in writing just that sentence. My claim is simply that we learn the intention lying behind Machiavelli's argument at this stage of his work, the intention being to challenge and repudiate an accepted moral commonplace.

III

I now turn to try to bring out the philosophical interest of my argument. This lies, as I have already hinted, in the suggestion that the argument I have now set out gives grounds for saying that the theses of the naturalists (C and D) as well as those of the anti-naturalists (A and B) may be mistaken. Consider first the two naturalist theses. Thesis C states that to redescribe an action is in no way to explain it. I have now sought to show, however, that for at least some actions there can be a unique form of redescription which, by way of recovering the agent's intended illocutionary act, may be capable of explaining at least certain features of their behaviour. This conclusion can be corroborated by reverting to

---

[28] Machiavelli 1960, p. 65: 'è necessario a uno principe ... imparare a potere essere non buono'.
[29] Gilbert 1977, p. 110.   [30] Gilbert 1977, pp. 111–12.

the example of the policeman saying 'The ice over there is very thin.' This episode might be witnessed by some puzzled bystanders who fail to grasp the policeman's primary intention in issuing his utterance. One request for an explanation might take the form of asking 'Why did he say that?' One reply might be 'He said it to warn the skater.' There seems no doubt, moreover, about the way in which such illocutionary redescriptions serve as explanations. It is one thing if the bystanders understand what the policeman's utterance to the skater means, so that they can give an account of what the policeman said. But it is another and further thing if they understand what the policeman's act of issuing an utterance with that meaning was itself intended to mean on the given occasion, so that they can give an account of why the policeman said what he said. Colloquially, we may say that what an illocutionary redescription will characteristically explain about a social action will be its *point*.

Critics have objected that the redescription only provides additional information about what the policeman was doing, not why he was doing it.[31] It is true that what the redescription serves to explain is not the occurrence of the policeman's action but the character of his utterance.[32] Nevertheless, my thesis about the explanation of action stands. To return to my imagined bystanders: as I have argued, one natural source of their puzzlement might stem from a failure to grasp the point of the policeman's utterance. To inform them that it was meant as a warning will remove their puzzlement. But to say that a sense of puzzlement about a state of affairs has been removed is to say that an explanation has been provided.

Consider next thesis D, which states that there is nothing in the fact that an action may have a meaning from which it follows that it may not be entirely explicable by the ordinary processes of causal explanation. I have now suggested that, while it may be essential in a wide range of cases to recover the meaning of an action in order to explain it, to supply this redescriptive form of explanation is to supply something other than a causal explanation. This can also be corroborated by reverting to my example of the policeman warning the skater. The explanation of the action is supplied by way of recovering what the policeman meant, in the non-natural sense of understanding not just what his utterance meant, but what his act of issuing that utterance meant in the circumstances. This is supplied by way of decoding the conventions governing the illocutionary force attaching to the utterance. But this can scarcely

<hr>

[31] See, for example, Graham 1988, p. 154; Hollis 1988, pp. 139, 141, 146.
[32] Freundlieb 1980, p. 436.

be to provide a causal explanation. For this is to focus on a feature of the policeman's action, not on an independently specifiable condition in the way that causal explanation requires.

Next consider the two anti-naturalist theses. Thesis A states that the reason why the concept of social meaning can be explanatory is because it tells us an agent's motives for acting. Drawing on my argument in chapter 5, however, I have now sought to show, first, that a sharp line needs to be drawn between motives and intentions in acting, and secondly that it is intentions, not motives, that we need to recover if we are to decode the meaning of social actions.

The need for this division does not seem to have been admitted by any of the philosophers I have quoted. The anti-naturalists (such as Melden, Rickman and Winch)[33] as well as the naturalists (such as Ayer, Davidson and MacIntyre)[34] write about motives and intentions in this connection – and often about reasons and purposes as well – as if they believe these terms to be virtually interchangeable. This seems a mistake in itself, but it also seems of some consequence when we try to explain social actions, since it encourages the elision of what I take to be a necessary stage in the process of explanation. The stage in question is the one at which it may be appropriate, before asking about someone's motives, or any deeper causes of their behaviour, to ask whether the performance of their action itself bears any conventional element of (non-natural) meaning or (illocutionary) force.

The significance of isolating this extra stage can be illustrated by examining the main instance of a social action offered by Ayer in his essay 'Man as a Subject for Science'. Ayer takes the case of someone drinking a glass of wine, and claims that this action might be explained, according to its context, either as '[1] an act of self-indulgence, [2] an expression of politeness, [3] a proof of alcoholism, [4] a manifestation of loyalty, [5] a gesture of despair, [6] an attempt at suicide, [7] the performance of a social rite, [8] a religious communication, [9] an attempt to summon up one's courage, [10] an attempt to seduce or corrupt another person, [11] the sealing of a bargain, [12] a display of professional expertise, [13] a piece of inadvertence, [14] an act of expiation, [15] the response to a challenge'.[35]

It is true that my argument is not altogether easy to make good in terms of Ayer's elaborate and eccentric list. In cases [3] and [13] it is

---

[33] Melden 1961, pp. 83–9; Rickman 1967, p. 69; Winch 1958, pp. 45–51.
[34] Davidson 1963, p. 699; Ayer 1967, p. 9; MacIntyre 1971, p. 226.
[35] Ayer 1967, pp. 9–10. I have added the numbers for ease of reference.

not clear that the *explicans* yields the explanation of anything that could be called a voluntary action. In cases [6], [10] and [12] it is not clear how the *explicans* is even to be understood. It is hard to see, that is, how any of these answers could be offered as possible explanations for the action simply of drinking a glass of wine. Furthermore, in cases [1], [5], [9] and [14] it is not clear that there is any separate question to ask about the meaning of the action. This still leaves us, however, with cases [2], [4], [7], [8], [11], and perhaps [15]. The explanation in these cases, *pace* Ayer's conflation of intentions and motives, seems to take the form of a redescription that directs us not primarily to the agent's motives, but rather to their intentions in drinking the glass of wine. Here it does seem necessary to begin by considering a stage of explanation prior to any attempt to elucidate the agent's motives. The stage in question is the one at which we attempt to recover the unique illocutionary redescription in terms of which the agent's performance of the action can be shown non-naturally to mean something. We might say, for example, in case [4] that what the agent was doing in drinking the glass of wine was confirming a bond of loyalty, or in case [11] that what they were doing was sealing a bargain. So it seems that the anti-naturalists must be mistaken when they equate the recovery of social meaning with the elucidation of motives.

Consider finally thesis B, which states that to account for an action by citing its meaning and the agent's motives is to provide a form of explanation incompatible with causality. This thesis is contradicted rather than sustained by the way in which I have sought to vindicate the possibility of giving non-causal explanations of action. I have sought to argue only that to explain an action in terms of the agent's intentions in performing it constitutes one stage in accounting for a certain range of social behaviour. I have not suggested that to provide such non-causal explanations is incompatible with the subsequent provision of further and arguably causal explanations of the same action. One such further stage might be to provide an explanation in terms of motives. A yet further stage might be to provide an explanation in terms of the grounds for the agent's possession of just those motives. It will normally be indispensable to move on to these further stages in order to provide anything like a complete explanation. And I should wish to claim that it is strongly arguable in the case of the first stage, and unquestionable in the case of the second, that to provide these further explanations will be to provide causal explanations for the performance of the action concerned.

IV

I turn finally to consider the practical implications of the thesis I have defended. For at least two reasons it seems to me of special interest to try to make this point. One is that there has been a tendency among philosophers of social science to deny that their views about the logic of explanation entail any methodological recommendations.[36] The other is that there has been a broader tendency among historians as well as social scientists to deny that the acceptance of any particular philosophical viewpoint has any bearing on the conduct of their disciplines. I now wish to suggest that, if the conceptual scheme I have set out is sound, it entails at least three methodological recommendations, all of which tend to be ignored or even repudiated in a good deal of current writing in history and social science. I concede, of course, the difficulty of deriving anything except negative methodological injunctions from my *a priori* arguments. I hope nevertheless that it may be possible to see in this section the beginnings of an answer to those who have refused to accept that the dispute over causal and rational explanation could have anything to do with the practice of the social sciences.

Consider first the classes (the non-linguistic as well as linguistic classes) of what Austin called 'ritual and ceremonial' actions. There are two methodological injunctions that seem, at least in these cases, to follow from the argument I have advanced. The first is that we need to raise questions about ritual beliefs in order to explain such actions. This suggestion has been rejected by a number of anthropologists,[37] and is certainly bypassed by those who have written as if they believe that ritual actions can sufficiently be explained in terms of their place in a social structure or by reference to their effects.[38] It is clear, however, that there is a link between the range of intentions it makes sense to ascribe to people and the nature of their beliefs. It follows that, in order to explain a ritual action by way of recovering the agent's intentions in performing it, we must be prepared to examine and refer to the ritual beliefs informing the intentions with which ritual actions are performed.

My second recommendation is that, as soon as we recognise the need to recover such beliefs, we need to raise questions about their rationality. A certain caution is admittedly required in developing this point. A clear

---

[36] See, for example, Winch 1964, p. 203.

[37] Jarvie and Agassi 1970, p. 179 go so far as to speak of the 'general criticism' in social anthropology of 'the entire assumption that people's actions can be explained by their beliefs'.

[38] Hollis 1970b, pp. 225–7 examines and criticises such explanations.

danger of conceptual imperialism lurks in the supposition that we can speak *tout court* of holding a rational belief as a matter of showing an adequate willingness to consider whether there is 'sufficient evidence in its favour', if it is 'based on good evidence', and so on.[39] We need to reckon with the fact that the question of what counts as good or sufficient evidence can never be free from cultural reference.

This objection has of late been increasingly voiced, especially by such followers of Wittgenstein as Peter Winch, and more recently by Richard Rorty and others.[40] They have insisted that, if we employ the concept of rationality to criticise our beliefs, we shall merely contaminate our social explanations with our own local standards of rationality. The objection has been developed as follows. We can readily imagine an alien system of beliefs in which the paradigms used to connect the system together are such that none of the evidence we should regard as evidence in favour of abandoning particular beliefs is held to count as decisive evidence for or against them. We can then imagine someone operating within the system who accepts these paradigms and canons of evidence, recognises and follows only the moves accepted as rational within the system, but never challenges the rationality of the system itself. We can hardly fail to concede that such people hold their beliefs in a rational way. But in that case the notion of employing the concept of rationality as a tool for the criticism of beliefs appears to lose any cutting edge.

This argument appears to me to embody a *non sequitur*. I have already given my reasons for this conclusion in chapter 3, but it may be worth reiterating my basic point. We can accept that what it means for someone to hold a rational belief is merely for the belief in question to be a suitable one to hold true in the circumstances in which they find themselves. But we can still apply the concept of rationality in the criticism of such an agent's beliefs. For it remains to be asked whether they held the belief in the light of, rather than in the face of, the criteria locally accepted as appropriate for the formation and testing of beliefs.

Why does this response matter for the purposes of my present argument? Because rational and irrational beliefs generate correspondingly different actions. In the first case, the investigator needs to find means to establish that the agent's beliefs were in fact rationally held, especially if they strike the investigator as obviously false. In the second case, a further and different type of investigation will be required if the agent's actions are to be explained. The investigator needs to discover why the agent

---

[39] Gibson 1960, p. 156.　　[40] Winch 1970, pp. 97–103; Rorty 1979, esp. pp. 174, 331.

continued to hold onto an unsuitable belief when the means to improve it were available. Unless the investigator is prepared to raise such questions, it may not be possible to identify what stands to be explained about the agent's beliefs and any actions undertaken in the light of them.

I turn lastly to consider the wider class of social actions which, I have suggested, can in part be explained by decoding the agent's (illocutionary) intentions in performing them. I wish to suggest that in these cases a further injunction follows from my general argument. The injunction is to think holistically, and thus to begin by focusing not on the individual action to be explained, but rather on the conventions surrounding the performance of such actions in the relevant social context.[41] The sense of grasping what is conventional is not limited to the case in which we speak of understanding that an action has been performed according to a convention that has self-consciously been followed. The relevant sense includes the wider notion of understanding the established assumptions and expectations of a given culture. We need to begin not by trying to recover the agent's motives by studying the context of social rules, but rather by trying to decode their intentions by situating their action within this larger structure of values and practices.

This injunction appears to hold good even in the case of the type of abnormal behaviour I have mentioned – such as the example from Laing and Esterson's work on schizophrenia. The question is what approach we should follow in attempting to discover whether the apparent autism of an allegedly schizophrenic adolescent may not be a case of deliberate and meaningful behaviour. The suggested answer is that we ought not to begin by making an intensive study of the particular case and its possible aetiology. We ought rather to begin by trying to relate the particular case to other instances of adolescent withdrawal. The aim will be to try to assess the extent to which the seeming autism may not represent a conventional form and degree of protest, rather than a set of pathological symptoms awaiting a straightforward causal explanation.

The same injunction applies even more clearly to the types of linguistic action I have mentioned. Consider again the passage I quoted from Machiavelli's *Il Principe*. Here there is not only a highly conventionalised genre of writing against which to measure Machiavelli's utterance. There is also a clear presumption that Machiavelli was aware of the genre and the conventions governing it. It seems unquestionable in this case that the appropriate route to follow, in attempting to recover what he meant,

---

[41] But for a criticism of this proposal see Mew 1971.

will be to begin not by making an intensive study of his text itself, but rather by trying to see what relations it bore to these existing conventions of discourse.

It is true that this injunction has been explicitly repudiated by those historians who have wished to insist that it must be possible, simply by reading such works 'over and over', to arrive at a sufficient understanding of them.[42] But it is surely clear (to keep to the Machiavelli example) that the fact that *Il Principe* was in part intended as an attack on the morality embodied in humanist advice-books to princes cannot be discovered by attending to Machiavelli's text, since this is not a fact contained in the text. It is also clear that no one can be said fully to understand Machiavelli's text who does not understand this cardinal fact about it. To fail to grasp this fact is to fail to grasp the point of Machiavelli's argument in the central chapters of his book. It seems, then, that some other form of study besides that of reading such texts 'over and over' is indispensable to understanding them. And it seems that this will need to take the form of adding a study of the general conventions and assumptions of the genre, from which the intentions of any particular contributor to it may then – by a combination of inference and scholarship – be decoded.

V

It will be clear by now that my thesis occupies a middle ground which has I believe been generally overlooked in recent philosophical debates about the explanation of action. I have not been particularly concerned with exegesis, but I believe that my position is similar to the one taken up – though by a different route – by Max Weber in his *Wirtschaft und Gesellschaft*. Those who have emphasised (correctly, I believe) the importance of intentions and conventions in the explanation of action have usually written as though it follows that the attempt to explain such actions causally must represent a confusion, even a 'pernicious confusion'; that it must in any case be 'wholly irrelevant'; and that the whole vocabulary of causality ought accordingly to be 'expunged' from discussions about the explanation of social action.[43] Conversely, those who have insisted (again correctly, I believe) on the absurdity of this commitment have usually written as though it follows that intentions and conventions must themselves be treated as causal conditions of actions.[44] What I have

[42] Plamenatz 1963, vol. 1, p. x.
[43] For these claims see respectively Louch 1966, p. 238; Melden 1961, p. 184; Abelson 1965, p. 541.
[44] See, for example, Davidson 1963, p. 699; Ayer 1967, p. 9.

sought to argue is that neither of these alleged implications follows, and that both of them appear to be mistaken.

It might finally be asked what relation these conclusions bear to the issue of determinism with respect to voluntary human action. This would be a vertiginous question even to broach, were it not that several proponents of the naturalist theses I have examined have suggested that they lend immediate strength to the thesis of determinism. This belief emerges, for example, at the end of A. J. Ayer's essay 'Man as a Subject for Science'. Ayer first recalls that we ordinarily explain human actions by citing the motives and intentions of agents and the social context of their behaviour. He then argues that all these conditions must be construed as causes of which their actions are effects. From this he concludes that there is 'no reason why the reign of law should break down' when we come to explain such actions. This is 'the strength of the determinists'.[45]

I have sought to argue, however, that although there can undoubtedly be successful causal explanations of voluntary human actions, there can also be successful explanations of such actions which are neither causal nor reducible to a causal form. If this argument is sound, it seems possible to suggest two conclusions about the relations between the naturalist theses I have examined and the idea of the social determinism of actions, without having to commit oneself on the vexed question of the meaning of the thesis of determinism itself. The first is that, if it is essential for the defence of the thesis of social determinism that all the mental states of agents should be construed as causes of their actions, then there may be something inherently doubtful about the thesis itself. But the main conclusion, which can I think be expressed more confidently, is that insofar as current arguments in favour of the thesis of social determinism depend upon the truth of thesis C and thesis D, the thesis of social determinism has not been strengthened at all.

[45] Ayer 1967, p. 24.

8

Moral principles and social change

I

We need to be particularly suspicious of politicians and other public figures who invoke high moral principles to explain their own behaviour.
Such, at least, is the view of the most hard-headed of our historians. It is
safe to assume, they tell us, that such professed ideals will be *ex post facto*
rationalisations, and that the actions of such dubious characters will
generally be undertaken for motives of a very different and often inad-
missible kind. Among recent historians, Sir Lewis Namier has perhaps
been the most influential proponent of this vision of politics, although it
is ironic that his arguments in defence of his position often sound very
like those of the Marxist historians whom he always professed to despise.
Like many Marxists, Namier was committed to two connected claims
about the interplay of principle and practice in public life. The first is that
we are indeed justified in dismissing the ideals professed by politicians
as so many attempts to invest their conduct with what Namier liked to
describe as a spurious air of morality and rationality.[1] The second is that
it follows from this that such principles play no causal role in bringing
about their actions, and do not therefore need to figure in our explanations of their behaviour. As Namier summarised, 'party names and cant'
are mere epiphenomena, providing us with no guide at all to the actual
motives and underlying realities of social and political life.[2]

Namier and his followers were assailed for their cynicism by less hard-
headed historians who wished to insist that, as Herbert Butterfield put it,
many public figures are 'sincerely attached to the ideals' for the sake of
which they claim to act.[3] According to historians of this persuasion, it will
usually be indispensable to refer to the professed principles of politicians

This chapter is effectively a new piece of work, but the germ of it can be found in my article 'Some
Problems in the Analysis of Political Thought and Action' in *Political Theory* 2 (1974), pp. 277–303.

[1] Namier 1930, p. 147.   [2] Namier 1957, p. vii.   [3] Butterfield 1957, p. 209.

if we wish to explain their behaviour. To explain an action is normally to cite the goal that an agent wishes to bring about – corresponding to their motive for acting – together with the belief that the performance of the action will conduce to the attainment of the goal. If someone professes to be acting for the sake of a moral principle, and if the principle is genuinely their motive for acting, then it is obvious that the principle makes a difference to the action and will need to be cited in any attempt to explain it.

One weakness of this response, it seems to me, is that those who have argued in these terms[4] have shown themselves unduly willing to endorse the basic premise of their adversaries. They have been willing, that is, to concede that the question of the relationship between principle and practice is equivalent to the question of whether people's professed ideals ever serve as the determining motives for their behaviour. They have thereby committed themselves to defending the generalisation that the sincere attachment of public figures to their professed principles constitutes their standard motive for action. This in turn has allowed their opponents to present an unrepentantly Namierite story in the form of a simple appeal to realism and common experience. They have taken their stand on the alternative empirical claim (which is usually taken to be far more plausible) that moral and political ideals, as one of Namier's disciples has declared, are 'rarely in themselves the determinants of human action'.[5] From this they have inferred that, since it is agreed that such ideals only make a difference if they are motives, and since it is intuitively clear that they are rarely motives, it is obvious that we do not usually need to refer to people's professed principles when we come to explain their behaviour.

It is this shared assumption, however, that seems to me worth questioning.[6] Even if we concede that principles rarely function as motives, we are still left with at least one type of situation in which an agent's professed ideals will nevertheless make a difference to their behaviour. This is the situation in which the agent is engaged in a course of action which is (as I shall put it) in some way questionable, and at the same time possesses a strong motive for attempting (in Weberian phrase) to legitimise it.[7]

---

[4] For examples see the discussion below in vol. 2, ch. 14, section III.   [5] Brooke 1963–4, p. 341.

[6] For a discussion of my ensuing argument see Gorman *et al.* 1987.

[7] I examine further examples of this predicament in volume 2 of the present work. I consider the development of early-modern theories of revolution from this perspective in volume 2 chapter 9, and I consider the opposition to the whig oligarchy in eighteenth-century England from the same

Consider, for example, the case in which Max Weber himself was principally interested, the case of those who devoted themselves to large-scale commercial undertakings in early-modern Europe.[8] The expected profits of these entrepreneurs gave them a recognisable motive for wanting to pursue their ventures unhindered. But the social and religious standards of their age were such that their conduct was liable to appear in a morally and even a legally dubious light.[9] Conservative moralists were all too ready to inveigh against usurious 'city cormorants' for their 'wicked and un-Christian-like dealing'.[10] As a result, the defenders of commerce were driven to retort that, as Lewes Roberts was to complain in his *Treasure of Traffic* in 1641, much more honour and respect are due to merchants than they ever receive.[11] Given this atmosphere of hostility, it was clearly desirable, perhaps even essential, for such entrepreneurs to be able to describe their behaviour in such a way as to repulse or at least to override the widespread accusation that they were behaving avariciously and dishonestly. They needed as a matter of some ideological urgency to legitimise what they were doing to those expressing such comprehensive doubts about the morality of their lives.

I next want to consider how the defenders of commercial society in seventeenth-century England set about this task of legitimising their conduct. My eventual aim will be to suggest that, if we examine the details of this historical case, we shall be able to uncover a further type of causal connection between the principles for the sake of which people profess to act and their actual courses of social or political action.

Before embarking on this enquiry, however, I need to concede that I have characterised the situation I want to investigate in an artificially simple way. I have implied that the sole reason for offering a legitimising description of a questionable action will be to commend it to others. I have thereby implied that there is no reason to suppose that we need to offer such descriptions for our own benefit, or even to believe in such descriptions at all. I have adopted this approach, however, only to avoid some complex empirical questions that in no way affect my general argument. It is obvious that anyone's motives in the type of situation I am describing will usually be mixed and complicated, and it is arguable that the need to sustain an appropriate self-image may be of

---

perspective in volume 2 chapter 13. For a critique of the assumptions underlying these discussions see Hollis 1974.

[8] Weber 1930, pp. 35–46.

[9] For Weber's discussion of these hostilities see Weber 1930, pp. 56–63.

[10] Fennor 1965, pp. 441, 445–6.   [11] Roberts 1952, p. 83.

paramount importance. To preserve simplicity, however, I shall restrict myself in what follows to what is, from my point of view, the hardest case: that of someone who never believes in any of their professed principles, and whose principles never serve in consequence as the motives of their actions. My aim will be to show that, even in this type of case, it still does not follow that there is no need to refer to their professed principles in order to explain their behaviour.

II

As my Weberian example will have made clear, the social actors in whom I am interested are those whom I shall describe (following Weber) as innovating ideologists. As I have indicated, I take their defining task to be that of legitimising some form of social behaviour generally agreed to be questionable. How can this task be successfully performed? As a preliminary to addressing this question, it will be helpful to focus attention on a body of words that perform an evaluative as well as a descriptive function in our language. They are used, that is, to describe individual actions[12] and to characterise the motives for which they are performed. Whenever they are used to describe actions, however, they have the effect of evaluating them at the same time. The special characteristic of this range of terms is thus that – to invoke the jargon of the philosophers of language – they have a standard application to perform one of two contrasting ranges of speech acts. They can be used, that is, to perform such acts as commending and approving – or else of condemning and criticising – whatever actions they are employed to describe. (Henceforth I shall inelegantly refer to them as 'evaluative-descriptive terms'.)

To focus on this body of words is to take over an insight developed by the so-called emotivists in moral philosophy, who contrasted the 'emotive' with the 'descriptive' components of ethical terms.[13] As J. O. Urmson pointed out, however, in making use of J. L. Austin's theory of speech acts to clarify their argument, the emotivists in effect elided the distinction that Austin had marked when he spoke of the 'illocutionary' as opposed to the 'perlocutionary' acts we are capable of performing by our use of evaluative-descriptive terms. I have already sought in chapter 6 to expound the distinctions that Austin drew by means of these neologisms.

---

[12] Or states of affairs. But I shall concentrate on actions.   [13] See especially Stevenson 1963.

Here I need only reiterate that, whereas an illocution is defined as an act performed *in* saying something, a perlocution is described as an effect, and hence as an act performed *as* a consequence of saying something.[14] The key contention (to which I shall return) is that it is possible to perform certain acts simply *in* speaking or writing in a certain way.

After these preliminaries, I am ready to revert to the figure of the innovating ideologist. The sort of perlocutionary effects that such figures normally aspire to achieve are effects such as inciting or persuading or convincing their hearers or readers to adopt some novel point of view. But the question of whether they succeed in realising such hopes is not primarily a linguistic matter, but simply a matter for historical investigation. By contrast, the sort of illocutionary effects they can hope to achieve will be effects such as evincing, expressing or soliciting approval or disapproval of the actions they describe. The question of whether they succeed in realising this sort of intention is essentially a linguistic matter, a matter of seeing how the terms in question are applied. This is what bestows on evaluative-descriptive terms their overwhelming ideological significance.

It is in large part by the rhetorical manipulation of these terms that any society succeeds in establishing, upholding, questioning or altering its moral identity. It is by describing and thereby commending certain courses of action as (say) honest or friendly or courageous, while describing and thereby condemning others as treacherous or aggressive or cowardly, that we sustain our vision of the social behaviour we wish to encourage or disavow. This being so, all innovating ideologists may be said to face a hard but obvious rhetorical task. Their goal is to legitimise questionable forms of social behaviour. Their aim must therefore be to show that a number of favourable terms can somehow be applied to their seemingly questionable actions. If they can bring off this rhetorical trick, they can hope to argue that the condemnatory descriptions otherwise liable to be applied to their behaviour can be overridden or set aside.

Two observations need to be added at this juncture, one emphatic, the other concessive. The point that perhaps needs to be emphasised is that, however revolutionary such ideologists may be, they will nevertheless be committed, once they have accepted the need to legitimise their actions, to showing that some *existing* favourable terms can somehow be applied as apt descriptions of their behaviour. All revolutionaries are to this extent

[14] Urmson 1968, pp. 24–37.

obliged to march backwards into battle.[15] To legitimise their conduct, they are committed to showing that it can be described in such a way that those who currently disapprove of it can be brought to see that they ought to withhold their disapproval after all. To achieve this end, they have no option but to show that at least some of the terms used by their ideological opponents to describe what they admire can be applied to include and thus to legitimise their own seemingly questionable behaviour.

The concessive point is that the situation in the real world is in at least one important respect more complicated than my model suggests. We cannot assume that innovating ideologists will necessarily apply to their behaviour whatever evaluative vocabulary is in fact best adapted to legitimising it. Rather they will apply the vocabulary that they happen to believe is best adapted to that purpose. But they may of course make a mistake or an irrational choice in assessing the best means to attain their ends.

We need to begin, however, by assuming their rationality. I have already explained in chapter 3 why this seems to me the right way to proceed, but it is perhaps worth recalling my central point. Suppose we begin by making this assumption and find it borne out. This will already provide us with an explanation for their behaviour. Suppose, on the other hand, we find on closer inspection that they were not behaving rationally. This will enable us to recognise that some further questions need to be answered if their behaviour is to be explained (the most obvious being: what prevented them from seeing that they were not behaving rationally?) Only if we begin by assuming rationality can we hope to identify what needs to be explained.

I now return to Max Weber and the innovating ideologists whom he discusses in *The Protestant Ethic and the Spirit of Capitalism*. Focusing on the early capitalists, Weber shows how they represented their behaviour in terms of the concepts normally used to commend an ideal of the religious life, emphasising their dedication to their calling and their careful and painstaking lives.[16] As he indicates, this was undoubtedly a rational choice for them to make. Not only were they right to see that, if they could apply such concepts to their own behaviour, this would provide them with a powerful legitimising device. They were also right to see that it was plausible to make the attempt. The Protestant conception

---

[15] Here I respond to those critics who complain that my approach involves 'the denial of the possibility of new insights' and blinds me to moments of creativity. For these objections see respectively Parekh and Berki 1973, p. 168 and Schochet 1974, pp. 270–1.

[16] Weber 1930, pp. 49–50 (quoting Benjamin Franklin); on the calling see pp. 79–84.

of the calling echoed their own worldly asceticism, and there were many affinities between the distinctively Protestant ideal of individual service and devotion to God and the commercial belief in the importance of duty, service and devotion to one's work.[17]

How did the early capitalists manage to exploit these affinities? Weber undertook no investigation into the rhetorical strategies of those who spoke for them, but it seems to me that two principal means are available to any innovating ideologist who aspires to apply a prevailing moral vocabulary to legitimise a questionable way of life. The first may be said to consist of manipulating the speech act potential of certain evaluative terms. The aim is to describe your actions in such a way as to make it clear to your ideological opponents that, although you may be employing a vocabulary generally used to express disapproval, you are using it to express approval or at least neutrality. The point of the strategy is to challenge your opponents to reconsider the feelings of disapproval they normally express when they use the terms concerned.

There are two broad tactics available to anyone attempting to bring off this first strategy. You can try in the first place to introduce new and favourable terms into the language. There are in turn two possibilities here. One is simply to coin new terms as the descriptions of allegedly new principles, and then apply them as descriptions of whatever questionable actions you wish to see commended. This appears to be the tactic that most commentators have had in mind when they have discussed the phenomenon of 'altered meanings and new words' in social and political debate.[18] But this is obviously an excessively crude device, and it is rare to find it employed in ideological argument. There is, however, one important instance of it in the case of the ideology with which Weber was concerned. The word *frugality* provides an example of an evaluative term that first came into widespread use towards the end of the sixteenth century to describe a motive and a form of behaviour for which approval was beginning to be widely sought.

I turn to the other and commoner version of the tactic. This consists of transforming a neutral into a favourable term (usually by meta-phorical extension) and applying it in virtue of its extended meaning to describe the course of action you wish to see commended. We encounter many instances of this sort of transformation among those who wrote in defence of early-modern commercial life. The metaphorical

---

[17] On the worldly asceticism of the early capitalists see Weber 1930, esp. pp. 42, 72, 80, 166, 180.
[18] See for example Parekh and Berki 1973, p. 168.

(and hence evaluative) uses of such words as *discerning* and *penetrating*, for example, first make their appearance in the language at the relevant time to describe a range of talents that many people had come to have a special reason for wishing to see commended.

The other broad tactic consists, more boldly, of seeking to vary the range of speech acts usually performed with existing unfavourable terms. Again there are two possibilities here. The more usual is to apply a term normally used to express disapproval in such a way as to neutralise it. One clear and ultimately successful instance of this tactic in the case of the ideology I am examining is provided by the word *ambition*. It was only in the course of the early-modern period that the word began to acquire its current neutral uses. It had previously been applied almost exclusively to express strong disapproval of whatever courses of action it had been employed to describe.

The other and more dramatic possibility is to reverse the speech act potential of an existing unfavourable term. An equally clear and successful example of this tactic in the case of the ideology I am examining is provided by the history of the words *shrewd* and *shrewdness*. Before the early seventeenth century these terms were almost always used to express disapproval and even contempt. During subsequent generations, however, their appraisive force began to be reversed, eventually leaving them with the standard use they continue to fulfil as terms of approbation, especially approbation of commercial good sense.

It is also possible to employ a mirror image of both these tactics. You can try in the first place to coin new and unfavourable terms to challenge accepted norms of behaviour. This happened in the case of the ideology I am considering with the associated ideas of *being a spendthrift* and *squandering one's substance*. Both these phrases came into widespread use towards the end of the sixteenth century to express a new distaste for the aristocratic ideal of conspicuous consumption and a new approval of what Richard Eburne in his treatise on colonies of 1624 was to call 'godly parsimony'.[19] You can also try to turn neutral into unfavourable terms by metaphorical extensions of their usage. A closely associated example from the same period is provided by the notion of behaving *exorbitantly*, a word that first acquired its metaphorical (and hence evaluative) applications in the early seventeenth century as a means of condemning obvious failures of godly parsimony. Finally, you can seek to reverse the speech act potential of existing commendatory

---

[19] Eburne 1962, p. 85.

terms, as happened in this period with such words as *obsequious* and *condescending.* These and associated descriptions were widely used throughout the sixteenth century to express approval, only mutating into terms of disapprobation once the underlying ideal of an aristocratic and hierarchical society began to be widely challenged.

I turn to the second strategy, which is at once much simpler and of very much greater significance. This consists of manipulating the criteria for applying an existing set of commendatory terms. The aim in this case is to insist, with as much plausibility as can be mustered, that in spite of contrary appearances a number of favourable terms can be applied as apt descriptions of your own apparently questionable behaviour. The aim is to challenge your ideological opponents to reconsider whether their use of the prevailing vocabulary of appraisal may not be socially insensitive. You urge them, in effect, to admit that they are failing to recognise that the ordinary criteria for applying a range of favourable descriptions are present in the very actions they see as questionable.

This particular rhetorical strategy has been little studied, but it seems to me to constitute one of the most widespread and important forms of ideological argument. Certainly it was extensively employed in the case of the ideology I am examining. It was essentially by these means that the attempt was made to connect the principles of Protestant Christianity with the practices of early-modern commercial life.[20] Consider, for example, the two most important words in the religious vocabulary of the age, the word *providence* and the word *religious* itself. During the latter part of the sixteenth century, it began to be suggested by those who wished to commend the successful exercise of care and foresight in monetary affairs that this apparently miserly conduct ought instead to be seen as a commendable working of providence and hence as a *provident* form of behaviour. At the same time, those anxious to propagate these values began to suggest that their characteristic interest in punctuality and exactitude ought not to be condemned as excessively rigorous and severe, but ought instead to be recognised and commended as a genuinely *religious* form of commitment.

The best proof of the ideological motives at work in these new patterns of social description is that the meanings of these words soon became stretched and confused. The term *providence* began to be applied to refer simply to acting with foresight about practical affairs. When, for

---

example, John Wheeler in his *Treatise of Commerce* of 1601 wrote in defence of the Merchant Adventurers, he praised their foresight in distributing 'the benefites, and commodities of the Companie to all the members of the same, so much, as is possible with great providence and equitie ordained'.[21] When William Alexander similarly wrote in defence of the Virginia settlers in his *Encouragement to Colonies* of 1624, he too singled out their 'provident forwardnes' as a cause of their 'good successe', adding that the recent settlers in New Plymouth were proving no less successful in learning to 'governe themselves after a very civill and provident manner'.[22] Soon afterwards we find Lewes Roberts speaking in similar terms in his *Treasure of Traffike* of 1641. He praises 'the care and industrious prudence' of rulers who encourage overseas trade, noting that their foresight is reflected in their 'provident decrees' and reminding us at the same time that 'want of this care, and provident foresight hath lost many kings the traffike of their Kingdomes'.[23]

Meanwhile the ideal of acting *religiously* began to be invoked simply to refer to instances of diligent and punctilious behaviour. We encounter this usage as early as John Wheeler's *Treatise of Commerce*, in which he praises the freedom of trade originally permitted to the English in the Low Countries. These 'auncient freedomes, and liberties of the Empire', he remarks, were 'freelie yielded, and so longe Religiouslie mainteyned, and kept as well towardes all the subjects, as towardes all the friendes, & Allies of the same'.[24] We encounter a yet clearer instance of the new usage in Thomas Mun's *Discourse of Trade* in 1621. Mun calls on his fellow-countrymen in his peroration 'to stirre up our minds, and diligence, to helpe the naturall commodities of this Realme by industrie, and encrease of Arts'. One way of exercising this thoughtfulness, he goes on to propose, will be to remind ourselves that 'for the better furtherance thereof, we ought religiously to avoid our common excesses of food and rayment'.[25] By the time we come to Lewes Roberts and his *Treasure of Traffike* in 1641, we find the new usage fully entrenched. Dedicating his treatise to the two Houses of Parliament, Roberts refers to their 'serious present affaires' and describes them as 'religious Pilots' who 'guide the helme of our Kingdome with your hand'.[26]

It might be objected that what I am illustrating is the failure of such propagandists as Wheeler, Mun and Roberts to present their activities

---

[21] Wheeler 1931, p. 272. [22] Alexander 1624, pp. 30–1.
[23] Roberts 1952, pp. 102, 105. [24] Wheeler 1931, pp. 179–80.
[25] [Mun] 1952, pp. 46–7. For the attribution see McCulloch 1952, p. v.
[26] Roberts 1952, p. 51.

as genuine embodiments of spiritual and God-fearing values, and hence as genuine instances of religious behaviour. Certainly the effect of their rhetoric is sometimes to leave the reader feeling not that they have successfully vindicated the pious character of their enterprises, but merely that they have employed a number of key religious terms in an idiosyncratic way. It is by no means clear, however, that they simply overreached themselves. If we consider the variety of ways in which the term *religious* came to be used in the later seventeenth century and beyond, we begin to appreciate the extent to which they scored an audacious success. Not only did people increasingly begin to speak of purely diligent and punctilious behaviour as religious. They began to do so in part because they evidently came to accept a broader sense of what might count as religious behaviour. The old watchword *laborare et orare* – that we must work and pray – yielded place to the more comforting suggestion that *laborare est orare* – that to work is to pray. By this stage, the sense of what it means to follow a genuinely religious life had been transformed. The rhetoric of the writers I have been considering helped to construct for their descendants a new and more comfortable world.

III

I turn to the general claim I take to be underpinned by my Weberian example. Those who have argued about the relations between moral principles and social behaviour in the manner popularised by such historians as Sir Lewis Namier have presented their readers, it seems to me, with a *non sequitur*. It does not follow, as they appear to believe, from the fact that someone's professed principles may be *ex post facto* rationalisations that those principles play no role in explaining their behaviour. As I have argued, this is to ignore the implications of the fact that people generally possess strong motives for seeking to legitimise any conduct liable to appear questionable. One implication is that they will generally find it necessary to claim that their actions were in fact motivated by some accepted principle. A further implication is that, even if they were not motivated by any such principle, they will find themselves committed to behaving in such a way that their actions *remain compatible* with the claim that their professed principles genuinely motivated them. To recognise these implications is to accept that the courses of action open to such agents will in part be determined by the range of existing principles they can hope to profess with some degree of plausibility.

There is a general and a more specific conclusion to be drawn out here. The general conclusion derives from the fact that any course of action will be inhibited to the degree that it cannot be legitimised. Any principle that helps to legitimise a course of action will therefore be among the enabling conditions of its occurrence. The more specific conclusion derives from the fact that the range of terms that innovating ideologists can hope to apply to legitimise their behaviour can never be set by themselves. The availability of such terms is a question about the prevailing morality of their society; their applicability is a question about the meaning and use of the terms involved, and about how far these can be plausibly stretched. These factors serve as rather specific constraints and directives to those considering what lines of conduct may afford them the best means of bringing their questionable behaviour in line with some accepted principle, thereby legitimising their conduct while at the same time getting what they want. They cannot hope to stretch the application of existing terms indefinitely; so they can only hope to legitimise, and hence to perform, a correspondingly restricted range of actions. To study the principles they invoke will thus be to study one of the key determinants of their behaviour.

Even if these conclusions seem acceptable, it might still be felt that in revisiting Max Weber's example I have chosen to illustrate them in an unfortunate way. It has become a commonplace to insist that we must reject any suggestion that the principles of Protestant Christianity played a causal role in the development of capitalist practices. As Hugh Trevor-Roper has dismissively remarked, any such theory 'is exploded by the simple fact' that 'large scale industrial production' already existed before the Protestant reformation.[27] It is true that, if Weber supposed that a pre-existing Protestant ethic constituted a necessary condition of the rise of capitalism, then his theory is undoubtedly refuted by showing that the emergence of capitalism predated the rise of Protestantism. But Weber was not greatly interested in such alleged connections,[28] although it must be admitted that R. H. Tawney's reworking of Weber's thesis in *Religion and the Rise of Capitalism* is more vulnerable to this line of attack.[29]

---

[27] Trevor-Roper 1967, pp. 21–2.

[28] Weber 1930, p. 91 explicitly rejects the thesis 'that capitalism as an economic system is a creation of the Reformation', pointing out that 'the fact that certain important forms of capitalistic business organisation are known to be considerably older than the Reformation is a sufficient refutation of such a claim'.

[29] See Tawney 1938, in which Lutheranism is viewed (pp. 92–5) as socially conservative, but in which the doctrines of Calvinism are claimed (pp. 111–27) to have given new and special encouragement to unfettered forms of business and commercial life.

Whereas Tawney may have viewed the Protestant reformation as a causal condition of capitalist development, however, Weber is I think more plausibly interpreted as claiming that the Protestant ethic was peculiarly well-adjusted to *legitimising* the rise of capitalism, and that it was in this way that it helped commercial society to develop and flourish.

My own argument can thus be read as an attempt to reinterpret what I take to have been one of Weber's underlying purposes in his celebrated series of articles. I do not wish, however, to press the point of interpretation here. I only wish to emphasise that, even if Trevor-Roper's strictures can be shown to point to a weakness in Weber's argument, they cannot be shown to point to any weakness in the argument I have myself tried to advance. My suggestion that Protestantism played a role in helping to legitimise (and thus to encourage) the rise of capitalism is based on assuming, not denying, that capitalism predated Protestantism. What I have tried to show is that it does not follow from this fact – as Trevor-Roper seems to believe – that Protestantism had no causal role to play in the development of capitalism. This is to ignore the fact that the earliest capitalists lacked legitimacy in the moral climate in which they found themselves. They therefore needed, as a condition of flourishing, to find some means of legitimising their behaviour. As I have shown, one of the means they found was to appropriate the evaluative vocabulary of the Protestant religion – greatly to the horror of the religious, who saw themselves as the victims of a trick.

If it was a trick, however, it certainly worked. The distinctive moral vocabulary of Protestantism not only helped to increase the acceptability of capitalism, but arguably helped to channel its evolution in specific directions, and in particular towards an ethic of industriousness. The relative acceptability of this new pattern of social behaviour then helped in turn to ensure that the underlying economic system developed and flourished. It is for this reason that, even if the early capitalists were never genuinely motivated by the religious principles they professed, it remains essential to refer to those principles if we wish to explain how and why the capitalist system evolved.

9

The idea of a cultural lexicon

I

What can we hope to learn about the processes of social innovation and legitimation by studying the key words we use to construct and appraise the social world itself? This is the question I confront in the course of the present chapter. The question is obviously a vast and intractable one, and in order to make it manageable I shall concentrate on one recent and highly influential study that has focused on the links between linguistic and social change. The work I have in mind – which I shall use as a stalking-horse in what follows – is Raymond Williams's *Keywords*.[1] It is Williams's central contention that a study of 'variations and confusions of meaning' may help us to improve our understanding of matters of 'historical and contemporary substance'.[2] If we take 'certain words at the level at which they are generally used' and scrutinise their developing structures of meaning 'in and through historical time', we may be able 'to contribute certain kinds of awareness' to current social and political debates, and in particular an 'extra edge of consciousness'.[3] But what kinds of awareness can we hope to attain from studying the history of key words? And how should we conduct our studies in order to ensure that this extra edge of consciousness is duly acquired? These are the questions I should like to examine at somewhat greater length.

This chapter is a revised version of an article that originally appeared under the same title in *Essays in Criticism* 29 (1979), pp. 205–24.

[1] Williams 1976 was reissued in a revised and extended form in 1983. My critique was originally published in 1979. Most of the claims in the 1976 version which I criticised in my article were modified or withdrawn in the 1983 edition. I have therefore had to give page references to both versions, referring to them as 'Williams 1976' and 'Williams 1983'.

[2] Williams 1976, p. 21; Williams 1983, p. 24.

[3] Williams 1976, pp. 20–1; Williams 1983, pp. 23–4.

158

II

Before proceeding, I need if possible to neutralise one serious doubt. It might be objected that, in singling out 'a shared body of words', we are focusing on the wrong unit of analysis altogether.[4] Williams's aim, he tells us, is to illuminate 'ways not only of discussing but at another level of seeing many of our central experiences'.[5] But if we wish to grasp how someone sees the world – what distinctions they draw, what classifications they accept – what we need to know is not what words they use but rather what concepts they possess.

It is true that this objection may appear a purely verbal one. For it might be replied – the claim has often been made – that possessing a concept is equivalently a matter of knowing the meaning of a word. This certainly seems to be Williams's own view, for in discussing the term *nature* he equates 'the word and the concept', and in speaking of *democracy* he explains how the 'concept' is 'embodied' in the word.[6]

To argue for any such equivalence, however, is undoubtedly a mistake. First of all, it cannot be a necessary condition of my possessing a concept that I need to understand the correct application of a corresponding term. Suppose, for example, that I am studying John Milton's thought, and want to know whether Milton considered it important that a poet should display a high degree of originality. The answer seems to be that he felt it to be of the utmost importance. When he spoke of his own aspirations at the beginning of *Paradise Lost*, what he particularly emphasised was his decision to deal with 'things unattempted yet in prose or rhyme'. But I could never have arrived at this conclusion by way of examining Milton's use of the word *originality*. For while the concept is central to his thought, the word did not enter the language until a century or more after his death. Although a history of the word *originality* and its various uses could undoubtedly be written, such a survey would by no means be the same as a history of the concept of originality – a consideration often ignored in practice by historians of ideas.

Moreover, it cannot be a sufficient condition of my possessing a concept that I understand the correct application of a corresponding term. There remains the possibility (explored by Kant and more recently by Wittgenstein) that I may believe myself to be in possession of a concept

---

[4] Williams 1976, p. 13; Williams 1983, p. 15.   [5] Williams 1976, pp. 12–13; Williams 1983, p. 15.
[6] Williams 1976, pp. 84, 189. But in Williams 1983, pp. 95, 224 these claims are deleted, and in his new Introduction Williams explicitly acknowledges (p. 21) 'the difficult relations between words and concepts'.

when this belief is mistaken. Consider, for example, the difficulties raised by certain highly general terms such as *being* or *infinity*. A whole community of language users may be capable of applying these terms with perfect consistency. Yet it might be possible to show that there is no concept that answers to any of their agreed usages.

What then is the relationship between concepts and words? We can scarcely hope to capture the answer in a single formula, but at least the following can be said. The surest sign that a group or society has entered into the self-conscious possession of a new concept is that a corresponding vocabulary will be developed, a vocabulary which can then be used to pick out and discuss the concept in question with consistency. This suggests that, while we certainly need to exercise more caution than Williams does in making inferences from the use of words to the understanding of concepts and back again, there is nevertheless a systematic relationship between words and concepts to be explored. To possess a concept is at least standardly to understand the meaning of a corresponding term (and to be able in consequence to think about the concept when instances are absent and recognise it when instances are present). As long as we bear in mind that 'standardly' here means something less than necessarily and sufficiently, I think we may legitimately proceed.

III

If our aim is to illuminate ideological disputes through the study of linguistic disagreements,[7] the first question we need to raise – as Williams acknowledges – is obviously the following. What exactly are we debating about a word when we find ourselves debating whether or not it ought to be applied as a description of a particular action or state of affairs?

Unfortunately, Williams's answer is confusingly vague. 'What is really happening in such encounters', he maintains, is a process whereby 'meanings are offered' and are then 'confirmed, asserted, qualified, changed'.[8] All such debates are thus taken to be about 'meanings'; about the 'historical origins and developments' which have issued in the 'present meanings' of the terms involved.[9]

This question-begging tendency to speak without further explication about 'changes of meaning' is due, I believe, to the fact that Williams at no point tries to isolate and analyse the class of terms in which he is chiefly interested. The class in question is the one that he describes as including

---

[7] For a discussion of this general issue see Norval 2000.
[8] Williams 1976, p. 9; Williams 1983, pp. 11–12.
[9] Williams 1976, pp. 13, 19–20; Williams 1983, pp. 15, 22–3.

the 'strong' and 'persuasive' words, the words that 'involve ideas and values'.[10] No consistent account of how certain words come to 'involve values' is presented. But it seems clear that, if any further progress is to be made in discussing the phenomenon of meaning change in ideological debates, the provision of such an analysis will have to be treated as a crucial preliminary step. As it happens, this is not as Herculean a labour as might be feared. A great deal of attention has been paid by theorists of language as well as moral philosophers to isolating and commenting on precisely these terms.[11] Drawing on their accounts, we may say, I think, that three main requirements need to be met if these 'persuasive' terms are to be understood and correctly applied.

It is necessary in the first place to know the nature and range of the criteria in virtue of which the word or expression is standardly applied. Suppose, for example, that I am unaware of the meaning of the appraisive term *courageous*, and ask someone to explain to me how to use the word properly. A good reply would surely mention various criteria that serve to mark the word off from similar and contrasting adjectives, so providing it with its distinctive role in our language of social description and appraisal. When listing these criteria, we would surely need to include at least the following: that the word can be used only in the context of voluntary actions; that the actor involved must have faced some danger; that they must have faced it with some consciousness of its nature; and that they must have faced it heedfully, with some sense of the probable consequences of undertaking the action involved. Summarising these criteria (in what is only apparently a tautology), we may say that the conditions under which the term *courageous* can be applied are such that the action involved must have been a courageous one.

Next, to apply an appraisive term correctly I also need to know its range of reference. I need, that is, to have a sense of the nature of the circumstances in which the word can properly be used to designate particular actions or states of affairs. The concept of reference has often been taken to be an aspect or feature of the meaning of a word. But it is perhaps more helpful to treat the understanding of the reference of a word as a consequence of understanding the criteria for applying it correctly. To grasp these criteria is to understand the sense of a word, its role in the language, and thus its correct use. Once I have acquired this understanding, I can expect to be able to exercise the further and

[10] Williams 1976, pp. 12, 15; Williams 1983, pp. 14, 17.

[11] Among moral philosophers I am most indebted to Foot 1958, Murdoch 1970 and Hampshire 1959, esp. pp. 195–222. Among philosophers of language, my approach owes most to Wittgenstein 1958, Austin 1980, and the analysis of Frege's views in Dummett 1973a, esp. pp. 81–109.

more mysterious skill of relating the word to the world. I can expect, for example, to be able to pick out just those actions which are properly to be called courageous, and to discuss the sorts of circumstance in which we might wish to apply that particular description, or might wonder whether we ought to apply it rather than a different one. For instance, someone might call it courageous if I faced a painful death with cheerfulness. However, it might be objected that strictly speaking no danger is involved in such circumstances, and thus that we ought not to speak of courage but rather of fortitude. Or again, someone might call it courageous if I stepped up from the circus audience to deputise for the lion tamer. But it might be countered that this is such a heedless action that it ought not to be viewed as courage but rather as sheer recklessness. Both these arguments are about the reference (but not the meaning) of the word *courageous*. Both are concerned with whether a given set of circumstances – what a lawyer would call the facts of the case – are such as to yield the agreed criteria for the application of the given appraisive term.

To apply any word to the world, we need to have a clear grasp of both its sense and its reference. But in the case of appraisive terms a further element of understanding is required. We need in addition to know what range of attitudes the term can standardly be used to express. For example, no one can be said to have grasped the correct application of the adjective *courageous* if they remain unaware of its standard use to commend, to express approval, and especially to express (and solicit) admiration for any action it is used to describe. To call an action courageous is not merely to describe it but to place it in a specific moral light. I can praise or rejoice at an action by calling it courageous, but I cannot condemn or sneer at it by describing it in this way.

If these are the three main things we need to know in order to isolate the class of appraisive terms and apply them correctly, we can now return to the question I raised at the beginning of this section. I asked what we might be debating about a key word if we found ourselves asking whether or not it ought to be applied in a particular case. As we have seen, Williams's answer is that such arguments must be about the senses or meanings of the words involved. As I have sought to show, however, we might be disagreeing about one of at least three different things, not all of which are self-evidently disagreements about meaning: about the criteria for applying the word; about whether the agreed criteria are present in a given set of circumstances; or about what range of speech acts the word can be used to perform.

IV

So far I have tried to isolate the principal debates that arise over the application of our appraisive vocabulary to our social world. I now turn to what I take to be the crucial question. In what sense are these linguistic disagreements also disagreements about our social world itself?

I have suggested that one type of argument over appraisive terms centres on the criteria for applying them. Now this is certainly a substantive social debate as well as a linguistic one. For it can equally well be characterised as an argument between two rival social theories and their attendant methods of classifying social reality.

As an illustration of such a dispute, recall the way in which Marcel Duchamp liked to designate certain familiar objects (coat-pegs, lavatory bowls) as works of art, thereby causing them to be framed and hung on the walls of galleries. Some critics have accepted that these are indeed significant works of art, on the grounds that they help us to sharpen our awareness and extend our appreciation of everyday things. But others have insisted that they cannot be works of art at all, on the grounds that we cannot simply *call* something a work of art, since works of art have to be deliberately created.

This disagreement arises at the linguistic level. It centres on whether or not a certain criterion (the exercise of skill) should or should not be regarded as a necessary condition for the application of a particular appraisive term (*a work of art*). But this is certainly a social dispute as well. What is at issue is whether or not a certain range of objects ought or ought not to be treated as having a rather elevated status and significance. And it is obvious that a great deal may depend on how this question is answered.

A number of the arguments in *Keywords* are primarily of this character. For example, the essays on 'literature' and 'science' largely fit this analysis, as does the useful discussion of 'the unconscious', in the course of which Williams actually points out that 'different theories' have generated 'confusions between different senses' of the term.[12] Moreover, Williams is surely right to claim that in these cases the argument is indeed about the senses or meanings of the words involved. It is true that some powerful voices – notably that of Hilary Putnam – have lately been raised against the contention that if we introduce a new theory relating to a given subject matter (for example, what constitutes a work of art) this will inevitably give rise to changes in the meanings of the constitutive

[12] Williams 1976, p. 272; Williams 1983, p. 322.

terms.[13] Putnam is surely right to protest that Paul Feyerabend and other post-empiricist philosophers tended to employ this assumption with excessive enthusiasm. Certainly we cannot say that any change of theory will automatically bring about a change in the meanings of all the words involved, if only because nouns and adjectives shift in meaning so much more readily than, say, conjunctions. Moreover, it seems unduly anarchistic to claim that the meaning of a word must have changed if we simply change our beliefs about whatever the word is customarily used to denote.[14] While accepting these cautions, however, I should still wish to insist that, if someone is mistaken about the criteria for applying a term, then they cannot be said to know its current meaning. And since I have argued that the question of whether Duchamp's coat-peg is a work of art is (at one level) an argument about the criteria for applying the term *a work of art*, I agree with Williams that in this type of argument about key words the disagreement really is about the meaning of the word concerned.

What Williams misses, however, in his account of these disputes is their almost paralysingly radical character. He remains content to suppose that in all discussions about 'meaning' we can 'pick out certain words of an especially problematical kind' and consider only 'their own internal developments and natures'.[15] This fails to recognise the implications of the fact that a term such as *art* gains its meaning from the place it occupies within an entire conceptual scheme. To change the criteria for applying it will thus be to change a great deal else besides. Traditionally, the concept of art has been connected with an ideal of workmanship, has been opposed to the 'merely useful', has been employed as an antonym for *nature*, and so on. If we now endorse the suggestion that an *objet trouvé* or a manufactured article can count as a work of art, we at once sever all these and many other conceptual links. So an argument over the

---

[13] For an attack on this line of thought see Putnam 1975, pp. 117–31.

[14] This objection of Putnam's, however, seems less well-argued. It is hard to think of clear cases in which meanings have remained constant in the face of changing beliefs, and Putnam's examples to the contrary strike me as unconvincing. Putnam 1975, pp. 127–8 takes the case of *gold* and argues that the meaning of the word would not be affected even if we were to find gold rusting and were thus obliged to change our beliefs about the substance. This seems dogmatic. Would we really go on saying things like 'It's as good as gold'? And if not, might we not have to concede that the meaning of *gold* had changed?

[15] Williams 1983, pp. 22–3, slightly revised from Williams 1976, p. 20. Williams 1983, p. 23 protests at the kind of reader who, in criticising his approach, is 'content to reassert the facts of connection and interaction from which this whole inquiry began'. Williams's new Introduction is thus explicit about the problems posed by a holistic (and in that sense a sceptical) approach to 'meanings'. But I cannot see that the implications of this scepticism have been accommodated even in the revised version of his text.

application of the term *art* is potentially nothing less than an argument over two rival (although not incommensurable)[16] ways of approaching and dividing up a large tract of our cultural experience. Williams appears, in short, to have overlooked the strongly holistic implications of the fact that, when a word changes its meaning, it alters its relationship with an entire vocabulary.[17] What this tells us about such changes is that we must be prepared to focus not on the 'normal structure' of particular words, but rather on their role in upholding complete social philosophies.

V

Even if we agree about the criteria for applying an appraisive term, I have suggested that a second type of dispute can arise over its use. We may instead find ourselves arguing over whether a given set of circumstances can be claimed to yield the criteria in virtue of which the term is normally employed. Again, such a disagreement will certainly be a social one, and not merely linguistic in character. For what is being contended in effect is that a refusal to apply the term in a certain situation may constitute an act of social insensitivity or a failure of social awareness.

As an illustration of this second type of argument, consider the contention that wives in ordinary middle-class families at the present time can properly be described as suffering *exploitation*, as being an exploited class. The social argument underlying this linguistic move might be spelled out somewhat as follows. It ought to be evident to all persons of goodwill that the circumstances of contemporary family life are such that this strongly condemnatory term does indeed (if you think about it) fit the facts of the case. Conversely, if you fail to acknowledge that the application of the term *exploitation* – in virtue of its agreed criteria – is indeed appropriate in the circumstances, you are wilfully refusing to perceive the institution of the modern family in its true and baleful light.

This is a dispute of an entirely different character from the first type of argument I singled out. Nevertheless, there has been a persistent tendency among moral and political philosophers to conflate the two. Consider, for example, the analysis offered by Stuart Hampshire in *Thought and Action* of an imagined debate between a Marxist and a liberal. According to Hampshire's account, the liberal will be likely to be 'startled to find that actions of his, to which he had never thought to attach political

---

[16] Otherwise it is hard to see how the disputants could be *arguing*.

[17] On this point see Dummett 1973b.

significance, in his sense of "political", are given a political significance'
by his Marxist opponent.[18]

As the above quotation already indicates, Hampshire classifies this
type of disagreement as one about the 'sense' of the word 'political'; as
'a disagreement about the criteria of application' of the term.[19] If this
is a genuine argument, however, it is obviously crucial that the Marxist
should be able to claim with some plausibility that he is employing the
term in virtue of its *agreed* sense. (I am following Hampshire in treating
both the Marxist and the liberal as male.) It is not clear that the Marxist
can even be said to be arguing with the liberal if he is simply content to
point out that, as Hampshire puts it, he has a different concept of 'the
political', with the result that he and the liberal are both confined to 'the
largely separated worlds of their thought'.[20] It is even less clear, if this
is all that the Marxist wishes to point out, why the liberal should feel in
the least discomfited by the argument, given that it amounts to nothing
more than a declaration of an intention to use a certain appraisive term in
an idiosyncratic way. If the Marxist is genuinely seeking to persuade the
liberal to share or at least acknowledge some political insight, he needs in
effect to make two points. One is that the term *political* can appropriately
be applied to a range of actions where the liberal has never thought of
applying it. But the other – which his application of the term challenges
the liberal to admit – is that this is not in the least due to a disagreement
about the meaning of the term, but rather to the fact that the liberal is
a person of blinkered political sensitivity and awareness.

The same confusion afflicts many of Williams's discussions about
key words. He gives examples of debates about, for example, whether
a certain procedure can be appraised as *empirical,* whether a particular
kind of household can be called a *family,* whether someone can be said to
have an *interest* in a particular state of affairs, and so on.[21] In each case he
classifies the dispute as one about the 'sense' of the term involved. Again,
however, it seems essential to the success of the social argument underlying such linguistic debates that the appraisive words in question should
be offered in virtue of their accepted sense as an apt way of describing
situations which have not hitherto been described in such terms.

It is true that, as a consequence of such arguments, new meanings
will often be generated. But the process by which this happens is the
opposite of the one Williams describes. When an argument of this nature

---

[18] Hampshire 1959, p. 197.   [19] Hampshire 1959, p. 196.   [20] Hampshire 1959, p. 197.
[21] Williams 1976, pp. 99, 109, 143; Williams 1983, pp. 115, 131, 171.

is successful, the outcome will hardly be the emergence of new meanings, save that the application of a term with a new range of reference may eventually put pressure on the criteria for applying it. The outcome will rather be the acceptance of new social perceptions, as a result of which the relevant appraisive terms will then be applied with unchanged meanings to new circumstances. It is only when such arguments fail that new meanings tend to arise.

This contention can readily be supported if we consider some of the ways in which a failure to persuade an interlocutor in this type of argument may be capable of leaving its traces on the language. Consider the case in which a particular social group seeks to insist that the ordinary criteria for applying a particular appraisive term are present in a much wider range of circumstances than has commonly been supposed. It is likely that other users of the language – not sharing the underlying social perceptions of the first group – will assume in good faith that a 'new meaning' has indeed been 'offered', and may simply accept it.

The history of our culture (and in consequence our language) has been punctuated with many such misunderstandings. One fruitful source has been the continuing efforts of the proponents of commercial society to legitimise their undertakings by reference to the most highly approved moral and spiritual values. I have already considered one such example in chapter 8: the use of the term *religious* that first emerged in the later sixteenth century as a means of commending merely diligent and punctilious forms of behaviour. The aim was clearly to suggest that the ordinary criteria for applying the strongly commendatory term *religious* were reflected in such actions, and thus that the actions themselves should be seen essentially as acts of piety and not merely as instances of administrative competence. This audacious move was partly successful, but only partly. The extent to which the proponents of commercial society may be said to have overreached themselves was eventually reflected in the emergence of a new meaning for the term *religious* – the meaning we still invoke when we say things like 'I attend my departmental meetings religiously.' It seems clear that the need for this new lexical entry originally arose out of the incapacity of many language users to see that the ordinary criteria for *religious* (including the notion of piety) were present in all the circumstances in which the term was beginning to be used.

There are many recent instances of the same phenomenon, some of which are cited and discussed in *Keywords*. For example, many industrial enterprises like to claim – with reference to their business strategies – that they have a certain *philosophy*. It is likewise common for firms to promise to supply prospective customers with their *literature* (meaning only their advertising brochures). Again a crude attempt is clearly being made to link the activities of commercial society with a range of 'higher' values. And again, the failure of such efforts often gives rise to genuine polysemy. Hearing that a firm has a certain philosophy, most language users have assumed that a new meaning must be involved, and have gone on to use the term accordingly. They have not in general come to feel that corporations can be said to have philosophies in the traditional sense of the term.

The language also supplies us with evidence of such ideological failures in a second and more decisive way. After a period of confusion about the criteria for applying a disputed term, the final outcome may not be polysemy but rather a reversion to the employment of the original criteria, together with a corresponding obsolescence of the newer usages. This can be observed, for example, in the history of the word *patriot*. During the eighteenth century, the enemies of the ruling oligarchy in England sought to legitimise their attacks on the government by insisting that they were motivated entirely by their reverence for the constitution, and thus that their actions deserved to be commended as patriotic rather than condemned as factious.[22] This at first bred such extreme uncertainty about the word *patriot* that it soon came to *mean* (according to one of the definitions in Dr Johnson's Dictionary) 'a factious disturber of the government'. With the gradual acceptance of party politics, however, this condemnatory usage eventually atrophied, and the word reverted to its original meaning and its standard application as a term of praise.

The same form of argument can also have a more equivocal outcome, an outcome that the language will again disclose. It may be that, after a similar period of semantic confusion, the original rather than the newer usage becomes obsolete. At first sight this may seem to indicate a success in the underlying campaign to change people's social perceptions. For this certainly makes it harder to invoke the primitive meaning of the word in order to insist that its newer applications may be nothing more than a deformation of its basic sense. But in fact such changes again tend to be indexes of ideological failure. For the standardisation of a new set of criteria will inevitably carry with it an alteration of the term's appraisive force. Sometimes the power of the word to evaluate what it is used to describe may be retained in a different (and usually weaker) form. A well-known instance is furnished by the word *naughty*, which has wholly

---

[22] For a fuller consideration of this example see below, volume 2 chapter 14.

lost the force it possessed when the Fool warned Lear in the course of the storm scene that 'Tis a naughty night to swim in'.[23] But often the process of acquiring a new meaning goes with total loss of appraisive force. A good example is provided by the history of the word *commodity*. Before the advent of commercial society, to speak of something as a commodity was to praise it, and in particular to affirm that it answered to one's desires, and could thus be seen as beneficial, convenient, a source of advantage. Later an attempt was made to suggest that an article produced for sale ought to be seen as a source of benefit or advantage to its purchaser, and ought in consequence to be described as a commodity. For a time the outcome of this further effort by the early English capitalists to legitimate their activities was that *commodity* became a polysemic word. But eventually the original applications withered away, leaving us with nothing more than the current and purely descriptive meaning of *commodity* as an object of trade. Although the capitalists inherited the earth, and with it much of the English language, they were unable in this case to persuade their fellow language users to endorse their attempted eulogy of their own commercial practices.

VI

Even if we agree about the criteria for applying an appraisive term, and also agree that a given set of circumstances can properly be said to answer to those criteria, a third type of dispute can still arise about its use. As I have suggested, this will be a dispute about the nature and range of the speech acts that the term can be used to perform. Once again this can certainly be characterised as a social dispute and not merely a linguistic one. For in this case what is at issue is the possibility that a group of language users may be open to the charge of having a mistaken or an undesirable social attitude.

We can distinguish two main routes by which an argument of this kind will be likely to issue in a contentious use of evaluative language. We may dissent from an orthodox social attitude by employing an appraisive term in such a way that its standard use to perform a particular range of speech acts is weakened or even abolished. This can in turn be achieved in one of two ways. If we do not share the accepted evaluation of some particular action or state of affairs, we may indicate our dissent simply by dropping the corresponding term from our vocabulary altogether. There are many

---

[23] Shakespeare 1988, *King Lear*, III. iv. 104–5, p. 961.

instances of this move in current social debates. Among terms hitherto used to commend what they describe, this appears to have happened some time ago in the case of *gentleman*. Among terms previously used to express an element of condescension or patronage, this has likewise happened with *native*, at least when used as a noun.

The other method of registering the same form of protest is more challenging. While continuing to employ an accepted term of social description and appraisal, we may make it contextually clear that we are using it merely to describe, and not at the same time to evaluate what is thereby described. There are many contemporary instances of this move as well. Among terms previously used to evince condescension or even hatred, the classic example is provided by the word *black* (used as the description of a person), whether employed as an adjective or a noun. So too with the word *queer*. Among terms previously used to commend, we may note the relatively new and carefully neutral applications of such words as *culture* and *civilisation*. As Williams himself observes,[24] these latter usages appear to have originated within the discipline of social anthropology, but have since come to be very generally accepted by those who wish to disavow any suggestion that one particular civilisation may be more deserving of study than another.

The second main way in which we can use our evaluative language to signal our social attitudes is more ambitious in character. I have already sought to illustrate it in chapter 8, in the course of examining early-modern debates about the values of commercial and capitalist society. It is possible to indicate, simply through our use of appraisive terms, not that we dissent from the idea of evaluating what they describe, but rather that we disagree with the direction of the evaluation and wish to see it reversed.

Again there are two possibilities here. We may use a term normally employed to condemn what is described in such a way as to make it contextually clear that, in our view, the relevant action or state of affairs ought instead to be commended. As Williams points out, one interesting example of this reversal can be seen in the history of the word *myth*. In a more confidently rationalist age, to describe an explanation as mythological was to dismiss it. But in recent times, as Williams observes, the term has often been used to extol the mythological 'version of reality' as 'truer' and 'deeper' than more mundane accounts.[25] Conversely, we may dislike a form of behaviour generally regarded as praiseworthy, and indicate our

---

[24] Williams 1976, pp. 50, 80; Williams 1983, pp. 59, 91.
[25] Williams 1976, pp. 176–8; Williams 1983, pp. 210–12.

disapproval by making it contextually clear that, although the term we are using is standardly employed to commend, we are employing it to condemn what is being described. Once again, there are many instances of this kind of struggle in current ideological debates. Think, for example, about the fortunes in recent times of that erstwhile commendatory term *elite*; or about the fate of those politicians who are regularly praised by one group of commentators for being *liberal* while others employ the same term to denigrate them.

Williams surveys a large number of disagreements that fall within this third general category, and in many cases his comments on them are extremely interesting and shrewd. But his discussion suffers throughout from a failure to distinguish this type of argument from the first type we considered, in which the primary point at issue was the proper sense or meaning of the terms involved. Indeed Williams not only fails but refuses to distinguish between the two types of argument. For example, he insists that the change involved in the move from condemning myths to commending them must be construed as a change in the 'sense' of the word *myth*.[26]

It would be perfectly possible, however, for both the sense and the reference of *myth* to remain stable in the face of the sort of changes in the use of the word that Williams is concerned to point out. It may be that all (and only) those theories and explanations which used to be called mythological are still called mythological, and that the *only* change involved in the use of the term derives from the shift from condemning myths to commending them. It is true that such a change of usage will be likely in due course to affect the sense of the word. But it is a mistake to suppose that this type of argument is primarily (or even necessarily) concerned with sense. What is changing – at least initially – is nothing to do with sense; what is changing is simply a social or intellectual attitude on the part of those who use the language.[27]

VII

I have now tried to furnish at least a preliminary response to the very large question I raised at the outset. I asked what kinds of knowledge and awareness we can hope to acquire about our social world through studying the vocabulary we use to describe and appraise it. I have answered that there are three main types of insight we can hope to achieve: insights

---

[26] Williams 1976, p. 117; Williams 1983, p. 211.
[27] Here I draw on the classic account in Searle 1962.

into changing social beliefs and theories; into changing social perceptions and awareness; and into changing social values and attitudes. I have thus attempted to supply at least a sketch of what seems to me most seriously lacking in Williams's book: an account of the sort of methodology we would need to develop in order to use the evidence of our social vocabulary as a clue to the improved understanding of our social world.

This in turn suggests a further and even more vertiginous question. Are we now in a position to say anything about the nature of the role played by our appraisive vocabulary in the process (and hence the explanation) of social change?

Williams clearly thinks that we are, and conveys this sense by alluding repeatedly to the image of language as a mirror of social reality. The process of social change is treated as the primary cause of developments in our vocabulary; conversely, such developments are treated as reflections of the process of social change.[28] Describing the emergence of capitalism as 'a distinct economic system', for example, Williams remarks that this gave rise to 'interesting consequent uses of language'.[29] Commenting more specifically on 'the economic changes of the Industrial Revolution', he notes that these produced a 'greatly sharpened' and extended 'vocabulary of class'.[30]

There is no doubt that this image serves to remind us of an important truth. Where we encounter a wide measure of agreement about the application of key social terms, we must be dealing with a strikingly homogeneous social and moral world; where there is absolutely no such agreement, we can expect total chaos. But it is arguable that the metaphor is also misleading in one crucial respect. It encourages us to assume that we are dealing with two distinct and contingently related domains: that of the social world itself, and that of the language we then apply in our attempts to delineate its character. This certainly seems to be the assumption underlying Williams's account. He sees a complete disjunction between 'the words' he discusses and 'the real issues' in the social world. And he sometimes speaks as if the gap between the two is one that we can scarcely hope to bridge. 'However complete the analysis' we offer at the linguistic level, he regretfully concludes, we cannot expect that 'the real issues' will be fundamentally affected.[31]

---

[28] Note, however, that Williams 1983, p. 22 now counters this criticism.
[29] Williams 1976, p. 43. But in Williams 1983 this claim is deleted.
[30] Williams 1976, p. 53; Williams 1983, p. 62.
[31] Williams 1976, pp. 13–14. But in Williams 1983, p. 16 this claim is modified.

To speak in this way is to forget something that Williams emphasises at other moments in *Keywords* with striking force. This is the fact that one of the most important uses of evaluative language is that of legitimising as well as describing the activities and attitudes of hegemonal social groups. The significance of this consideration can be brought out if we revert for a moment to the principal example I examined in chapter 8. I considered the case of the entrepreneurs of early-modern England who were anxious to persuade their contemporaries that, although their commercial enterprises might appear morally questionable, they were in fact deserving of respect. One device they adopted was to argue that their characteristically punctual and conscientious behaviour could properly be seen as religious in character, and hence as motivated by pious and not merely by self-seeking principles. Their underlying purpose was of course to legitimise their behaviour by insisting on the propriety of describing it in these highly commendatory terms.

Now it may seem – and this is evidently Williams's view – that this sort of example precisely fits the metaphor of language as the mirror of a more basic social reality. The merchant is perceived to be engaged in a more or less dubious way of life which he has strong motives for wishing to exhibit as legitimate. So he professes just those principles, and offers just those descriptions, that serve to present what he is doing in a morally acceptable light. Since the selection of the principles and their accompanying descriptions both relate to his behaviour in an obviously *ex post facto* way, it hardly seems that an explanation of his behaviour need depend in the least on studying the moral language he may elect to use. His choice of vocabulary appears to be entirely determined by his prior social needs.

It seems to me, however, that this is to misunderstand the role of the normative vocabulary that any society employs for the description and appraisal of its social life. The merchant cannot hope to describe *any* actions he may choose to perform as being 'religious' in character, but only those which can be claimed with some show of plausibility to meet such agreed criteria as there may be for the application of the term. It follows that, if he is anxious to have his conduct appraised as that of a genuinely religious man, he will find himself restricted to the performance of only a certain range of actions. So the problem facing the merchant who wishes to be seen as pious rather than self-interested cannot simply be the instrumental one of tailoring his account of his principles in order to fit his projects. It must in part be the problem of tailoring his projects in order to make them answer to the pre-existing language of moral principles.[32]

The story of the merchant suggests two morals, and I shall end by drawing them. One is that it must be a mistake to portray the relationship between our social vocabulary and our social world as a purely external and contingent one. It is true that our social practices help to bestow meaning on our social vocabulary. But it is equally true that our social vocabulary helps to constitute the character of those practices. To recognise the role of our evaluative language in helping to legitimate social action is to recognise the point at which our social vocabulary and our social fabric mutually prop each other up. Perhaps we can even go further (as Charles Taylor has done) and add that, although 'we can speak of mutual dependence if we like', what we really need to recognise 'is the artificiality of the distinction between social reality and the language of description of that social reality'.[33]

The other moral is that, if there are indeed causal linkages between social language and social reality, to speak of the one as mirroring the other may be to envisage the causal arrows pointing in the wrong direction. To recover the nature of the normative vocabulary available to us for the description and appraisal of our conduct is at the same time to identify one of the constraints on our conduct itself. This in turn suggests that, if we wish to explain why social agents concentrate on certain courses of action while avoiding others, we are bound to make reference to the prevailing moral language of the society in which they are acting. This language, it now appears, will figure not as an epiphenomenon of their projects, but as one of the determinants of their behaviour.

To conclude with these morals is to issue a warning to literary critics and social historians alike to avoid a prevalent but impoverishing form of reductionism. But it is also to suggest that the special techniques of the literary critic have – or ought to have – a central place in the business of cultural criticism which a work like Williams's *Keywords* has scarcely begun to recognise.

---

[32] Here I draw on Skinner 1978b, vol. 1, pp. xi–xiii.   [33] Taylor 1971, p. 24.

10

Retrospect: Studying rhetoric and conceptual change

I have been concerned in several of the previous chapters with the prospect of treating the study of changing concepts as a distinct form of historical enquiry. As I have sought to stress, if we wish to write this kind of history it seems to me that we shall do well to concentrate in particular on the concepts we employ to describe and appraise what Hobbes called our artificial world, the world of politics and morality. This in turn means that we shall need to focus on the various terms – the entire normative vocabulary – in which such concepts are habitually expressed. As I argued in chapters 8 and 9, these terms, the paradigms of which are the names of the virtues and vices, are those which perform evaluative as well as descriptive functions in natural languages. They are basically used to describe actions and the motives for which they are performed. But if the criteria for applying one or other of these terms can plausibly be claimed to be reflected in some given action or state of affairs, then the application of the term serves not only to describe but at the same time to evaluate it.

I began to make such normative vocabularies a subject of my own historical research in the 1970s, and it was during those years that the original versions of chapters 8 and 9 were published. One reason for writing those articles was my wish to dispute the view – then prevalent in Anglophone philosophy – that we can validly speak (as T. D. Weldon had done in the title of a classic text) of *the* vocabulary of politics[1] and that we can likewise speak (as R. M. Hare had done in an even more influential book) of *the* language of morals.[2] This assumption seemed to me well worth disputing in the name of a more historically-minded acknowledgement that different societies may conceptualise these domains in different and

This chapter is a revised and extended version of an article that originally appeared under the title of 'Rhetoric and Conceptual Change' in *The Finnish Yearbook of Political Thought*, 3 (1999), pp. 60–73.

[1] Weldon 1953.   [2] Hare 1952.

175

possibly even incommensurable ways. Those two essays may thus be said to have embodied an advance (or at least a change of mind) from the position I had earlier adopted in the essay reprinted here as chapter 4, in which I had still been content to assume that moral and political theory possess their own distinct and relatively stable vocabularies.

I had a second and more basic motivation for wishing to study the changing use of concepts. I wanted to question the assumption influentially propagated by Arthur Lovejoy and his disciples about the proper task of the historian of ideas. Lovejoy had argued that, beneath the surface of ideological debate, there will always be a range of perennial and unchanging 'unit ideas' which it becomes the task of the intellectual historian to uncover and trace.[3] Against this contention I tried once more to speak up for a more radical contingency in the history of thought.[4] This part of my programme (if I may speak in such elevated terms) was already announced in the original version of the article reprinted here as chapter 4. Drawing on a suggestion made by Wittgenstein in his later work, I argued that there cannot be a history of unit ideas as such, but only a history of the various uses to which they have been put by different agents at different times. There is nothing, I ventured to suggest, lying beneath or behind such uses; their history is the only history of ideas to be written.

One way of expressing my underlying commitment would thus be to say that I wanted to treat the understanding of concepts as always, in part, a matter of understanding what can be done with them in argument. In announcing this belief, as I initially did in the essay reprinted here as chapter 4, I declared my allegiance to one particular tradition of twentieth-century social thought. The tradition may perhaps be said to stem from Nietzsche, although I originally encountered it myself in the social philosophy of Max Weber, as my discussions in chapters 7 and 8 will have made clear. Like Nietzsche, Weber believed that our concepts not only alter over time, but are incapable of providing us with anything more than a series of changing perspectives on the world in which we live and have our being. Our concepts form part of what we bring to the world in our efforts to make sense of it. The shifting conceptualisations to which this process gives rise constitute the very stuff of ideological

<hr>

3 Lovejoy 1960.
4 But Lovejoy's approach has been valuably restated and defended in Oakley 1984, pp. 15–40. For Oakley's reaction to my own remarks on Lovejoy see Oakley 1984, pp. 28–31.

debate, so that it makes no more sense to regret than to deny that such conceptual changes continually take place.

If we endorse this vision of politics, as I do, we place a question-mark against all those neo-Kantian projects of our time in which we encounter an aspiration to halt the flux of politics by trying definitively to fix the analysis of key moral terms. I continue to harbour a special prejudice against those who, in adopting this approach, imagine an ideal speech situation in which everyone (*everyone?*) would make the same moral and cognitive judgements.[5] There are no moral or cognitive judgements which are not mediated by our concepts, and it seems to me that even our most apparently abstract concepts are historical through and through.

I have been less concerned with questioning this approach, however, than with considering what kind of history needs to be written if the phenomenon of conceptual change is to be fruitfully explored. It is worth adding that the view at which I have arrived is in some respects similar to the one embodied in Reinhart Koselleck's now celebrated programme for the study of *Begriffsgeschichte*, histories of concepts.[6] Koselleck and I both assume that we need to treat our normative concepts less as statements about the world than as tools and weapons of ideological debate. Both of us have perhaps been influenced by Foucault's Nietzschean contention that 'the history which bears and determines us has the form of a war'.[7]

One reason why it is perhaps worth identifying my original targets in this way is that a number of my critics have supposed that what I was aiming to discredit was Koselleck's project of writing *Begriffsgeschichte*. But this was never the case. It is no doubt deplorable, but it is nevertheless a fact, that when in the late 1960s and 1970s I wrote the essays of which I have been speaking, I had no knowledge of Koselleck's research programme. I did not come to appreciate the distinctiveness and magnitude of his achievement until Melvin Richter made his work available to Anglophone readers in his articles of the 1980s[8] and later in his important study, *The History of Social and Political Concepts*, published as recently as 1995.[9]

---

5 Commenting on this commitment, Geuss 1981 p. 66 remarks that 'I find it quite hard to burden pre-dynastic Egyptians, ninth-century French serfs and early-twentieth-century Yanomamö tribesmen with the view that they are acting correctly if their action is based on a norm on which there would be universal consensus in an ideal speech situation.'

6 See, for example, Koselleck 1985, esp. pp. 73–91 and Koselleck 1989. See also the discussion in Richter 1995, esp. pp. 26–57.

7 Foucault 1980, p. 114.   8 See in particular Richter 1986 and Richter 1987.   9 Richter 1995.

How far one can hope to capture the historicity of concepts by adopting Koselleck's approach remains a question.[10] But if there are any remaining doubts, these ought not in my view to be doubts about the very idea of writing conceptual histories – or not, at least, if these are histories of how concepts have been put to use over time. It is perhaps worth adding that I have even attempted to write some such histories myself, and two of these studies are included in the present work: in volume 2 I reprint (in a much revised form) an essay originally published in 1989 on the acquisition of the concept of the State, and in volume 3 I reprint an associated essay of 1999 on the relationship to this tradition of Hobbes's argument in *Leviathan*. I have also written – in my book *Liberty Before Liberalism* – about the rise and fall within Anglophone political theory of a particular view about the concept of liberty, a view according to which our freedom should be seen not merely as a predicate of our actions but as an existential condition in contrast with that of servitude.[11] I do not consider these studies to be in tension with anything I have written about the need to understand what can be done with concepts as an element in the process of recovering their meaning and significance. On the contrary, part of my aim in each of these studies was to indicate why the concept in question first came to prominence at a particular historical period by way of indicating what could be done with it that could not be done in its absence.

As these remarks will already have made clear, I strongly endorse the belief that we must be ready as historians of philosophy not merely to admit the fact of conceptual change but to make it central to our research. Not only is our moral and social world held in place by the manner in which we choose to apply our inherited normative vocabularies, but one of the ways in which we are capable of reappraising and changing our world is by changing the ways in which these vocabularies are applied. As I have already tried to show in chapters 8 and 9, there is in consequence a genealogy of all our evaluative concepts to be traced, and in tracing their changing applications we shall find ourselves looking not merely at the reflections but at one of the engines of social change. Since I have always sought to emphasise that innovating ideologists may in consequence be no less preoccupied with wresting an available moral language to their own ends than with seeking at the same time to challenge conventional

---

[10] Schmidt 1999 makes some interesting criticisms of Koselleck's project along these lines, questioning in particular his reliance on dictionaries as sources. For an excellent survey of the issues see Hampsher-Monk 1988.

[11] Skinner 1998, pp. 59–99.

beliefs, I am startled to find myself accused by a recent critic of failing to acknowledge the first of these possibilities.[12] Chapter 8 of the present volume is largely given over to considering this issue, and one of my aims in discussing the phenomenon of rhetorical redescription below will be to show that the first possibility as well as the second will always be in play.

I have already gestured in chapter 9 at what I take to be the fundamental point we need to grasp if we are to study the phenomenon of conceptual change, but I should like to enlarge on it here. My almost paradoxical contention is that the various transformations we can hope to chart will not strictly speaking be changes in concepts at all. They will be transformations in the applications of the terms by which our concepts are expressed. These changes will in turn be of various kinds, but in my own research I have chiefly focused on what Kari Palonen in a recent appraisal of my work has helpfully labelled a rhetorical perspective.[13] I have mainly been interested in the kinds of debate that take place when we ask whether a given action or state of affairs does or does not license us to apply some particular evaluative term as an apt description of it. While this has been my principal interest, however, I should not want it to be thought that I take this to be the sole or even the most significant way in which the process of conceptual change can be initiated. Before turning to consider the rhetorical case in more detail, I should like to mention two other ways in which the phenomenon of conceptual change can be historically mapped.

We can hope in the first place to trace the changing extent or degree to which a particular normative vocabulary is employed over time. There are obviously two contrasting possibilities here. The rise within a given society of new forms of social behaviour will generally be reflected in the development of corresponding vocabularies in which the behaviour in question will then be described and appraised. I have already considered the early-modern European development of commercial society from this perspective in chapter 8, focusing on the growing salience of an appraisive vocabulary centred on such novel values as *frugality, industriousness, punctuality, conscientiousness* and the like. The alternative possibility is that a given society may gradually lose its sense that some particular style of behaviour deserves to be singled out and valorised. This kind of change of heart will generally be registered in the atrophying of the corresponding normative vocabulary. An instructive example is offered by the

---

[12] See Bevir 1999, pp. 49–50 and cf. also Bevir 1997. For a summary restatement of Bevir's position see Bevir 2001.

[13] For an appraisal of this perspective see Palonen 1997 and 1999.

disappearance in contemporary English of a complex vocabulary widely used in earlier generations to describe and commend an ideal of *gentlemanly* conduct, and at the same time to stigmatise any behaviour liable to undermine it. Such terms as *cad* and *bounder* – together with the contrasting concept of *gentlemanliness* – are still included in historical dictionaries of the English language, but they are obsolete as terms of appraisal now that the patterns of conduct they were used to evaluate have lost their social significance.

Such examples arguably provide the best evidence in favour of the claim that concepts have a history – or rather, that the terms we use to express our concepts have a history. They rise and fall, and in some cases they finally disappear from sight. I confess, however, that this kind of long-term shift in the *fortuna* of concepts has not remained one of my primary interests. Here my approach differs markedly from that of Koselleck and his associates, who have chiefly been preoccupied with the slower march of time and much less concerned than I have been with the pointillist study of sudden conceptual shifts.[14] One reason why I have been less interested in such broader chronologies is that, in the examples I have given, the shifting vocabularies are little more than indexes or reflections of deeper transformations in social life. This in turn means that, if a history of these conceptual changes were to have any explanatory value, the explanations would have to be given at the level of social life itself. But I have no general theory about the mechanisms of social transformation, and I am somewhat suspicious of those who have. Certainly I am deeply suspicious of any theories in which Time itself appears as an agent of change. As John Dunn remarked in a classic article long ago, such metaphors have a nasty habit of reappearing as objectifications, thereby encouraging a discredited form of intellectual history in which Tradition is always doing battle with Progress, Enlightenment with Superstition, and so forth.[15]

I next want to build on what I said in chapter 9 about a second form of conceptual change, or rather a second way in which the vocabularies we use to describe and appraise our social world continually wrinkle and slide. This further process occurs when the capacity of a normative vocabulary to perform and encourage particular acts of appraisal alters either in direction or in intensity. Changes of this kind will usually reflect

[14] See, for example, Richter's discussion of the handling of the concept of *Herrschaft* and its history in Koselleck's *Geschichtliche Grundbegriffe* in Richter 1995, pp. 58–78. For a fuller comparison between my approach and that of Koselleck see Guilhaumou 2000.

[15] Dunn 1980, esp. p. 13.

an underlying attempt to modify existing social perceptions and beliefs, and these efforts will in turn be featured in the language of evaluation in one of two principal ways. A term generally used to commend an action or state of affairs may be used instead to express and solicit disapproval, or else a condemnatory term may be used to suggest that, contrary to received assumptions, what is being described is deserving of praise.

What is being proposed in such cases is that a society should reconsider and perhaps transvalue some of its moral values. Sometime we can even pinpoint such dramatic suggestions at specific moments within individual texts. Consider, for example, Machiavelli's evident desire in chapter 16 of *Il Principe* to insist that the virtue of liberality, so highly prized in the courtly societies of Renaissance Europe, may actually be the name of a dangerous vice.[16] Or consider Baldassare Castiglione's contrasting desire in his *Libro del Cortegiano* of 1528 to single out the quality he labels *sprezzatura* – the quality of nonchalantly refusing to set a high price on anything – and to commend it as one of the leading virtues of civilised life.[17] The unsettling implications of the latter suggestion can be seen at their clearest in the English version of the *Cortegiano* first issued by Sir Thomas Hoby in 1561. Faced with the need to find a translation for *sprezzatura*, Castiglione's invented term, Hoby chose to render it as *recklessness*.[18] He thereby confronted his puritan contemporaries with the unsettling thought that a deliberate refusal to act with foresight and conscientiousness might be deserving of the highest praise.[19]

Whenever such suggestions are widely taken up, a whole society may eventually come to alter its attitude towards some fundamental value or practice and alter its normative vocabulary accordingly. We could therefore say that these are examples of conceptual change in perhaps its purest sense. However, I have again paid little attention to the long-term social transformations that cause such appraisive terms to lose – or to alter the direction of – their evaluative force. This lack of interest again contrasts strongly with Koselleck's approach. The reason for my neglect is the same as before. I lack any talent for writing the kind of social history that would be required. I also plead guilty to the further charge – levelled, for example, by Palonen[20] – that in contrast to Koselleck I have made no attempt to investigate the possibility that Time itself may need to be

---

[16] Machiavelli 1960, pp. 66–8.
[17] See Castiglione 1981, pp. 59–60 *et passim* on the need 'usar in ogni cosa una certa sprezzatura'.
[18] Castiglione 1994, p. 53.
[19] On the language of Hoby's translation see Burke 1995, pp. 66–72. On *sprezzatura* see Saccone 1983.
[20] Palonen 1999, pp. 53–5.

included in the very meaning of certain concepts. I do indeed neglect this possibility, but only because I cannot make sense of it.

I turn finally to re-examine the form of conceptual change in which I have chiefly been interested, the form I have described as rhetorical in character. Such changes originate when an action or state of affairs is described by means of an evaluative term that would not normally be used in the given circumstances. The aim is to persuade an audience that, in spite of appearances, the term can properly be applied – in virtue of its ordinary meaning – to the case in hand. The effect of successfully persuading someone to accept such a judgement will be to prompt them to view the behaviour in question in a new moral light. An action they had previously regarded as commendable may come to seem worthy of condemnation, while an action they had previously condemned may seem worthy of praise.

When, in the early 1970s, I first discussed this technique of rhetorical redescription, I operated with the assumption that for every evaluative term there will at any one time be a standard and accepted meaning and use. This remains the key assumption on which my historical analysis in chapter 8 is based. As a result, I portray the figure of the innovating ideologist in that chapter as someone engaged in the manipulation of a normative vocabulary by a series of what I describe as sleights of hand. Since that time, however, I have immersed myself in the writings of the classical theorists of eloquence who originally described the relevant techniques of rhetorical redescription. As a result I have come to share their more sceptical understanding of normative concepts and the fluid vocabularies in which they are habitually expressed. I have found myself increasingly adopting their assumption that it makes little sense to speak of evaluative terms as having accepted denotations that can either be followed or, with varying degrees of disingenuousness, effectively manipulated. I have come to appreciate their sense that there will always be a degree of 'neighbourliness', as they liked to call it, between apparently conflicting evaluative terms. It now seems to me, in short, that all attempts to legislate about the 'correct' use of normative terms must be regarded as equally ideological in character. Whenever such terms are employed, their application will always reflect a wish to impose a particular moral vision on the workings of the social world.

I should like to end by offering some general reflections about this crucial technique of rhetorical redescription, a technique to which I return in greater detail in volume 2 chapter 10, and again in discussing Hobbes's reactions to it in volume 3 chapter 4. It will be best to begin with the analysis furnished by the ancient rhetoricians themselves.[21] One of the clearest accounts is supplied by Quintilian, although he owes an obvious debt to Cicero, while both of them are in turn influenced by the pioneering discussion to be found in Book II of Aristotle's *Art of Rhetoric*. Quintilian's main discussion of the technique – to which he gives the name *paradiastole* – appears in Book IV of his *Institutio Oratoria* as part of his advice on how to present a narrative of facts. Suppose you find yourself in a court of law facing an advocate who has managed to describe an act 'in such a way as to rouse up the judges and leave them full of anger against your side'.[22] Suppose too that you cannot hope to deny what happened. How should you proceed? Quintilian's answer is that 'you should restate the facts, but not at all in the same way; you must assign different causes, a different state of mind and a different motive for what was done'.[23] Above all, 'you must try to elevate the action as much as possible by the words you use: for example, prodigality must be more leniently redescribed as liberality, avarice as carefulness, negligence as simplicity of mind'.[24]

Quintilian had already put forward this last and crucial suggestion in Book II, in which he had quoted (although without acknowledgement) three examples of the same technique mentioned by Aristotle in *The Art of Rhetoric*: 'slander can pass for frankness, recklessness for courage, extravagance for copiousness'.[25] Aristotle had added that the same technique can equally well be used not merely to extenuate the vices but to depreciate the virtues, as when we denigrate the behaviour of a habitually cautious man by claiming that he is really a person of cold and designing temperament.[26]

As Quintilian emphasises, the essence of the technique may thus be said to consist of replacing a given evaluative description with a rival term that serves to picture the action no less plausibly, but serves at the same time to place it in a contrasting moral light. You seek to persuade your audience to accept your new description, and thereby to adopt a new attitude towards the action concerned. As Quintilian explicitly adds, this means that strictly speaking we ought not to describe the technique as a case of substituting one word for another. 'For no one supposes that the words prodigality and liberality mean the same thing; the difference

---

[21] All ensuing translations from classical texts are my own.
[22] Quintilian 1920–2, IV. II. 75, vol. 2, p. 90.　　[23] Quintilian 1920–2, IV. II. 76–7, vol. 2, p. 90.
[24] Quintilian 1920–2, IV. II. 77, vol. 2, pp. 90–2.
[25] See Aristotle 1926, I. IX. 28–9, pp. 96–8 and cf. Quintilian 1920–2, II. XII. 4, vol. 1, p. 284.
[26] Aristotle 1926, I. IX. 28, p. 96.

is rather that one person calls something prodigal which another thinks of as liberality.'[27] What we are really claiming is that the *res* – the actual behaviour – possesses a different moral character from that which our dialectical opponents may have assigned to it.

Quintilian also explains what makes the use of paradiastolic redescription a perennial possibility. Drawing once more on Aristotle, he reiterates that this is due to the fact that many of the vices are 'neighbours' of the virtues. Cicero had already put forward the same explanation in his *De Partitione Oratoria*. 'Cunning imitates prudence, insensibility imitates temperance, pride in attaining honours and superciliousness in looking down on them both imitate magnanimity, extravagance imitates liberality and audacity imitates courage.'[28] Such a large number of the vices, in short, stand in 'neighbourly relations' with the virtues that a clever orator will always be able to challenge the proffered evaluation of any action whatsoever with some show of plausibility.

One of the defining achievements of Renaissance culture was to revive and reassess the rhetorical philosophy of the ancient world. This in turn means that, if we wish to see the techniques perfected by the ancient rhetoricians put to work again, we need to turn to the moral philosophy of the Renaissance. Among moralists of that period, it was Machiavelli who arguably took the lessons of the ancient rhetoricians most profoundly to heart. Certainly he uses the technique of paradiastolic redescription with unparalleled audacity in challenging the political morality of his age. He first employs it in chapter 16 of *Il Principe* to question the so-called 'princely' virtue of liberality. Two contrasting rhetorical strategies are at work in this passage. As we have already seen, one is Machiavelli's astonishing suggestion that liberality may not be the name of a virtue. But his other strategy depends on assuming that liberality and generosity are undeniably the names of good qualities. While conceding the point, however, he adds that much of the behaviour usually described and commended as liberal and generous ought rather to be redescribed and condemned as *suntuosità*, mere ostentatiousness.[29] Machiavelli's next chapter questions the princely virtue of clemency in the same way. He begins by acknowledging that cruelty is of course a vice, but he insists that many of the actions usually celebrated as contrasting instances of clemency ought rather to be redescribed in much less favourable terms.[30] The avoidance of cruelty

---

[27] Quintilian 1920–2, VIII. VI. 36, vol. 3, p. 322.　　[28] Cicero 1942, II. XXIII. 81, p. 370.
[29] Machiavelli 1960, p. 66.　　[30] Machiavelli 1960, p. 68.

for which the Florentines congratulated themselves when they refused to punish the leaders of the uprising at Pistoia was really an instance of *troppa pietà*, mere over-indulgence.[31] Likewise, the clemency for which Scipio Africanus became famous in his campaigns against Hannibal was really an example of his *natura facile*, his laxity of character.[32]

Nietzsche offers a yet more emphatic account of how easy it is for vices to present themselves as virtues. This is one of the chief topics he examines – with an almost horrified fascination – in the opening essay of *The Genealogy of Morality*. The passage is a famous one, but his commentators seem unaware of the fact that the technique he is analysing and illustrating is precisely that of paradiastolic redescription. Nietzsche begins by asking whether anyone would like 'to have a little look down into the secret of how *ideals are fabricated* on this earth':

What's happening down there? Tell me what you see, you with your most dangerous curiosity – now *I* am the one who's listening. –
– 'I cannot see anything but I can hear all the better. There is a guarded, malicious little rumour-mongering and whispering from every nook and cranny. I think people are telling lies; a sugary mildness clings to every sound. Lies are turning weakness into an *accomplishment*, no doubt about it – it's just as you said.' –
– Go on!
– 'and impotence which doesn't retaliate is being turned into "goodness"; timid baseness is being turned into "humility"; submission to people one hates is being turned into "obedience" (actually towards someone who, they say, orders this submission – they call him God.) The inoffensiveness of the weakling, the very cowardice with which he is richly endowed, his standing-by-the-door, his inevitable position of having to wait, are all given good names such as "patience", which is also called *the* virtue; not-being-able-to-take-revenge is called not-wanting-to-take-revenge, it might even be forgiveness ("for *they* know not what they do – but we know what *they* are doing!"). They are also talking about "loving your enemy" – and sweating while they do it.'
– Go on! . . .
'But enough! enough! I can't bear it any longer. Bad air! Bad air! This workshop where *ideals are fabricated* – it seems to me just to stink of lies.'[33]

It is Nietzsche's contention, in short, that the slave morality of the Christians succeeded in overturning the moral world of antiquity by rhetorically redescribing a number of vices as their neighbouring virtues.

For a contrasting example of how a virtue can come to be recognised as a vice, consider an example recently discussed by Ian Hacking, that of the history of the concept of *child abuse*. What appeared as wholesome

---

[31] Machiavelli 1960, p. 69.   [32] Machiavelli 1960, p. 71.   [33] Nietzsche 1994, pp. 30–1.

discipline in the rearing of children in one generation may come to be viewed as cruelty in the next. Nothing in the conduct of adults towards children need in the intervening period have changed. What will have altered, if the new evaluation is accepted, is the sensibility of a community. The intervening process, in Hacking's words, will have been one of 'inventing new descriptions, providing new ways to see old acts'.[34] A number of practices previously regarded as acceptable and perhaps even taken for granted will come to seem morally intolerable. This is not of course to say that the process is one of coming to see things as they really are. As before, it is merely a matter of substituting one social philosophy for another, both of which may have seemed rationally defensible at different times.

It might appear, however, that in talking in this way about rhetorical redescription we are precisely *not* talking about conceptual change. I certainly agree that a number of philosophers have been too ready to say that what is happening in such disputes is that each party must 'have a different concept' of (say) what constitutes child abuse. But if the disputants are genuinely arguing, they must have the *same* concept of what constitutes child abuse. The difference between them will not be about the meaning of the relevant evaluative term, but merely about the range of circumstances in which they are prepared to apply it. This caution strikes me as correct and important, but the fact remains that the outcome of such debates will nevertheless be a form of conceptual change. The more we succeed in persuading people that a given evaluative term applies in circumstances in which they may never have thought of applying it, the more broadly and inclusively we shall persuade them to employ the given term in the appraisal of social and political life. The change that will eventually result is that the underlying concept will acquire a new prominence and a new salience in the moral arguments of the society concerned.

It is true that I have again been less interested in these long-term changes than in the kind of epiphanic moments dramatised by Nietzsche. But I acknowledge, of course, that if we are interested in mapping the rise and fall of particular normative vocabularies we shall also have to devote ourselves to examining the *longue durée*. So I am not unhappy with Palonen's recent suggestion[35] that much of my own research might be regarded as a contribution to one aspect of the vastly more ambitious

---

[34] Hacking 1995, p. 56. Hacking 1995 pp. 55–68 is partly a paraphrase of the fuller discussion in Hacking 1991.

[35] Palonen 1999, pp. 56–7.

programme pursued by Reinhart Koselleck and his associates. Koselleck is interested in nothing less than the entire process of conceptual change; I am chiefly interested in one of the techniques by which it takes place. But the two programmes do not strike me as incompatible, and I hope that both of them will continue to flourish as they deserve.

Bibliography

Aaron, Richard I. (1955). *John Locke*, 2nd edn, Oxford.

Abelson, Raziel (1965). 'Because I Want To', *Mind* 74, pp. 540–53.

Abrams, Philip (1967). Introduction to John Locke, *Two Tracts on Government*, ed. Philip Abrams, Cambridge, pp. 3–111.

Adkins, A. W. H. (1960). *Merit and Responsibility: A Study in Greek Values*, Oxford.

Adler, M. J. (1967). Foreword to Otto A. Bird, *The Idea of Justice*, New York.

Aiken, Henry David (1955). 'The Aesthetic Relevance of Artists' Intentions', *Journal of Philosophy* 52, pp. 742–53.

Alexander, William (Earl of Stirling) (1624). *An Encouragement to Colonies*, London.

Allport, Floyd H. (1955). *Theories of Perception and the Concept of Structure*, New York.

Ammirato, Scipio (1846–9). *Istorie Fiorentine*, ed. Ferdinando Ranalli, 6 vols., Florence.

Anglo, Sydney (1966). 'The Reception of Machiavelli in Tudor England: A Reassessment', *Il Politico* 31, pp. 127–38.

  (1969). *Machiavelli: A Dissection*, London.

  (1973). 'Melancholia and Witchcraft: The Debate between Wier, Bodin and Scot' in *Folie et déraison à la Renaissance*, ed. Alois Gerlo, Brussels, pp. 209–22.

Anscombe, G. E. M. (1957). *Intention*, Oxford.

Aristotle (1926). *The 'Art' of Rhetoric*, ed. and trans. J. H. Freese, London.

Armstrong, Robert L. (1965). 'John Locke's "Doctrine of Signs": A New Metaphysics', *Journal of the History of Ideas* 26, pp. 369–82.

Arnold, Thomas Clay (1993). *Thoughts and Deeds: Language and the Practice of Political Theory*, New York.

Aubrey, John (1898). *'Brief Lives', chiefly of Contemporaries, set down by John Aubrey, between the years 1669 & 1696*, ed. Andrew Clark, 2 vols., Oxford.

Austin, J. L. (1980). *How To Do Things With Words*, ed. J. O. Urmson and Marina Sbisà, 2nd edn with corrections, Oxford.

Avineri, Shlomo (1968). *The Social and Political Thought of Karl Marx*, Cambridge.

Ayer, A. J. (1967). 'Man as a Subject for Science' in *Philosophy, Politics and Society*, 3rd series, ed. Peter Laslett and W. G. Runciman, Oxford, pp. 6–24.

Ayers, Michael (1978). 'Analytical Philosophy and the History of Philosophy' in *Philosophy and its Past*, ed. Jonathan Rée, Michael Ayers and Adam Westoby, Brighton, pp. 41–66.

Bach, Kent and Harnish, Robert M. (1979). *Linguistic Communication and Speech Acts*, Cambridge, Mass.

Bailyn, Bernard (1967). *The Ideological Origins of the American Revolution*, Cambridge, Mass.

Barnard, F. M. (1965). *Herder's Social and Political Thought*, Oxford.

Barnes, Barry (1974). *Scientific Knowledge and Sociological Theory*, London.

Barnes, Barry and Bloor, David (1982). 'Relativism, Rationalism and the Sociology of Knowledge' in *Rationality and Relativism*, ed. Martin Hollis and Steven Lukes, London, pp. 21–47.

Baron, Hans (1961). 'Machiavelli: the Republican Citizen and the Author of *The Prince*', *English Historical Review* 76, pp. 217–53.

Bartelson, Jens (1995). *A Genealogy of Sovereignty*, Cambridge.

Barthes, Roland (1979). 'From Work to Text' in *Textual Strategies*, ed. Josué V. Harari, Ithaca, N.Y., pp. 73–81.

Bateson, F. W. (1953). 'The Function of Criticism at the Present Time', *Essays in Criticism* 3, pp. 1–27.

Baumgold, Deborah (1981). 'Political Commentary on the History of Political Theory', *American Political Science Review* 75, pp. 928–40.

Baxter, Andrew (1745). *An Enquiry into the Nature of the Human Soul*, 3rd edn, 2 vols., London.

Beardsley, Monroe C. (1958). *Aesthetics*, New York.

(1970). *The Possibility of Criticism*, Detroit, Mich.

(1992). 'The Authority of the Text' in *Intention and Interpretation*, ed. Gary Iseminger, Philadelphia, Penn., pp. 24–40.

Bevir, Mark (1994). 'Are There any Perennial Problems in Political Theory?' *Political Studies* 42, pp. 662–75.

(1997). 'Mind and Method in the History of Ideas', *History and Theory* 36, pp. 167–89.

(1999). *The Logic of the History of Ideas*, Cambridge.

(2001). 'Taking Holism Seriously: A Reply to Critics', *Philosophical Books* 42, pp. 187–95.

Bird, Otto A. (1967). *The Idea of Justice*, New York.

Blackburn, Simon (1984). *Spreading the Word*, Oxford.

Bloom, Allan (1980). 'The Study of Texts' in *Political Theory and Political Education*, ed. Melvin Richter, Princeton, N.J., pp. 113–38.

Bloom, Allan and Jaffa, Harry C. (1964). *Shakespeare's Politics*, New York.

Bloor, David (1976). *Knowledge and Social Imagery*, London.

Bluhm, William T. (1965). *Theories of the Political System*, Englewood Cliffs, N.J.

Bodin, Jean (1595). *La Demonomanie des Sorciers*, Paris.

Boucher, David (1985). *Texts in Contexts: Revisionist Methods for Studying the History of Ideas*, Dordrecht.

Bracken, Harry M. (1965). *The Early Reception of Berkeley's Immaterialism, 1710–1733*, The Hague.

Brailsford, H. N. (1961). *The Levellers and the English Revolution*, London.

Brodbeck, May (1963). 'Meaning and Action', *Philosophy of Science* 30, pp. 309–24.

Bronowski, Jacob and Mazlish, Bruce (1960). *The Western Intellectual Tradition*, London.

Brooke, John (1963–4). 'Namier and Namierism', *History and Theory* 3, pp. 331–47.

Burke, Peter (1995). *The Fortunes of the 'Courtier': The European Reception of Castiglione's 'Cortegiano'*, Cambridge.

Bury, J. B. (1932). *The Idea of Progress*, London.

Butterfield, Herbert (1957). *George III and the Historians*, London.

Carr, E. H. (1961). *What is History?* London.

Cassirer, Ernst (1946). *The Myth of the State*, New Haven, Conn.

    (1954). *The Question of Jean-Jacques Rousseau*, trans. Peter Gay, Bloomington, Ind.

    (1955). *The Philosophy of the Enlightenment*, trans. Fritz C. A. Koelln and James P. Pettegrove, Beacon edn, Boston, Mass.

Castiglione, Baldassare (1981). *Il Libro del Cortegiano* [1528], ed. Nicola Longo, Milan.

    (1994). *The Book of the Courtier* [1561], trans. Thomas Hoby, ed. Virginia Cox, London.

Castoriadis, Cornelius (1987). *The Imaginary Institution of Society*, trans. Kathleen Blamey, Cambridge.

Catlin, G. E. G. (1950). *A History of Political Philosophy*, London.

Chapman, J. W. (1956). *Rousseau – Totalitarian or Liberal?* New York.

Cherel, Albert (1935). *La Pensée de Machiavel en France*, Paris.

Cicero (1942). *De Partitione Oratoria*, ed. and trans. H. Rackham, London.

Cioffi, Frank (1976). 'Intention and Interpretation in Criticism' in *On Literary Intention*, ed. David Newton-De Molina, Edinburgh, pp. 55–73.

Clark, Stuart (1980). 'Inversion, Misrule and the Meaning of Witchcraft', *Past and Present* 87, pp. 98–127.

    (1997). *Thinking with Demons: The Idea of Witchcraft in Early Modern Europe*, Oxford.

Close, A. J. (1972). '*Don Quixote* and "The Intentionalist Fallacy"', *British Journal of Aesthetics* 12, pp. 19–39.

Cobban, Alfred (1941). *The Crisis of Civilization*, London.

Cochrane, Eric W. (1961). 'Machiavelli: 1940–1960', *Journal of Modern History* 33, pp. 113–36.

Cohn, Norman (1976). *Europe's Inner Demons*, London.

Colish, Marcia L. (1971). 'The Idea of Liberty in Machiavelli', *Journal of the History of Ideas* 32, pp. 323–50.

Collingwood, R. G. (1939). *An Autobiography*, Oxford.

    (1940). *An Essay on Metaphysics*, Oxford.

    (1946). *The Idea of History*, Oxford.

Coltman, Irene (1962). *Private Men and Public Causes: Philosophy and Politics in the English Civil War*, London.

Corwin, Edward S. (1928–9). 'The "Higher Law" Background of American Constitutional Law', *Harvard Law Review* 42, pp. 149–85, 365–409.

    (1948). *Liberty against Government*, Baton Rouge, La.

Cox, Richard H. (1960). *Locke on War and Peace*, Oxford.

Cranston, Maurice (1964). 'Aquinas' in *Western Political Philosophers*, ed. Maurice Cranston, London, pp. 29–36.

Cropsey, Joseph (1962). 'A Reply to Rothman', *American Political Science Review* 56, pp. 353–9.

Curley, E. M. (1978). *Descartes Against the Skeptics*, Oxford.

Dahl, Robert A. (1963). *Modern Political Analysis*, Englewood Cliffs, N.J.

Danto, Arthur C. (1965). *Analytical Philosophy of History*, Cambridge.

Davidson, Donald (1963). 'Action, Reason and Cause', *Journal of Philosophy* 60, pp. 685–700.

(1967). 'The Logical Form of Action Sentences' in *The Logic of Decision and Action*, ed. Nicholas Rescher, Pittsburgh, Penn., pp. 81–95.

(1984). 'On the Very Idea of a Conceptual Scheme' in *Inquiries into Truth and Interpretation*, Oxford, pp. 183–98.

(1986). 'A Coherence Theory of Truth and Knowledge' in *Truth and Interpretation*, ed. Ernest LePore, Oxford, pp. 307–19.

Davies, E. T. (1964). *The Political Ideas of Richard Hooker*, London.

Defoe, Daniel (1965). 'The Shortest-Way with the Dissenters' [1702] in *Daniel Defoe*, ed. James T. Boulton, London, pp. 88–99.

D'Entrèves, A. P. (1939). *The Medieval Contribution to Political Thought*, Oxford.

Derrida, Jacques (1976). *Of Grammatology*, trans. Gayatri Chakravorty Spivak, Baltimore, Md.

(1978). *Writing and Difference*, trans. Alan Bass, London.

(1979). *Spurs: Nietzsche's Styles*, trans. Barbara Harlow, Chicago, Ill.

Dibon, Paul (1959). 'Redécouverte de Bayle' in *Pierre Bayle: Le Philosophe de Rotterdam: Etudes et documents*, ed. Paul Dibon, Amsterdam, pp. vii–xvii.

Dickens, Charles (1985). *Hard Times* [1854], ed. David Craig, Penguin Classics edn, London.

Donagan, Alan (1957). 'Explanation in History', *Mind* 66, pp. 145–64.

Dray, William (1957). *Laws and Explanations in History*, Oxford.

Dummett, Michael (1973a). *Frege: Philosophy of Language*, London.

(1973b). 'The Justification of Induction', *Proceedings of the British Academy* 59, pp. 201–32.

Dunn, John (1969). *The Political Thought of John Locke: An Historical Account of the Argument of the 'Two Treatises of Government'*, Cambridge.

(1980). *Political Obligation in its Historical Context: Essays in Political Theory*, Cambridge.

(1996). *The History of Political Theory and Other Essays*, Cambridge.

Durkheim, Emile (1964). *The Rules of Sociological Method*, trans. S. A. Solovay and J. H. Mueller, New York.

Eburne, Richard (1962). *A Plain Pathway to Plantations* [1624] in *Folger Documents of Tudor and Stuart Civilization*, ed. Louis B. Wright, Ithaca, N.Y., pp. 3–154.

Edling, Max and Mörkenstam, Ulf (1995). 'Quentin Skinner: from Historian to Political Scientist', *Scandinavian Political Studies* 18, pp. 119–32.

Elster, Jon (1978). *Logic and Society*, New York.

   (1982). 'Belief, Bias and Ideology' in *Rationality and Relativism*, ed. Martin Hollis and Steven Lukes, London, pp. 123–48.

Elton, G. R. (1969a). *The Practice of History*, rev. edn, London.

   (1969b). *England 1200–1640*, Cambridge.

   (1970). *Political History: Principles and Practice*, London.

   (1991). *Return to Essentials*, Cambridge.

Elyot, Sir Thomas (1962). *The Book Named the Governor* [1531], ed. S. E. Lehmberg, London.

Evans, Richard J. (1997). *In Defence of History*, London.

Femia, Joseph V. (1988). 'An Historicist Critique of "Revisionist" Methods for Studying the History of Ideas' in *Meaning and Context: Quentin Skinner and his Critics*, ed. James Tully, Cambridge, pp. 156–75.

Fennor, William (1965). *The Counter's Commonwealth* [1617] in *The Elizabethan Underworld*, ed. A. V. Judges, London, pp. 423–87.

Fish, Stanley (1980). *Is There a Text in this Class?* Cambridge, Mass.

Foord, Archibald S. (1964). *His Majesty's Opposition, 1714–1830*, Oxford.

Foot, Philippa (1958). 'Moral Arguments', *Mind* 67, pp. 502–13.

Forster, E. M. (1924). *A Passage to India*, London.

Forster, Michael N. (1998). 'On the Very Idea of Denying the Existence of Radically Different Conceptual Schemes', *Inquiry* 41, pp. 133–85.

Foucault, Michel (1979). 'What is an Author?' in *Textual Strategies*, ed. Josué V. Harari, Ithaca, N.Y., pp. 141–60.

   (1980). *Power/Knowledge*, ed. Colin Gordon, Brighton.

Freundlieb, Dieter (1980). 'Identification, Interpretation, and Explanation: Some Problems in the Philosophy of Literary Studies', *Poetics* 9, pp. 423–40.

Friedrich, C. J. (1964). 'On Re-reading Machiavelli and Althusius: Reason, Rationality and Religion' in *Rational Decision*, ed. C. J. Friedrich, New York.

Gadamer, Hans-Georg (1960). *Wahrheit und Methode*, Tübingen.

   (1975). *Truth and Method*, London.

Gang, T. M. (1957). 'Intention', *Essays in Criticism* 7, pp. 175–86.

Gardiner, Patrick (ed.) (1959). *Theories of History*, New York.

Garfinkel, Alan (1981). *Forms of Explanation*, New Haven, Conn.

Gay, Peter (1974). *Style in History*, New York.

Geertz, Clifford (1980). *Negara: The Theater State in Nineteenth-Century Bali*, Princeton, N.J.

   (1983). *Local Knowledge*, New York.

   (2000). *Available Light: Anthropological Reflections on Philosophical Topics*, Princeton, N.J.

Geuss, Raymond (1981). *The Idea of a Critical Theory: Habermas and the Frankfurt School*, Cambridge.

Gibson, Quentin (1960). *The Logic of Social Enquiry*, London.

Gilbert, Felix (1977). *History: Choice and Commitment*, Cambridge, Mass.

Gombrich, E. H. (1962). *Art and Illusion: A Study in the Psychology of Pictorial Representation*, rev. edn, London.

Goodman, Nelson (1978). *Ways of Worldmaking*, Brighton.
Gorman, David, *et al.* (1987). 'Provocation on Belief', *Social Epistemology* 1, pp. 97–108.
Gough, J. W. (1950). *John Locke's Political Philosophy: Eight Studies*, Oxford.
  (1957). *The Social Contract*, 2nd edn, Oxford.
Graham, Keith (1977). *J. L. Austin: A Critique of Ordinary Language Philosophy*, Brighton.
  (1980). 'The Recovery of Illocutionary Force', *Philosophical Quarterly* 30, pp. 141–8.
  (1981). 'Illocution and Ideology' in *Issues in Marxist Philosophy* 4, ed. John Mepham and D. H. Ruben, Brighton, pp. 153–94.
  (1988). 'How Do Illocutionary Descriptions Explain?' in *Meaning and Context: Quentin Skinner and his Critics*, ed. James Tully, Cambridge, pp. 147–55.
Greene, John C. (1957–8). 'Objectives and Methods in Intellectual History', *Mississippi Valley Historical Review* 44, pp. 58–74.
Greenleaf, W. H. (1972a). 'Hobbes: The Problem of Interpretation', in *Hobbes and Rousseau*, ed. Maurice Cranston and R. S. Peters, New York, pp. 5–36.
  (1972b). 'Hume, Burke and the General Will', *Political Studies* 20, pp. 131–40.
Grice, H. P. (1957). 'Meaning', *Philosophical Review* 66, pp. 377–88.
  (1969). 'Utterer's Meaning and Intentions', *Philosophical Review* 78, pp. 147–77.
Guilhaumou, Jacques (2000). 'De l'histoire des concepts à l'histoire linguistique des usages conceptuels', *Genèses* 38, pp. 105–18.
Gunn, J. A. W. (1988–9). 'After Sabine, After Lovejoy: The Languages of Political Thought', *Journal of History and Politics* 6, pp. 1–45.
Gunnell, John G. (1979). *Political Theory: Tradition and Interpretation*, Cambridge, Mass.
  (1982). 'Interpretation and the History of Political Theory: Apology and Epistemology', *American Political Science Review* 76, pp. 317–27.
Gwyn, W. B. (1965). *The Meaning of the Separation of Powers*, New Orleans.
Hacker, Andrew (1954). '*Capital* and Carbuncles: the "Great Books" Reappraised', *American Political Science Review* 48, pp. 775–86.
  (1961). *Political Theory: Philosophy, Ideology, Science*, New York.
Hacking, Ian (1982). 'Language, Truth and Reason' in *Rationality and Relativism*, ed. Martin Hollis and Steven Lukes, London, pp. 48–66.
  (1991). 'The Making and Molding of Child Abuse', *Critical Inquiry* 17, pp. 253–88.
  (1995). *Rewriting the Soul: Multiple Personality and the Sciences of Memory*, Princeton, N.J.
Hampsher-Monk, Iain (1988). 'Speech Acts, Languages or Conceptual History?' in *History of Concepts: Comparative Perspectives*, ed. Iain Hampsher-Monk, Karen Tilmans and F. Van Free, Amsterdam, pp. 37–50.
  (2001). 'The History of Political Thought and the Political History of Thought' in *The History of Political Thought in National Context*, ed. Dario Castiglione and Iain Hampsher-Monk, Cambridge, pp. 159–74.

194   *Bibliography*

Hampshire, Stuart (1959). *Thought and Action*, London.

Hancher, Michael (1972). 'Three Kinds of Intention', *Modern Language Notes* 87, pp. 827–51.

Hare, R. M. (1952). *The Language of Morals*, Oxford.

Harlan, David (1989). 'Intellectual History and the Return of Literature', *American Historical Review* 94, pp. 581–609.

Harrison, W. (1955). 'Texts in Political Theory', *Political Studies* 3, pp. 28–44.

Hart, Jeffrey P. (1965). *Viscount Bolingbroke, Tory Humanist*, London.

Hawthorn, Geoffrey (1979). 'Characterising the History of Social Theory', *Sociology* 13, pp. 475–82.

Hearnshaw, F. J. C. (1928). 'Henry St John, Viscount Bolingbroke' in *The Social & Political Ideas of Some English Thinkers of the Augustan Age A.D. 1650–1750*, ed. F. J. C. Hearnshaw, London, pp. 210–47.

Hempel, Carl (1942). 'The Function of General Laws in History', *Journal of Philosophy* 39, pp. 35–48.

Hesse, Mary (1970a). 'Hermeticism and Historiography: An Apology for the Internal History of Science' in *Minnesota Studies in the Philosophy of Science* 5, ed. Roger H. Stuewer, Minneapolis, Minn., pp. 134–60.

  (1970b). 'Is There an Independent Observation Language?' in *The Nature and Function of Scientific Theories*, ed. R. G. Colodny, Pittsburgh, Penn., pp. 35–77.

  (1973). 'Reasons and Evaluations in the History of Science' in *Changing Perspectives in the History of Science*, ed. Mikulás Teich and Robert Young, London, pp. 127–47.

  (1974). *The Structure of Scientific Inference*, London.

Hexter, J. H. (1964). 'The Loom of Language and the Fabric of Imperatives: the Case of *Il Principe* and *Utopia*', *American Historical Review* 69, pp. 945–68.

  (1971). *The History Primer*, London.

Hirsch, E. D., Jr (1967). *Validity in Interpretation*, New Haven, Conn.

  (1976). 'In Defense of the Author' in *On Literary Intention*, ed. David Newton-De Molina, Edinburgh, pp. 87–103.

Hobbes, Thomas (1996). *Leviathan, or The Matter, Forme, & Power of a Commonwealth Ecclesiasticall and Civill* [1651], ed. Richard Tuck, Cambridge.

Holdcroft, David (1978). *Words and Deeds*, Oxford.

Hollinger, David A. (1985). *In the American Province: Studies in the History and Historiography of Ideas*, Bloomington, Ind.

Hollis, Martin (1970a). 'The Limits of Irrationality' in *Rationality*, ed. Bryan R. Wilson, Oxford, pp. 214–20.

  (1970b). 'Reason and Ritual' in *Rationality*, ed. Bryan R. Wilson, Oxford, pp. 221–39.

  (1972). 'Witchcraft and Winchcraft', *Philosophy of the Social Sciences* 2, pp. 89–103.

  (1974). 'My Role and its Duties' in *Nature and Conduct*, ed. R. S. Peters, London, pp. 180–99.

  (1982). 'The Social Destruction of Reality' in *Rationality and Relativism*, ed. Martin Hollis and Steven Lukes, London, pp. 67–86.

(1988). 'Say it with Flowers', in *Meaning and Context: Quentin Skinner and his Critics*, ed. James Tully, Cambridge, pp. 135–46.

Hood, F. C. (1964). *The Divine Politics of Thomas Hobbes*, Oxford.

Hooker, Richard (1989). *Of the Laws of Ecclesiastical Polity* [1594], ed. A. S. McGrade, Cambridge.

Hough, Graham (1966). *An Essay on Criticism*, London.

(1976). 'An Eighth Type of Ambiguity' in *On Literary Intention*, ed. David Newton-De Molina, Edinburgh, pp. 222–41.

Hoy, David (1985). 'Jacques Derrida' in *The Return of Grand Theory in the Human Sciences*, ed. Quentin Skinner, Cambridge, pp. 43–64.

Hudson, Liam (1972). *The Cult of the Fact*, New York.

Hume, Robert D. (1999). *Reconstructing Contexts: The Aims and Principles of Archaeo-Historicism*, Oxford.

Humphrey, Lawrence (1563). *The Nobles, or Of Nobility*, London.

Hylton, Peter (1984). 'The Nature of the Proposition and the Revolt against Idealism' in *Philosophy in History*, ed. Richard Rorty, J. B. Schneewind and Quentin Skinner, Cambridge, pp. 375–97.

Inglis, Fred (2000). *Clifford Geertz: Culture, Custom and Ethics*, Cambridge.

Iser, Wolfgang (1972). 'The Reading Process: A Phenomenological Approach', *New Literary History*, 3, pp. 279–99.

Jacob, James R. and Jacob, Margaret C. (1980). 'The Anglican Origins of Modern Science: the Metaphysical Foundations of the Whig Constitution', *Isis* 7, pp. 251–67.

Jacob, Margaret C. (1976). *The Newtonians and the English Revolution, 1689–1720*, Ithaca, N.Y.

James, Susan (1984). *The Content of Social Explanation*, Cambridge.

Jarvie, I. C. (1970). 'Understanding and Explanation in Sociology and Social Anthropology' in *Explanation in the Behavioural Sciences*, ed. Robert Borger and Frank Cioffi, Cambridge, pp. 231–48.

Jarvie, I. C. and Agassi, Joseph (1970). 'The Problem of the Rationality of Magic' in *Rationality*, ed. Bryan Wilson, London, pp. 172–93.

Jaspers, Karl (1962). *The Great Philosophers*, vol. 1, London.

Jauss, Hans Robert (1970). 'Literary History as a Challenge to Literary Theory', *New Literary History* 2, pp. 7–37.

Jenssen, Peter L. (1985). 'Political Thought as Traditionary Action: the Critical Response to Skinner and Pocock', *History and Theory* 24, pp. 115–46.

Jones, Robert A. (1977). 'On Understanding a Sociological Classic', *American Journal of Sociology* 83, pp. 279–319.

Jones, W. T. (1947). *Machiavelli to Bentham* in *Masters of Political Thought*, ed. Edward M. Sait, 3 vols., London, vol. 2.

Joyce, James (1969). *Ulysses* [1922], Harmondsworth.

Juhl, P. D. (1976). 'Can the Meaning of a Literary Work Change?' in *The Uses of Criticism*, ed. A. P. Foulkes, Frankfurt, pp. 133–56.

(1980). *Interpretation*, Princeton, N.J.

Kaufman, Arnold S. (1954). 'The Nature and Function of Political Theory', *Journal of Philosophy* 51, pp. 5–22.

Keane, John (1988). 'More Theses on the Philosophy of History' in *Meaning and Context: Quentin Skinner and his Critics*, ed. James Tully, Cambridge, pp. 204–17.

Kenny, Anthony (1963). *Action, Emotion and Will*, London.

King, Preston (1983). 'The Theory of Context and the Case of Hobbes' in *The History of Ideas*, ed. Preston King, London, pp. 285–315.

  (1995). 'Historical Contextualism: The New Historicism?' *History of European Ideas* 21, pp. 209–33.

Kiremidjian, G. D. (1969–70). 'The Aesthetics of Parody', *Journal of Aesthetics and Art Criticism* 28, pp. 231–42.

Kjellström, Peter (1995). 'The Narrator and the Archaeologist: Modes of Meaning and Discourse in Quentin Skinner and Michel Foucault', *Statsvetenskaplig Tidskrift*, 98, pp. 21–41.

Koselleck, Reinhart (1985). *Futures Past: On the Semantics of Historical Time*, trans. Keith Tribe, London.

  (1989). 'Linguistic Change and the History of Events', *Journal of Modern History* 61, pp. 649–66.

Kuhn, Thomas S. (1962). *The Structure of Scientific Revolutions*, Chicago, Ill.

  (1977). *The Essential Tension*, Chicago, Ill.

Labrousse, Elisabeth (1964). *Pierre Bayle*, vol. 2: *Hétérodoxie et rigorisme*, The Hague.

LaCapra, Dominick (1980). 'Rethinking Intellectual History and Reading Texts', *History and Theory* 19, pp. 245–76.

Ladurie, E. Le Roy (1974). *The Peasants of Languedoc*, trans. John Day, London.

Laing, R. D. and Esterson, A. (1970). *Sanity, Madness, and the Family*, 2nd edn, London.

Lakatos, Imre (1978). *The Methodology of Scientific Research Programmes: Philosophical Papers*, vol. 1, ed. John Worrall and Gregory Currie, Cambridge.

Lakoff, Sanford A. (1964). *Equality in Political Philosophy*, Cambridge, Mass.

Laski, Harold J. (1961). *Political Thought in England: Locke to Bentham*, Oxford.

Laslett, Peter (1965). Introduction to *The Library of John Locke*, ed. John Harrison and Peter Laslett (Oxford Bibliographical Society Publications 13), Oxford.

Laudan, Larry (1977). *Progress and its Problems*, Berkeley, Calif.

Lear, Jonathan (1982). 'Leaving the World Alone', *Journal of Philosophy* 79, pp. 382–403.

  (1983). 'Ethics, Mathematics and Relativism', *Mind* 92, pp. 38–60.

Leeuwen, T. M. van (1981). *The Surplus of Meaning*, Amsterdam.

Lemon, M. C. (1995). *The Discipline of History and the History of Thought*, London.

Lerner, Max (1950). Introduction to *Machiavelli, The Prince and The Discourses*, New York.

Leslie, Margaret (1970). 'In Defence of Anachronism', *Political Studies* 18, pp. 433–47.

Levine, Joseph M. (1986). 'Method in the History of Ideas: More, Machiavelli and Quentin Skinner', *Annals of Scholarship* 3, pp. 37–60.

Lewis, David (1969). *Convention*, Cambridge, Mass.

  (1974). 'Radical Interpretation', *Synthèse* 27, pp. 331–44.

Locke, John (1988). *Two Treatises of Government* [1690], ed. Peter Laslett, Cambridge.

Lockyer, Andrew (1979). '"Traditions" as Context in the History of Political Theory', *Political Studies* 27, pp. 201–17.

Louch, A. R. (1966). *Explanation and Human Action*, Oxford.

Lovejoy, Arthur O. (1960). *The Great Chain of Being: A Study of the History of an Idea*, Torchbook edn, New York.

Lukes, Steven (1973). 'On the Social Determination of Truth' in *Modes of Thought*, ed. Robin Horton and Ruth Finnegan, London, pp. 230–48.

(1977). *Essays in Social Theory*, London.

Macdonald, Graham and Pettit, Philip (1981). *Semantics and Social Science*, London.

Machiavelli, Niccolò (1960). *Il Principe e Discorsi Sopra La Prima Deca di Tito Livio*, ed. Sergio Bertelli, Milan.

(1962). *Istorie Fiorentine* [1525], ed. Franco Gaeta, Milan.

MacIntyre, Alasdair (1962). 'A Mistake about Causality in Social Science' in *Philosophy, Politics and Society*, 2nd series, ed. Peter Laslett and W. G. Runciman, Oxford, pp. 48–70.

(1966). *A Short History of Ethics*, London.

(1971). *Against the Self-Images of the Age*, London.

Macpherson, C. B. (1962). *The Political Theory of Possessive Individualism: Hobbes to Locke*, Oxford.

Makkreel, Rudolf A. (1990). 'Traditional Historicism, Contemporary Interpretations of Historicity and the History of Philosophy', *New Literary History* 21, pp. 977–91.

Mandelbaum, Maurice (1965). 'The History of Ideas, Intellectual History, and the History of Philosophy', *History and Theory* 5, pp. 33–66.

(1967). 'A Note on History as Narrative', *History and Theory* 6, pp. 413–19.

Mandell, David Paul (2000). 'The History of Political Thought as a "Vocation": A Pragmatist Defense' in *Vocations of Political Theory*, ed. Jason A. Frank and John Tambornino, Minneapolis, Minn., pp. 118–42.

Mansfield, Harvey (1965). *Statesmanship and Party Government: A Study of Burke and Bolingbroke*, Chicago, Ill.

Marsilius of Padua (1951–6). *The Defender of Peace* [*Defensor Pacis* 1324], 2 vols., ed. and trans. Alan Gewirth, New York.

Martin, Kingsley (1962). *French Liberal Thought in the Eighteenth Century*, London.

Martinich, A. P. (1992). *The Two Gods of Leviathan: Thomas Hobbes on Religion and Politics*, Cambridge.

McCloskey, Robert G. (1957). 'American Political Thought and the Study of Politics', *American Political Science Review* 51, pp. 115–29.

McCoy, Charles R. N. (1963). *The Structure of Political Thought*, New York.

McCullagh, C. Behan (1984). 'The Intelligibility of Cognitive Relativism', *Monist* 67, pp. 327–40.

(1998). *The Truth of History*, London.

McCulloch, J. R. (1952). Preface to *Early English Tracts on Commerce*, ed. J. R. McCulloch, Cambridge, pp. iii–xv.

McGinn, Colin (1977). 'Charity, Interpretation, and Belief', *Journal of Philosophy* 74, pp. 521–35.

McGrade, Arthur S. (1963). 'The Coherence of Hooker's Polity: the Books on Power', *Journal of the History of Ideas* 24, pp. 163–82.

Melden, A. I. (1961). *Free Action*, London.

Merkl, Peter H. (1967). *Political Continuity and Change*, New York.

Mew, Peter (1971). 'Conventions on Thin Ice', *Philosophical Quarterly* 21, pp. 352–6.

Mintz, Samuel I. (1962). *The Hunting of Leviathan*, Cambridge.

Monter, E. William (1969). 'Inflation and Witchcraft: the Case of Jean Bodin' in *Action and Conviction in Early Modern Europe*, ed. Theodore K. Rabb and Jerrold Seigel, Princeton, N.J., pp. 371–89.

Morgenbesser, Sidney (1966). 'Is it a Science?' *Social Research* 33, pp. 255–71.

Morgenthau, Hans J. (1958). *Dilemmas of Politics*, Chicago, Ill.

Morris, Christopher (1953). *Political Thought in England: Tyndale to Hooker*, Oxford.
  (1966). 'Montesquieu and the Varieties of Political Experience' in *Political Ideas*, ed. David Thomson, London, pp. 79–94.

Morris Jones, Huw (1964). 'The Relevance of the Artist's Intentions', *British Journal of Aesthetics* 4, pp. 138–45.

Mortimore, G. W. and Maund, J. B. (1976). 'Rationality in Belief' in *Rationality and the Social Sciences*, ed. S. I. Benn and G. W. Mortimore, London, pp. 11–33.

Mulligan, Lotte, Richards, Judith and Graham, John (1979). 'Intentions and Conventions: A Critique of Quentin Skinner's Method for the Study of the History of Ideas', *Political Studies* 27, pp. 84–98.

[Mun, Thomas] (1952). *A Discourse of Trade from England unto the East Indies* [1621] in *Early English Tracts on Commerce*, ed. J. R. McCulloch, Cambridge, pp. 1–47.

Murdoch, Iris (1970). *The Sovereignty of Good*, London.

Murphy, N. R. (1951). *The Interpretation of Plato's Republic*, Oxford.

Namier, L. B. (1930). *England in the Age of the American Revolution*, London.
  (1957). *The Structure of Politics at the Accession of George III*, 2nd edn, London.

Nehamas, Alexander (1985). *Nietzsche: Life as Literature*, Cambridge, Mass.

Nelson, Leonard (1962). 'What is the History of Philosophy?' *Ratio* 4, pp. 122–35.

Newton-Smith, W. H. (1981). *The Rationality of Science*, London.

Nietzsche, Friedrich (1994). *On the Genealogy of Morality* [1887], ed. Keith Ansell-Pearson, trans. Carol Diethe, Cambridge.

Norval, Aletta J. (2000). 'The Things We Do with Words – Contemporary Approaches to the Analysis of Ideology', *British Journal of Political Science* 30, pp. 313–46.

Novick, Peter (1988). *That Noble Dream: The 'Objectivity Question' and the American Historical Profession*, Cambridge.

Oakley, Francis (1984). *Omnipotence, Covenant, and Order: An Excursion in the History of Ideas from Abelard to Leibniz*, Ithaca, N.Y.

(1999). *Politics and Eternity: Studies in the History of Medieval and Early-Modern Political Thought*, Leiden.

Owen, David (1999). 'Political Philosophy in a Post-imperial Voice', *Economy and Society* 28, pp. 520–49.

Palonen, Kari (1997). 'Quentin Skinner's Rhetoric of Conceptual Change', *History of the Human Sciences* 10, pp. 61–80.

(1999). 'Rhetorical and Temporal Perspectives on Conceptual Change', *Finnish Yearbook of Political Thought* 3, pp. 41–59.

Papineau, David (1978). *For Science in the Social Sciences*, London.

Parekh, B. and Berki, R. N. (1973). 'The History of Political Ideas: A Critique of Q. Skinner's Methodology', *Journal of the History of Ideas* 34, pp. 163–84.

Parkin, Charles (1956). *The Moral Basis of Burke's Political Thought*, Cambridge.

Petrey, Sandy (1990). *Speech Acts and Literary Theory*, London.

Plamenatz, John (1963). *Man and Society*, 2 vols., London.

Plucknett, Theodore F. T. (1926–7). 'Bonham's Case and Judicial Review', *Harvard Law Review* 40, pp. 30–70.

Pocock, J. G. A. (1962). 'The History of Political Thought: A Methodological Enquiry' in *Philosophy, Politics and Society*, 2nd series, ed. Peter Laslett and W. G. Runciman, Oxford, pp. 183–202.

(1965). 'Machiavelli, Harrington, and English Political Ideologies in the Eighteenth Century', *William and Mary Quarterly* 22, pp. 549–83.

(1973). 'Verbalizing a Political Act: Towards a Politics of Speech', *Political Theory* 1, pp. 27–45.

(1980). 'Political Ideas as Historical Events: Political Philosophers as Historical Actors' in *Political Theory and Political Education*, ed. Melvin Richter, Princeton, N.J., pp. 139–58.

(1985). *Virtue, Commerce, and History: Essays on Political Thought and History, Chiefly in the Eighteenth Century*, Cambridge.

(1987). *The Ancient Constitution and the Feudal Law: A Study of English Historical Thought in the Seventeenth Century: A Reissue with a Retrospect*, Cambridge.

Popkin, Richard H. (1953). 'Joseph Glanvill: A Precursor of David Hume', *Journal of the History of Ideas* 14, pp. 292–303.

(1969). 'The Sceptical Origins of the Modern Problem of Knowledge' in *Perception and Personal Identity*, ed. Norman S. Care and Robert H. Grimm, Cleveland, Ohio, pp. 3–24.

(1979). *The History of Scepticism from Erasmus to Spinoza*, Berkeley, Cal.

Popper, K. R. (1962). *The Open Society and Its Enemies*, 4th edn, 2 vols., London.

Pratt, Mary Louise (1977). *Toward a Speech Act Theory of Literary Discourse*, Bloomington, Ind.

Prezzolini, Giuseppe (1968). *Machiavelli*, trans. G. Savini, London.

Price, Russell (1973). 'The Senses of *Virtù* in Machiavelli', *European Studies Review* 3, pp. 315–45.

Prudovsky, Gad (1997). 'Can We Ascribe to Past Thinkers Concepts They Had No Linguistic Means to Express?' *History and Theory* 36, pp. 15–31.

Putnam, Hilary (1975). *Mind, Language and Reality*, Cambridge.
  (1981). *Reason, Truth and History*, Cambridge.
Quine, W. V. O. (1960). *Word and Object*, New York.
  (1961). *From a Logical Point of View*, rev. edn, Cambridge, Mass.
Quintilian (1920–2). *Institutio Oratoria*, ed. and trans. H. E. Butler, 4 vols., London.
Raab, Felix (1964). *The English Face of Machiavelli: A Changing Interpretation 1500–1700*, London.
Rée, Jonathan (1991). 'The Vanity of Historicism', *New Literary History* 22, pp. 961–83.
Reid, Thomas (1941). *Essays on the Intellectual Powers of Man*, ed. A. D. Woozley, London.
Richards, I. A. (1929). *Practical Criticism*, London.
Richter, Melvin (1986). 'Conceptual History (*Begriffsgeschichte*) and Political Theory', *Political Theory* 14, pp. 604–37.
  (1987). '*Begriffsgeschichte* and the History of Ideas', *Journal of the History of Ideas* 48, pp. 247–63.
  (1995). *The History of Social and Political Concepts: A Critical Introduction*, Oxford.
Rickman, H. P. (1967). *Understanding and the Human Studies*, London.
Ricoeur, Paul (1973). 'The Model of the Text: Meaningful Action Considered as a Text', *New Literary History* 5, pp. 91–117.
  (1981). *Hermeneutics and the Human Sciences*, ed. and trans. John B. Thompson, Cambridge.
Roberts, Geoffrey (1996). 'Narrative History as a Way of Life', *Journal of Contemporary History* 31, pp. 221–8.
Roberts, Lewes (1952). *The Treasure of Traffike or a Discourse of Forraigne Trade* [1641] in *Early English Tracts on Commerce*, ed. J. R. McCulloch, Cambridge, pp. 49–113.
Robinson, Howard (1931). *Bayle the Sceptic*, New York.
Rorty, Richard (1972). 'The World Well Lost', *Journal of Philosophy* 69, pp. 649–65.
  (1979). *Philosophy and the Mirror of Nature*, Princeton, N.J.
  (1983). 'Postmodernist Bourgeois Liberalism', *Journal of Philosophy* 80, pp. 583–9.
  (1985). 'Solidarity or Objectivity' in *Post-Analytic Philosophy*, ed. John Rajchman and Cornel West, New York, pp. 3–19.
Rosebury, Brian (1997). 'Irrecoverable Intentions and Literary Interpretation', *British Journal of Aesthetics* 37, pp. 15–27.
Russell, Bertrand (1946). *History of Western Philosophy*, New York.
Ryan, Alan (1965). 'John Locke and the Dictatorship of the Bourgeoisie', *Political Studies* 13, pp. 219–30.
Sabine, George H. (1951). *A History of Political Theory*, 3rd edn, London.
Saccone, Eduardo (1983). '*Grazia, Sprezzatura, Affettazione* in the *Courtier*' in *Castiglione: The Ideal and the Real in Renaissance Culture*, ed. Robert W. Hanning and David Rosand, London, pp. 45–67.

Sampson, R. V. (1956). *Progress in the Age of Reason*, Cambridge, Mass.
Schiffer, Stephen R. (1972). *Meaning*, Oxford.
Schmidt, James (1999). 'How Historical is *Begriffsgeschichte?*' *History of European Ideas* 25, pp. 9–14.
Schochet, Gordon (1974). 'Quentin Skinner's Method', *Political Theory* 2, pp. 261–76.
Schutz, Alfred (1960). 'The Social World and the Theory of Social Action', *Social Research* 27, pp. 203–21.
Searle, John R. (1962). 'Meaning and Speech Acts', *Philosophical Review* 71, pp. 423–32.
  (1969). *Speech Acts*, Cambridge.
Seidman, Steven (1983). 'Beyond Presentism and Historicism: Understanding the History of Social Science', *Sociological Inquiry* 53, pp. 79–94.
Seliger, Martin (1968). *The Liberal Politics of John Locke*, London.
Shakespeare, William (1988). *The Complete Works*, ed. Stanley Wells and Gary Taylor, Oxford.
Shapiro, Ian (1982). 'Realism in the Study of the History of Ideas', *History of Political Thought* 3, pp. 535–78.
Shirley, F. J. (1949). *Richard Hooker and Contemporary Political Ideas*, London.
Sibley, Mulford Q. (1958). 'The Place of Classical Theory in the Study of Politics' in *Approaches to the Study of Politics*, ed. Roland Young, Chicago, Ill.
Skinner, Quentin (1966). 'The Limits of Historical Explanations', *Philosophy* 41, pp. 199–215.
  (1970). 'Conventions and the Understanding of Speech-acts', *Philosophical Quarterly* 20, pp. 118–38.
  (1971). 'On Performing and Explaining Linguistic Actions', *Philosophical Quarterly* 21, pp. 1–21.
  (1974) 'Some Problems in the Analysis of Political Thought and Action', *Political Theory* 23, pp. 277–303.
  (1975). 'Hermeneutics and the Role of History', *New Literary History* 7, pp. 209–32.
  (1978a). 'Action and Context', *Proceedings of the Aristotelian Society*, supp. vol. 52, pp. 57–69.
  (1978b). *The Foundations of Modern Political Thought*, vol. I: *The Renaissance*, Cambridge.
  (1996). 'From Hume's Intentions to Deconstruction and Back', *Journal of Political Philosophy* 4, pp. 142–54.
  (1998). *Liberty Before Liberalism*, Cambridge.
Skorupski, John (1976). *Symbol and Theory*, Cambridge.
  (1978). 'The Meaning of Another Culture's Beliefs' in *Action and Interpretation*, ed. Christopher Hookway and Philip Pettit, Cambridge, pp. 83–106.
Smith, R. Jack (1948). 'Intention in an Organic Theory of Poetry', *Sewanee Review* 56, pp. 625–33.
Spitz, J. F. (1989). 'Comment lire les textes politiques du passé? Le Programme méthodologique de Quentin Skinner', *Droits* 10, pp. 133–45.

Stark, Werner (1960). *Montesquieu: Pioneer of the Sociology of Knowledge*, London.

Stern, Laurent (1980). 'On Interpreting', *Journal of Aesthetics and Art Criticism* 39, pp. 119–29.

Stevenson, C. L. (1963). *Facts and Values*, New Haven, Conn.

Stewart, John B. (1963). *The Moral and Political Philosophy of David Hume*, New York.

Stout, Jeffrey (1981). *The Flight from Authority*, Notre Dame.

Stove, D. C. (1982). *Popper and After*, Oxford.

Strauss, Leo (1952). *Persecution and the Art of Writing*, Glencoe, Ill.

  (1953). *Natural Right and History*, Chicago, Ill.

  (1957). *What is Political Philosophy?* Glencoe, Ill.

  (1958). *Thoughts on Machiavelli*, Glencoe, Ill.

Strauss, Leo and Cropsey, Joseph (1963). *The History of Political Philosophy*, Chicago, Ill.

Strawson, P. F. (1971). *Logico-Linguistic Papers*, London.

Strout, Cushing (1992). 'Border Crossings: History, Fiction, and *Dead Certainties*', *History and Theory* 31, pp. 153–62.

Supple, B. E. (1959). *Commercial Crisis and Change in England 1600–1642: A Study in the Instability of a Mercantile Economy*, Cambridge.

Talmon, J. L. (1952). *The Origins of Totalitarian Democracy*, London.

Tarlton, Charles D. (1973). 'Historicity, Meaning and Revisionism in the Study of Political Thought', *History and Theory* 12, pp. 307–28.

Tawney, R. H. (1938). *Religion and the Rise of Capitalism*, Pelican Books edn, Harmondsworth.

Taylor, A. E. (1938). 'The Ethical Doctrine of Hobbes', *Philosophy* 13, pp. 406–24.

Taylor, Charles (1964). *The Explanation of Behaviour*, London.

  (1971). 'Interpretation and the Sciences of Man', *Review of Metaphysics* 25, pp. 3–51.

  (1981). 'Understanding and Explanation in the *Geisteswissenschaften*' in *Wittgenstein: To Follow a Rule*, ed. Steven Holtzman and Christopher Leich, London, pp. 191–210.

  (1982). 'Rationality' in *Rationality and Relativism*, ed. Martin Hollis and Steven Lukes, London, pp. 87–105.

  (1988). 'The Hermeneutics of Conflict' in *Meaning and Context: Quentin Skinner and his Critics*, ed. James Tully, Cambridge, pp. 218–28.

Thomas, Keith (1971). *Religion and the Decline of Magic*, London.

Thompson, Martyn P. (1993). 'Reception Theory and the Interpretation of Historical Meaning', *History and Theory* 32, pp. 248–72.

Thorne, S. E. (1938). 'Dr Bonham's Case', *Law Quarterly Review* 54, pp. 543–52.

Travis, Charles (1975). *Saying and Understanding*, Oxford.

Trevor-Roper, H. R. (1967). *Religion, the Reformation and Social Change*, London.

Tuck, Richard (1993). 'The Contribution of History' in *A Companion to Contemporary Political Philosophy*, ed. Robert E. Goodin and Philip Pettit, Oxford, pp. 72–89.

Tucker, Robert C. (1961). *Philosophy and Myth in Karl Marx*, Cambridge.

Tully, James (1988). 'The Pen is a Mighty Sword: Quentin Skinner's Analysis of Politics' in *Meaning and Context: Quentin Skinner and his Critics*, ed. James Tully, Cambridge, pp. 7–25.

(1993). *An Approach to Political Philosophy: Locke in Contexts*, Cambridge.

(1995). *Strange Multiplicity: Constitutionalism in an Age of Diversity*, Cambridge.

Turner, Stephen (1983). '"Contextualism" and the Interpretation of the Classical Sociological Texts', *Knowledge and Society* 4, pp. 273–91.

Urmson, J. O. (1968). *The Emotive Theory of Ethics*, London.

Vanderveken, Daniel (1990). *Meaning and Speech Acts*, 2 vols., Cambridge.

Vile, M. J. C. (1967). *Constitutionalism and the Separation of Powers*, Oxford.

Villari, Pasquale (1892). *The Life and Times of Niccolò Machiavelli*, trans. Linda Villari, new edn, 2 vols., London.

Viroli, Maurizio (1987). '"Revisionisti" e "Ortodossi" Nella Storia delle Idee Politiche', *Rivista di Filosofia* 78, pp. 121–36.

Vossenkuhl, Wilhelm (1982). 'Rationalität und historisches Verstehen. Quentin Skinner's Rekonstruktion der politischen Theorie', *Conceptus* 16, pp. 27–43.

Warrender, Howard (1957). *The Political Philosophy of Hobbes: His Theory of Obligation*, Oxford.

(1979). 'Political Theory and Historiography', *The Historical Journal* 22, pp. 931–40.

Watkins, J. W. N. (1965). *Hobbes's System of Ideas*, London.

Weber, Max (1930). *The Protestant Ethic and the Spirit of Capitalism*, trans. Talcott Parsons, London.

(1968). *Economy and Society: An Outline of Interpretive Sociology*, ed. Guenther Roth and Claus Wittich, 3 vols., New York.

Weldon, T. D. (1946). *States and Morals*, London.

(1953). *The Vocabulary of Politics*, Harmondsworth.

Weston, Corinne Comstock (1965). *English Constitutional Theory and the House of Lords*, London.

Wheeler, John (1931). *A Treatise of Commerce* [1601], ed. G. B. Hotchkiss, New York.

Whitfield, J. H. (1947). *Machiavelli*, Oxford.

Williams, Raymond (1976). *Keywords: A Vocabulary of Culture and Society*, London.

(1983). *Keywords: A Vocabulary of Culture and Society*, rev. and expanded, London.

Wimsatt, K. C. (1954). *The Verbal Icon*, Lexington, Ky.

Wimsatt, W. K. and Beardsley, Monroe C. (1976). 'The Intentional Fallacy' in *On Literary Intention*, ed. David Newton-De Molina, Edinburgh, pp. 1–13.

Winch, Peter (1958). *The Idea of a Social Science*, London.

(1964). 'Mr Louch's Idea of a Social Science', *Inquiry* 7, pp. 202–8.

(1970). 'Understanding a Primitive Society' in *Rationality*, ed. Bryan R. Wilson, Oxford, pp. 78–110.

Winiarski, Warren (1963). 'Niccolo Machiavelli' in *History of Political Philosophy*, ed. Leo Strauss and Joseph Cropsey, Chicago, Ill., pp. 247–76.

Wittgenstein, Ludwig (1958). *Philosophical Investigations*, trans. G. E. M. Anscombe, 2nd edn, Oxford.

Wokler, Robert (2001). 'The Professoriate of Political Thought in England since 1914: A Tale of Three Chairs' in *The History of Political Thought in National Context*, ed. Dario Castiglione and Iain Hampsher-Monk, Cambridge, pp. 134–58.

Wolin, Sheldon S. (1961). *Politics and Vision*, Boston, Mass.

Woodhouse, A. S. P. (1938). *Puritanism and Liberty*, London.

Wootton, David (1986). Preface and Introduction to *Divine Right and Democracy*, Harmondsworth, pp. 9–19, 22–86.

Yolton, John W. (1975). 'Textual vs Conceptual Analysis in the History of Philosophy', *Journal of the History of Philosophy* 13, pp. 505–12.

Zuckert, Michael P. (1985). 'Appropriation and Understanding in the History of Political Philosophy: On Quentin Skinner's Method', *Interpretation* 13, pp. 403–24.

Index

actions
  causes of, 128, 131–2, 143, 145, 147, 174
  descriptions of, 107–8, 148–9, 182
  evaluative descriptions of, 148, 149–50,
    151–5, 160–2
  explanation of, 128–30, 137–8, 139–40
  legitimation of, 146–9, 150–5, 156–7, 158,
    167–9, 173–4
  'social meaning' of, 128–32, 134, 138–9
  motives for, 146, 147–8, 151, 155, 157
Acton, John Emerich Dalberg, Lord, 15
Adkins, A. W. H., 126
Adler, M. J., 69n.
Alexander, William, Earl of Stirling, 154
Ammirato, Scipio, 39
anachronism, 50–1, 60–1
Anglo, Sydney, 28n., 39n.
Anscombe, G. E. M., 98n.
Aquinas, St Thomas, 52, 65
Aristotle, 28, 60, 107, 183, 184
Aubrey, John, 82
Augustine, St, 86
Austin, J. L.
  How to Do Things with Words, 103, 133
  and Collingwood, 115–16
  on illocutionary acts, 98, 105–6, 108, 109–10,
    134
  meaning and use, 2, 82, 104
  performatives, 113
  speech acts, 2, 115–16, 135, 148
  'uptake', 106n., 107–8, 114, 124
  and Wittgenstein, 2, 82, 103, 106
author, the
  'death of', 90–1, 117, 119
  'ill-health of', 118
Ayer, A. J., 131, 138–9, 144

Bacon, Francis, 84
Barnes, Barry, 34–5, 37, 44n., 53–4
Bartelson, Jens, 34n.
Barthes, Roland, 90, 117, 118

Bateson, F. W., 101
Baxter, Andrew, 79
Bayle, Pierre, 80–2, 87
Beardsley, Monroe C., 90, 91, 93, 94, 95–6
beliefs
  and facts, 44–6
  formation of, 53–5
  identification of, 49–51
  and rationality, 31–3, 35–8, 40, 42–5, 54–6,
    140–1, 150
  and truth, 1–2, 51–3
Berkeley, George, 63, 78, 79–80
Bevir, Mark, 5n., 67n., 109n., 112n., 179n.
Blackburn, Simon, 47n.
Bloor, David, 34–5, 37, 44n., 53–4
Bodin, Jean, 28, 43, 51
Boethius, 49
Bolingbroke, Henry St John, Viscount, 69, 75
Boucher, David, 109n.
Buchanan, George, 63
Burke, Edmund, 68, 75
Butterfield, Herbert, 145

Carr, E. H., 20n.
Castiglione, Baldassare, 181
Castoriadis, Cornelius, 102
causes
  and explanation, 4, 9–12, 128–31, 137–9,
    143, 147, 174
  historians on, 11–12
  motives as, 131, 144
  and reasons, 33–5, 41
Cervantes Saavedra, Miguel de, 122–3
Chatsworth House, 17, 19, 20, 21, 25
Cicero, 49, 183, 184
Cioffi, Frank, 96n., 97
Clark, Stuart, 28n., 36n.
classic texts, canon of, 2–3, 57, 59, 72, 79, 88
classification, problems of, 15, 58–9, 74, 163
Close, A. J., 123 and n.
Cohen, L. Jonathan, 114

Printed by Integrated Books International,
United States of America